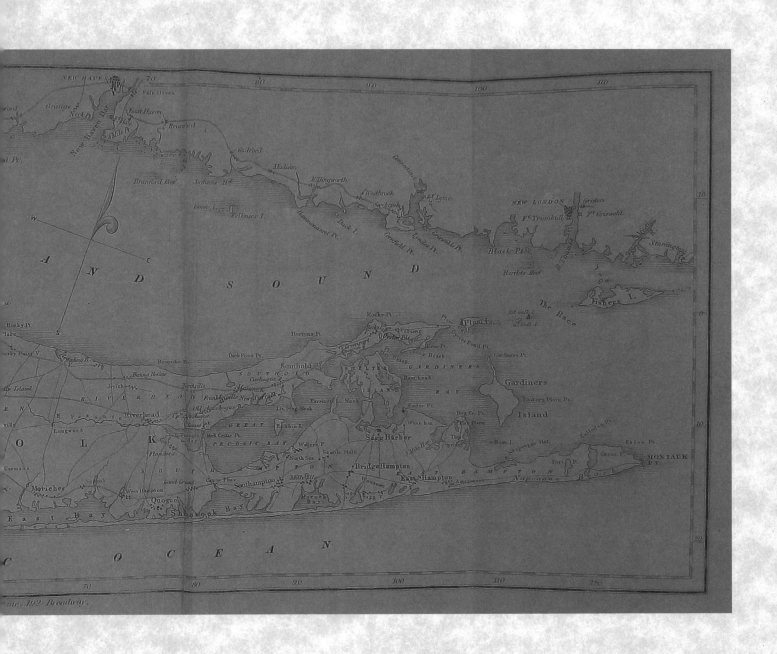

Water & Ice

The Wreck of the *Bristol*
Late 1830s—Unknown Artist

Dreadful Wreck of the *Mexico* on Hempstead Beach (1837)
Detail
Nathaniel Currier

WATER AND ICE

The Tragic Wrecks
Of the *Bristol* and the *Mexico*
On the South Shore of Long Island

Arthur S. Mattson

Lynbrook Historical Books
28 Hart Street
Lynbrook, New York 11563
2009

Printed in the United States of America.

FIRST EDITION

Library of Congress Control Number: 2009904238

Mattson, Arthur, S.
Water and Ice : The Tragic Wrecks of the *Bristol* and the *Mexico*
on the South Shore of Long Island /
Arthur S. Mattson

Includes bibliographic references and index.
ISBN 978-0-615-29439-1 (alk. paper)
1. Sailing ships—United States—History. 2. Immigrants – United States –
History – 19th century. 3. Merchant Mariners—History.

Also by Arthur S. Mattson

The History of Lynbrook

Cover:
The Wreck of the *Mexico*
Unknown artist
Thomas Bingley's *Tales of Shipwrecks and other Disasters at Sea* (1842).

This book is dedicated to the memory of my sister

Irene Kristine Bates

Born December 27, 1948
Mineola, Long Island, New York

B.A. Bethel College '68

M.A. SUNY Albany '70

Marine Archaeologist

Died June 30, 1972
in the Bay of Biscay,
in the wreck of a tall ship.

"The history of the world cannot furnish two more awful calamities of a similar nature, following each other in such quick succession."

——"Two Late Awful Shipwrecks off Sandy Hook,"
New York Sun, January 12, 1837, Supplement.

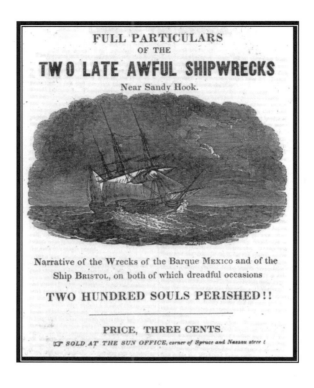

Contents

Contents

(continued)

Preface

A tall, marble obelisk rises from the center of the Rockville Cemetery in Lynbrook, Long Island, surrounded by a plot of land named "The Mariners Burying Ground." The monument stands atop a grassy mound and reaches a total height of eighteen feet. Thus, it is easily visible from the two adjacent, heavily-traveled roads, Ocean Avenue and Merrick Road. Yet, few of the thousands of daily passersby have any idea of the awful tragedies to which this cold stone and earthen mound remain the last testimony; nor are they aware of the strong connection this monument has to the history of Long Island, New York State, and the United States.

Carved, weathered letters on the obelisk's mottled white base tell of two shipwrecks in the winter of 1836-37, and of a mass grave containing 139 of the 215 victims of those wrecks. The engravings say that the *Bristol* and the *Mexico* were both American vessels, and that the passengers were emigrants from Ireland and England. The captains' names are listed—Alexander McKown of the ship *Bristol*, and Charles Winslow of the barque *Mexico*. A Bible verse proclaims, "Lord save us, we perish," and some weary doggerel tells us, "In this grave, from the wide Ocean doth sleep, / The bodies of those that had crossed the deep. . ." There is a concluding, sobering note: "This monument was erected partly by the money found upon their persons."

When I first read those inscriptions over thirty years ago, I was curious to know more, but my search for the story behind the two catastrophes was more difficult than I ever imagined. It took decades. Along the way I acquired an interest in local history, and that led me to become the Historian for the Village of Lynbrook. In 2005, I included a short chapter about the two shipwrecks in my first book, *The History of Lynbrook*. But the research for that chapter only whetted my appetite. The trail had not run cold.

Far from it. The story had become increasingly compelling and the leads kept accumulating.

My quest steered a motorcycling vacation in the United Kingdom to Liverpool, not because of the riding terrain or an interest in the *Beatles*, but because I had learned that both ships sailed from that city in 1836, only days apart, on their final voyages. The Prince's Dock, where the two ships tied up side by side, is still there. Best of all, the Merseyside Maritime Museum and the Liverpool Library had valuable information in their files. A ski trip to Salt Lake, Utah became a good "cover" for a hunt for genealogical information about the ships' captains. And so it went; years of such off-and-on research, which accelerated once I retired from banking, and culminated in this book. The result is a story of early nineteenth-century Ireland, England, Long Island, and New York City, combined with two fascinating, interconnected sea stories that begin in Liverpool and end in disaster on sand bars off Long Island's South Shore. The nautical terms used in this book may be unfamiliar to some readers. As a result, a Glossary is provided near the back of the book.

The search for 170-year-old facts was more than an academic exercise, for I am the son of immigrants who sailed to America in the 1920s. I also served in the U.S. Naval Reserve at the Freeport station, crossed the Atlantic on a destroyer, and sailed a tall ship from New York to Cape May and Provincetown. Fifty years of skin-diving, sailing, fishing, and clamming in Long Island waters, and motorcycling almost every road on the Island, added to my interest. In addition, two personal, traumatic experiences made the account of the two wrecks truly *my story*.

In 1972—the same year that I first came upon the mass grave and monument in Lynbrook—my sister, Irene Bates, then twenty-three, drowned in the wreck of her restored, nineteenth-century tall-ship, the *Lefteria* ("freedom" in Greek). It happened in a nighttime collision with a French weather ship, *France II*, in the Bay of Biscay.

That accident involved Sir Francis Chichester, the famous, singlehanded-around-the-world sailor. At age seventy, and seriously ill with spinal cancer, Chichester attempted one final, ill-advised, long-distance sail on the *Gypsy Moth V*, with tragic results. In a confused state because of his illness and prescription drugs, Chichester alternately radioed for help, gave an incorrect position, gave the correct position, waved help away, accepted it, and even had a minor collision with a vessel that had come to his aid. At some point during the confusion on this dark night, the French weather ship made a rapid course change and plowed into my sister's yacht, just as it approached to help the unfortunate Sir Francis. The low-lying *Lefteria* and her wine-colored sails were not visible at night, and the French ship's watch was not paying attention to either their own radar or *Lefteria's* running lights.

The yacht was struck amidships. The much larger weather ship rode atop the wooden vessel for a few moments before breaking her back and sending *Lefteria* and her several tons of stone ballast toward the bottom.

The impact probably threw Irene from her bunk. In total blackness, with water pouring in around her, she somehow managed to fight her way to a ladder and escape the ship, but it was too late. Disoriented, and too far below the surface, she had no chance. She drowned, but her body was recovered. Of the *Lefteria's* crew of eleven American, Swedish, Danish, and Dutch young people, only four survived. Two months later, Chichester succumbed to his disease.

Irene's death by drowning echoed in my mind as I read the nineteenth-century newspaper stories on microfilm. I could see her struggle in the accounts of men, women, and children fighting for their lives in the hold of the *Bristol* as tons of water rushed down on them through an open hatch. Moreover, as those responsible for the wrecks of the *Bristol* and the *Mexico* gradually revealed themselves from dusty archives, it became clear that Sir Francis is far from alone in the history of mariners and shipowners who in the pursuit of their own ends discount the lives of innocent people around them.

There is yet another reason why the wrecks are *my wrecks*. Like John Lawson, a Scottish ship's doctor who is quoted in the chapter entitled "The Wreck of the *Bristol*," I had my own near-drowning experience, one that validates much of what the good doctor wrote. This recollection has made the memory of my sister's death more painful, and has added a sense of personal horror to each reading of the contemporaneous accounts of the mass drownings in 1836.

As a young teenager, I spent most summers at my parents' cottage on the North Shore of Long Island, at Sound Beach. I became an avid and highly skilled spear-fisherman, capable of harvesting twenty or more pounds of *tautog* (blackfish) a day and selling the catch to less fortunate rod-and-reel fishermen. My expertise was such that I was able to spear every fish in the head, so as not to damage the meat. Unsuccessful fisherman bought fish from me that I had skinned, gutted, and filleted. They sought me out because there were no spear-holes through my fillets, and thus nothing to betray the fish's actual means of capture when they brought their "catch" home.

One bright summer day, at age sixteen and fit as a dolphin, I swam out on a solo, spear-fishing expedition 300 yards from shore. My objective was a cluster of rocks that barely broke the surface. Once there, I descended fifteen feet to the bottom, where blackfish and sea bass lurked among the cracks and crevices of a massive array of boulders. I poked my head into a three-foot wide opening, and allowed my eyes to get used to the dim light. I had looked into this very crevice dozens of times before, but today was different. There before me, instead of a fish, was one of the few lobsters I had ever seen in the wild. Determined to catch it and have it for dinner, or better yet, sell it, I eased in and slowly extended my hand toward the backward-retreating crustacean. When the creature raised its claws in a fighting mode, I decided that perhaps my thin skin was not up to such a battle. It was time for *me* to retreat.

Because of my eagerness, I was farther into the crevice than I thought. I began to paddle backward with my free arm, the one not holding the spear-gun. But my diving fins, which were designed to propel me forward, restricted my ability to back up. Moreover, the buoyancy of my upper torso had floated me upward into a narrower space. I began to panic.

My only thought was *not to die here* in an underwater crevice, as a meal for a lobster. Since the sloping walls were too slippery to push against, in desperation I jammed the four-foot-long spear-gun up and forward into the crevice and was lucky to strike a flat surface. I shoved against the gun and forced my upper body down and backward. So forceful was this move that the spear-gun discharged its steel shaft, further propelling me down and out. At last, I pushed myself free.

I was still fifteen feet below the surface and starving for air. My lungs were burning, and my throat and chest began involuntarily to gulp for air, even though my mouth was closed. The Scotsman I referred to, Dr. Lawson, called his own automatic reaction in a similar event a "laryngospasm." Whatever it is called, I vividly remember the sounds from my throat and chest, clearly audible underwater, like a hog rooting around in a sty.

I dropped the spear-gun, and kicked off from the rocky bottom. As I neared the surface I was unable to stop myself from taking an involuntary, full gulp of seawater. I clambered onto a nearly submerged rock, half in and half out of the water, choking, and sputtering.

During those horrific two minutes underwater, I did not experience anything close to Dr. Lawson's idyllic "falling about in a green field in early summer," and there was no "sight of the Grampians," or of the Catskills, for that matter. I was at war with the elements, fighting panic, disorientation, and physical pain. It may well have been the same for my sister, for the six others of the *Lefteria's* crew who drowned, and for the one hundred passengers on the *Bristol* who suffered the same fate.

The pain and suffering of the passengers aboard the barque *Mexico*, a few weeks after the wreck of the *Bristol*, may have been greater. One hundred fifteen men, women, and children clung to the mast and railings of the stranded barque just two hundred yards off Long Beach, as sea spray blasted them and gradually froze them to death inside crystalline shells of ice.

Introduction

It was New Year's Day, 1837, and bitterly cold at five degrees above zero. Massive ice-floes drifted through New York Harbor from their spawning grounds in the Hudson River, rhythmically rising and falling as they met the ocean swells at Sandy Hook. Captain Charles Winslow stood on the open deck of the barque *Mexico*, anxiously scanning the horizon. In the gray light of the fading day, he counted more than thirty other tall ships standing off the Hook, all waiting for harbor pilots to take them in. None had appeared since dawn.

Each of the captains faced a similar decision: give up for the day, or attempt to navigate into the harbor that very afternoon, with no pilot to guide the ship past rocks, sandbars, and shoals. Winslow, an experienced captain out of the Port of Philadelphia, had entered New York Harbor before, but unlike some of the other captains, he had never gone in without a pilot. His calculation was even more difficult because he had to take into account his "white cargo" of 111 emigrants housed on the *Mexico's* steerage deck. [1] These passengers, most of them women and children, were literally starving after sixty-nine days at sea, more than twice the expected time to cross from Liverpool. Moreover, most of the members of the undermanned crew of his three-masted, 279-ton barque were suffering from frostbite, and were refusing to come on deck.

If Winslow attempted to cross the shoals of New York Harbor without a pilot, and wrecked his ship, owner Samuel Broom of New York would ensure that he would never sail again as master of a tall ship. The

---

[1] In the 1830s, the word "emigrant" was used on both sides of the Atlantic when referring to people seeking a new life in North America. That usage will be followed in this book in preference to the word "immigrant." The use of the phrase "white cargo" to describe poor emigrants from the United Kingdom and Ireland is discussed in the chapter, "White Cargo."

captain also had to consider the owner's teenage brother who was aboard. Young master Broom could be counted on to report to his older brother every mistake the captain might make.

The wind began to rise strongly from the southeast, pushing shoreward, and making it ever more dangerous for the barque to remain anywhere near Sandy Hook. This new threat would require the captain to ask untrained passengers to help move the ship out to sea. Winslow later said that at this moment he experienced "a degree of anxiety that was not to be expressed." Reluctantly, he decided to head out into the New York Bight—the wide "V" between the coasts of Long Island and New Jersey. The result was a disaster for his ship, his cargo, his passengers, and his crew when the vessel grounded on a sandbar, in a blizzard, off Long Beach, Long Island.

Winslow could not have known that he was retracing the path of Captain Alexander McKown of the ship *Bristol*. A few weeks earlier, McKown sailed home to New York from Liverpool and found no pilots at the Hook. He, like Captain Winslow, sailed out into the New York Bight. The *Bristol's* voyage ended in catastrophe when the ship grounded at Rockaway Beach, only a few hundred yards from shore, and was engulfed by a freak wave. Two hundred fifteen people, mostly emigrants from Ireland, England, Scotland, and Wales, died in the two wrecks. These two catastrophes off Long Island's South Shore, taken together or separately, were the largest, accidental mass-deaths in the history of the United States up to that time.

The disasters had a profound effect locally and nationally. Thrilling newspaper accounts of the wrecks set the stage for New York's eventual leading role in journalistic investigative reporting. Newspaper exposés of the harbor pilot monopoly stirred calls for massive changes in that corrupt system. A Supreme Court decision involving the *Bristol's* wreck-robbers significantly extended the reach of the federal government's powers. The haphazard nature of the rescues from shore resulted in a redefinition of the job of lighthouse keepers to be life savers as well, and the U.S. Coast Guard permanently added sea-rescues to its mission.

The arts were affected too. Print-makers from Nathaniel Currier to an anonymous Welshman produced dramatic scenes from the wrecks. More importantly, a seventeen-year-old Long Islander who later said he was "almost an observer" of the wrecks was so profoundly moved by the twin tragedies that he later, as a mature poet, joined the themes of *death* and *the sea* in his works. He also included dramatic yet accurate details of one of the wrecks in what is probably his most haunting poem, "The Sleepers," in *Leaves of Grass*. The young poet was Walt Whitman.

The Sleepers
Stanza Four in *Leaves of Grass*

The beach is cut by the razory ice-wind, the wreck-guns sound,
The tempest lulls, the moon comes floundering through the drifts.

I look where the ship helplessly heads end on, I hear the burst as
    she strikes, I hear the howls of dismay, they grow fainter
    and fainter.

I cannot aid with my wringing fingers,
I can but rush to the surf and let it drench me and freeze upon me.
I search with the crowd, not one of the company is wash'd to us
    alive,
In the morning I help pick up the dead and lay them in rows in
    a barn.

Whitman wrote in a prose work, *Specimen Days*, that the *Mexico* was indeed the ship that he was referring to in "The Sleepers." It was not necessary for him to name the ship in the poem itself. All the major and minor New York City and Long Island newspapers had printed detailed stories of the wreck, and "The Sleepers" matched those accounts with such precision that there could be no doubt about the reference. When Whitman published "The Sleepers" in the 1850s, New Yorkers still had clear memories of the twin tragedies. They recalled the contrasts of joyous anticipation and suffering, of altruism and self-interest, of steadfastness and dereliction of duty, and of bravery and cowardice that characterized the *Bristol* and the *Mexico* disasters.

Over the next 170 years, however, the deaths of 215 passengers and crewmen by sudden drowning in the hold of the *Bristol*, and by agonizingly slow freezing on the deck of the *Mexico*, went from the biggest news story of the years 1836 and 1837 to oblivion. The role of Captain McKown of the *Bristol* as an inspiration for the maritime traditions of "women and children first" and "the captain is the last to leave his ship" disappeared from memory. The silver cup awarded to the brave rescuers of the *Mexico* was melted down. The saber of Captain Winslow was stolen and fenced. The Currier prints became arcane collectors' items. The record of dereliction of duty of the harbor pilots, the racism and cowardly self-interest of Captain Winslow, and the outrageous conduct of the body-robbers of the *Bristol* were all reduced to hazy, unwanted—and ultimately lost—memories.

Here, from the archived, microfilmed pages of long-disintegrated newspapers, the *New York Herald, New York American, New York Times* (unrelated to today's newspaper of the same name)*, Liverpool Albion,*

Liverpool Mercury, Dublin Evening Post, New York Sunday Morning News, New York Sun, New York Gazette and General Advertiser, Morning Courier and New York Express, Long Island Democrat, and *Hempstead Inquirer,* from maritime museum archives, from manuscripts, and books is the story of drowning and freezing—of water and ice—and of the victims Walt Whitman called:

> These waifs from the deep, cast high and dry
> Wash'd on America's shores.
> —Walt Whitman, "As Consequent, Etc.," *Leaves of Grass.*

"No one can do anything lasting for Long Island who has not lived there, who does not know and love its geology, topography, its waters and its people, who is unacquainted with its history as well as its immediate past."

—Robert Moses' remarks at a conference at Hofstra University in 1955.
Reprinted in the *Long Island Historical Journal* – Vol. 19, (Fall 2006/Spring 2007): 173.

The Two Ships – A Summary

	Bristol	*Mexico*
Type of vessel	Ship	Barque
Rigging	3 square-rigged masts	2 square-rigged masts, 1 fore-and-aft-rigged mizzen
Year built	1835	1825
Tons	450	279
Captain	Alexander McKown	Charles Winslow
Owner	Woodhull & Minturn	Samuel Broom
Cost of passage (Approx.)	First cabin £25 Second cabin £7 Steerage £5 (£5 is about $550 today)	£3 - 10s for steerage (one class). (About $400 today)
Provisions	Hot and cold meals of chicken, lamb, pork, wine, tea, and "stores of every description" in 1st class. One hot meal a day in 2nd. Cold meals in steerage.	A supply of salt meat and hard biscuits, which the passengers had to allocate among themselves.
Crew	17 Includes the captain and two mates.	12 Includes the captain, one mate, and a supercargo.
Passengers: First cabin Second cabin Steerage	10 49 68	-- -- 111
Total passengers	127	111
Deaths: Passengers Crew	95 5	108 7
Total deaths	100	115
Cause of death	100 by drowning	114 by freezing 1 by drowning
Cargo	250 tons of railroad iron, 50 tons of coal, dry goods, and crates.	200 tons of iron bars, 100 tons of coal, 200 tons of crates.
Sailed	October 15, 1836	October 23, 1836
Days at sea	35	71
Wrecked	November 21, 1836	January 2, 1837

Part I

The Wreck of the *Bristol*

Merchant Shipping in the 1830s

Church Sexton Thomas Shore paced back and forth in the cemetery behind the Old Sand Hole Methodist Church in Near Rockaway, Long Island. It was Wednesday, January 11, 1837, the day set for the dedication of the new Mariners Burying Ground, and for the mass burial of the victims of a recent shipwreck, the *Mexico*, off Hempstead Beach. Shore was supervising a team of volunteers as they extended the ends of a six-foot-deep, six-foot-wide trench. It was finally long enough, he hoped, to accommodate all the coffins arranged side by side.[2]

Shore had reason to be concerned that the trench would not be long enough. The Rev. William M. Carmichael, D.D., of Hempstead, who was scheduled to lead the funeral procession and deliver the graveside oration, had stopped by earlier on his way to Lott's barn, where the bodies were being prepared for burial. Carmichael informed the sexton that more frozen bodies had washed up on Hempstead Beach, making the latest count fifty-three. Moreover, if the *Mexico's* official papers were correct, there were potentially 115 victims in all—108 passengers and seven crew members—so more bodies could be expected. Whatever the count, the work had to be completed by 11 AM, when the procession was scheduled to arrive at the cemetery.

---

[2] Many local place names have changed over the years: *Hempstead Beach* is now Long Beach; *Near Rockaway*, which encompassed today's East Rockaway, Lynbrook, Rockville Centre, and Oceanside, has disappeared from use; *The Old Sand Hole Methodist Church* has been gone for over 100 years; *The Old Sand Hole Cemetery* (in today's Lynbrook) has been renamed the Rockville Cemetery. See the Appendix (page 259) for a brief discussion of some of the local place names used in this book.

Most of the burial details come from the unpublished diary of coffin-maker Peter T. Hewlett of East Rockaway.

The task was not easy. The hard-frozen ground had resisted the men's efforts for days, but they were determined to finish on time. Some of the more powerful workers wielded pickaxes to tear away at opposite ends of the trench and bite down through the first two feet of frozen soil. Others worked behind them, using shovels to remove the lower layers of softer sand down to the desired six-foot depth.

Close by, just barely within the paced-off dimensions of the Mariners Burying Ground, some other men were working. They were black men from the neighborhood, applying the finishing touches to a smaller grave, one intended for the three black sailors to be interred. For thousands of sea-miles these sailors had worked alongside the white sailors aboard the *Mexico*, they had taken their meals from the same pot, and they had slept side by side in hammocks in the forecastle. But when the only rescue boat came out, the captain did not allow them in. Now, in death, they could not even share the same trench with the whites.

At ten o'clock on this bitterly-cold morning, three hundred wagons, perhaps the largest procession of horse-drawn wagons ever seen on Long Island before or since, began a stately, three-mile march to the cemetery from what is today the village of Baldwin. In the lead were the clergy followed by the Committee of Arrangements. Next were the coffin wagons, carrying white bodies ahead and black bodies to the rear. The coffins of rough-sawn hemlock lay one to a wagon, each with a frozen body inside. Each, that is, but one. The exception was the coffin of Judy Pepper and her husband William, the parents of six young children who also had died aboard the *Mexico*. The couple's bodies had been pulled from the surf locked in each other's arms and encased in a six-inch-thick coat of ice. The two Peppers would now be buried together in that final embrace. Mourners followed at the rear, mostly local farmers and baymen along with a few friends and relatives of the deceased.

Once the procession reached the Burying Ground and the coffins were lowered into the two graves, the Rev. Carmichael began his oration. Tears had been flowing even before he began, not because the victims were known to the residents of Near Rockaway—indeed, the dead were strangers to most of the mourners—but because one-third of the coffins were small. They contained the bodies of children.

The Rev. Carmichael quoted from Matthew 8:25, "Lord save us, we perish," and declared that these deaths just a few yards off Long Island's South Shore were tragedies beyond any human understanding, that they were part of God's unknowable plan. However, these deaths were not the result solely of forces beyond men's control. They were the product of pernicious merchant shipping practices that favored the rich and the powerful, and assigned a lower value to the lives of emigrants and sailors—particularly when they were poor, or Irish, or Catholic, or black—than it did to the crates, barrels, iron bars, and coal in a ship's cargo hold.

The years 1836 and 1837 were very much in the "The Age of Sail," even though the American-built steamship *Savannah* had crossed the Atlantic seventeen years before, using a combination of sail and steam power. In 1836, Dr. Dionysius Lardner, Professor of Natural Philosophy at University College, London, presented calculations to prove that a steamboat could never cross the Atlantic under continuous steam power. His argument was that such a ship would need more coal than she could possibly carry. The good professor was proven wrong just two years later when two British ships, the *Sirius* and the *Great Western,* steamed all the way from Bristol, England to New York.

It would, however, take more than these minor successes with steam power to change the mind of the vast majority American shipowners who disliked the high risks and questionable economics of transatlantic steaming. They not only saw little future for ocean-going steamships, they believed that sail-power's best days were yet to come. Indeed, when the three-masted tall ships *Bristol* and *Mexico* set sail on their fateful voyages in the autumn of 1836, the U.S. was the builder of the best sailing ships in the world, and better ones *were* yet to come.

The nation had come a long way since 1607, when its shipbuilding industry got a tenuous start. Some early settlers in Maine were so anxious to return home to England that they constructed the first American-built ship, the clunky, barely seaworthy *Virginia*. During the Revolutionary War, American shipbuilding received wide notice when the British found reason to curse at—and admire—the patriots' ability to outrun enemy frigates, owing to the lightness and speed of their colonial schooners. These two- and three-masted, lightly-crewed ships dispensed completely with the square rig in favor of fore-and-aft schooner rigs, and they were the fastest ships afloat.

After the Revolution it became America's desire, positioned as it was between the Atlantic and the Pacific, and newly freed from British dominion, to sail not only fast but far—to China and beyond. Speed became important for trips around the Horn because of the vast distances involved, and also across the North Atlantic where a few extra knots allowed ships to outrun a storm. The American clipper ships of the 1810s, which were named for their ability to "clip it along" at a rapid rate, suited this purpose well. The poet John Dryden used the old English verb "clip" in this way and may have inspired the name "clipper," in his poem about the British Royal Navy:

Have you not seen, when, whistled from the fist,
Some falcon stoops at what her eye designed,
And, with her eagerness the quarry missed,
Straight flies at check, and clips it down the wind.

—Dryden, *In thriving arts long time had Holland grown.*

In the War of 1812, American clippers continually eluded the British naval blockade and raided British commercial shipping, even brazenly seizing prizes in the English Channel. Because shipyards in the city of Baltimore furnished the largest clipper fleet during the war—fifty-eight vessels—any fast, narrow, American vessel with a sharp prow became know as a "Baltimore clipper," regardless of where it was built.

Perversely, the same design characteristics that served America so well in the War of 1812 and on trips around the Horn of South America also lent themselves to the slave trade. In the awful logic of the slavers, speed was necessary to get their perishable "black ivory" to market. Even after Congress banned the importation of slaves in 1808, American clippers continued to supply slaves to the Caribbean for another dozen years until 1820, when U.S. law declared international slave trading to be *piracy*, punishable by death. The purchase and sale of slaves and their children already in the U.S. remained legal in some states until the Civil War.

After the international slave trade was banned, American shipowners realized that they could use the speed and reliability of their clipper ships to gain a competitive advantage in transporting cargo and passengers across the Atlantic, even if it meant sacrificing capacity. These progressive owners developed the *packet lines,* using ships based on the Baltimore clipper. The innovation of the packet lines was not so much in their vessels' construction and rigging as it was in their use. They sailed regularly between specific ports, *on a schedule.* Later, as competition mounted, there was also a requirement for flat-out speed.

The first packet line was the Black Ball Line out of New York, which advertised:

In order to furnish frequent and regular conveyance of GOODS
and PASSENGERS the subscribers have undertaken to establish
a line of vessels between NEW YORK and LIVERPOOL, to sail
from each place on a certain day in every month of the year.

—*New York Commercial Advertiser*, October 24, 1817.

Soon the Black Ball Line had two sailings from New York to Liverpool, on the first and sixteenth of every month. The owners posted notices in the newspapers promising "a regular succession of vessels, which will positively sail, full or not full." New York merchants saw proof that the Black Ball Line's owners were determined to keep to their posted schedules when, in January 1818, the 427-ton merchantman *James Monroe* set sail in a snowstorm from her dock on South Street. She had only eight passengers—despite accommodations for twenty-eight—and in her hold were 1,500 barrels of apples, 860 barrels of flour, 200 barrels of potash, 85 bales of cotton and wool, and a mail pouch—despite room for a thousand more barrels. Any other ship of the day would have waited for the weather to improve and for the ship's hold to be filled, but the *James Monroe* sailed on schedule, casting her lines when the stroke of ten o'clock rang from St. Paul's church steeple in downtown Manhattan.

Most packets of the 1830s were in the mold of the Baltimore clippers, but in the 1850s and 1860s, they evolved into the magnificent, sharp-hulled, massively-canvassed clippers of the Gold Rush and the China Trade. This was an era that produced such awe-inspiring vessels as the American-built *Flying Cloud* and the British-built *Cutty Sark*. But the earlier clippers of the 1830s also looked impressively fast. And indeed they were fast, with raked-to-stern masts, fore-and-aft rigging, and square topsails. They also were strong-hulled and built for safety. These ships earned America an unparalleled international reputation, even though there were probably never more than fifty such clippers afloat, a small fraction of the American deep-water tonnage of that day.

Between 1820 and 1860, American shipbuilding reigned supreme. Northern forests provided pine masts and oak planks, while the southern states provided live-oak knee timbers. So many ships were built that eastern forests were virtually depleted of high-quality trees. America also led in navigation. Nathaniel Bowditch of Salem, Massachusetts, a self-educated mathematical genius, published his *Practical Navigator* in 1802. His book not only revealed eight thousand errors in the standard British book on navigation, but it remains, after seventy-five editions, the standard American work, even into the twenty-first century.

The cumulative impression of all this shipbuilding and navigation excellence led, in 1837, to a British Parliamentary committee report stating:

> [T]he American ships frequenting the ports of England are stated by several witnesses to be superior to those of a similar class among the ships of Great Britain, the commanders and officers being generally considered to be more competent as seamen and navigators and more uniformly persons of education than the commanders and officers of British ships of a similar size and class trading from England to America.
>
> —— Paine, Ralph D. *The Old Merchant Marine* (1919).

American-built vessels, especially the packets, were also considered to be the safest afloat. Between 1824 and 1844, only six out of one hundred thousand passengers sailing on the New York packets lost their lives in accidents. What is even more remarkable about this record is that the packets sailed twelve months a year, in all kinds of weather.

Sadly, almost all of the praise for American ships was based on the performance of the packets. It did not apply to the vessels that are the subjects of this book, the *Bristol* and the *Mexico*, or ships like them. These second-tier merchant ships attracted cargo and passengers that did not require the speed or firm scheduling of the packets, along with their higher prices. To keep costs down and prices low, most shipowners operated slower, bulkier vessels that could carry far more weight and volume of cargo for their tonnage and crew-size than did the faster, narrower clippers. These second-tier ships got little attention, but they were the workhorses of the Atlantic and handled over ninety percent of the cargo shipped.

Demand for vessels such as the *Bristol* and the *Mexico* was huge. While the number of packets increased from 36 vessels in 1830 to only 48 in 1840, New York area shipbuilders launched 98 ships and barques, 94 brigs, and 497 schooners in the year 1834 alone. Unlike the packets, which contained specifically-designed passenger quarters, these merchant vessels were primarily designed as cargo carriers, with little if any allowance for the safety and comfort of large numbers of passengers. Indeed, the twelve-year-old *Mexico* should never have carried more than half-a-dozen passengers and the newer, larger *Bristol* perhaps twenty. Yet each of these vessels carried more than one hundred people across the North Atlantic on what were essentially cargo ships. To understand the imprudence of this, one has only to imagine putting one hundred men, women, and children on an oil tanker or container ship today. It took a series of disasters such as the *Mexico* and the *Bristol* shipwrecks for maritime laws to be substantially changed to prevent such tragedies.

In contrast to the stellar safety record of the packets, the dismal record of merchant cargo vessels in the 1830s shows how dangerous those ships were. Shipwrecks were reported in the *Liverpool Mercury* and the *New York Sun* almost every week. Sometimes there were five or six in a single week. Bad weather was usually the direct cause, but badly-maintained ships and poorly trained captains and officers were often the underlying problem.

The 279-ton barque *Mexico* was built in Falmouth, Massachusetts, and was a year or two past the mid-point of the usual twenty-year lifespan of a square-rigged vessel. The 450-ton ship *Bristol* was built in New York, and was almost new. She was about to complete her third voyage to England. The *Mexico* and the *Bristol* were typical ocean-going merchant vessels of the

18

1830s, but the two ships were far from being large vessels. The packets, for example, were twice the tonnage of the *Bristol* or the *Mexico*, and military ships were even larger.

While the term *ship* has always applied in general to any large vessel regardless of design, to "real salts" of the 1830s, a *ship* had exactly three masts, all square-rigged. The *Bristol* was a ship. The *Mexico*, on the other hand, had her two forward masts square-rigged like the *Bristol*, but her mizzenmast (near the stern) was rigged fore-and-aft. The *Mexico* was a barque. Barques and ships could sail from New York to Liverpool in three to four weeks, helped by the prevailing westerly winds, and make the return trip in four to five weeks. This was not as fast as the packets, which cut at least a week off the trip in both directions, but demand for these slower ships was high, and business was good.

Richard Dana's *Alert*, a 398-ton merchant ship.
Three square-rigged masts, similar to the *Bristol*.

Oil painting by Sidney Chase.

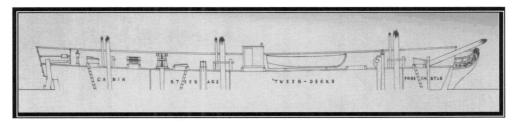

Hull Cross-Section of the *Alert*
From Richard Dana's *Two Years before the Mast*.
The ship *Alert* was one of the two vessels Dana sailed on from Boston to California and back in 1834-5. A cookhouse and ship's boat are on deck. There are steep ladders leading below.

Barque Similar to the *Mexico*
Note the square-rigged foremast and main, and fore-and-aft-rigged mizzen.
Two double-stacked ship's boats are on deck, amidships,
and a small cookhouse is just abaft of the boats.
Anonymous

The Owners of the *Bristol*

**Robert Bowne Minturn,
Owner of the *Bristol***

www.centralparkhistory.com

In the 1830s, American entrepreneurs were actively building new and exciting maritime businesses such as coastal steamboat lines and ocean-crossing packet lines. Some of these shipowners amassed incredible wealth, while others barely got by. The owners of the *Bristol* and the owner of the *Mexico* were New York City merchant shippers, but they remained worlds apart. Samuel Broom (no dates known) was a minor player. He was a confectionery merchant, newly arrived from Philadelphia, and the owner of a single ship, the *Mexico*. There is no record of him as a shipowner after the destruction of the *Mexico*. By contrast, Robert Bowne Minturn (1805-1866), a principal owner of the *Bristol*, was a partner in a huge shipping conglomerate. Despite the wreck of his ship, he continued acquiring a large fortune and went on to become a respected industry leader and benefactor.

In 1836, the year when the *Bristol* was wrecked, Robert Minturn was a partner in Grinnell, Minturn & Company, located at 134 Front Street. That partnership operated several top-of–the-line packet ships under the unimaginative name, The Line of Packets. Minturn was also a partner in a smaller firm, Woodhull & Minturn, the direct owner of the *Bristol*, one of the latest ships to be built specifically for that company. Woodhull & Minturn's offices were at 89 South Street, which today is the address of the South Street Seaport Café, at Pier 17. The *Bristol's* berth was located a few blocks north, at the foot of Dover Street, just south of where the Brooklyn Bridge is today.

Sailing Notices for the *Bristol* and "The Line of Packets"
—Liverpool Mercury, September 30, 1836

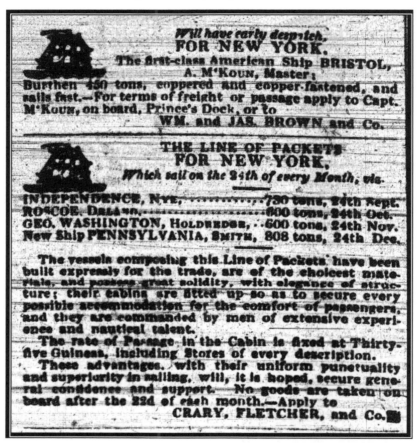

Bristol, A. M'Koun, master – 450 tons

Independence, Nye – 730 tons, 24th Sept.
Roscoe, Delano – 600 tons, 24th Oct.
George Washington, Holdredge – 600 tons, 24th Nov.
Pennsylvania, Smith – 808 tons, 24th Dec.

On September 30, 1836, a notice appeared in the *Liverpool Mercury* newspaper for "The first-class American Ship *Bristol*." Just below that advertisement was another one for "The Line of Packets." Agents in Liverpool were soliciting passengers and freight for the vessels' return trips to New York. Although Robert Minturn had significant partnership interests in both the *Bristol* and The Line of Packets, his agents were careful to market them separately. The *Bristol's* advertisement doesn't even identify the owner or the line—only the passenger/freight broker, Wm. and Jas. Brown and Co. Despite the two listings' adjacency in the sailing notice, the difference in the service offered was significant. The Line of Packets provided a service level considerably higher than that of the *Bristol*, and the owners wanted to avoid any confusion in the minds of prospective customers.

- The four packets in the sailing notice averaged 700 tons—250 tons larger than the *Bristol's* 450 tons.

- The packets sailed on a fixed schedule from Liverpool— the 24th of each month. The *Bristol* had no fixed schedule, and sailed at the convenience of her captain and owners.

- The packets emphasized their "elegance of structure," and offered "every possible accommodation for the comfort of passengers." The *Bristol* merely advertised "passage."

- The packets' target customers were well-to-do cabin passengers, with a fixed price of £35, considerably above the *Bristol's* primary customers—second cabin and steerage—at about £7 and £5 respectively.[3]

- The packet lines had a shipping broker with a sales office in Liverpool. The *Bristol's* broker directed all inquiries for passage or freight to the ship's captain (using a variant spelling on McKown) down at the Prince's Dock.

The Bristol's owner (Woodhull & Minturn) and The Line of Packets' owner (Grinnell, Minturn & Company) were descended from a transatlantic shipping business named Fish and Grinnell. That firm was founded in 1815 when Joseph Grinnell (1789-1885), a twenty-six-year-old merchant from New Bedford, Massachusetts, realized that New York City was fast

---

[3] The website, Measuringworth.org <http://www.measuringworth.com/exchange/>, provides £/$ conversions for historical periods. For example, one pound (£1) in 1836 = $113.11 in 2007, the latest period given. As a rule of thumb, one can add two zeros to the number of £'s in 1836 to get the dollars today.

becoming the merchant shipping capital not only of the United States, but of the world. Instead of fighting the highly competitive New York shippers from far off New Bedford, he moved to New York. Once there, he joined up with Thaddeus Phelps and a man with the improbable name of Preserved Fish, to form the firm of Fish and Grinnell. [4]

The new company quickly recognized that the future of transatlantic shipping lay with speedy packet lines making regularly scheduled runs to Liverpool. They saw that this arrangement was bringing great profits to the previously established Black Ball Line, and they decided to compete head to head. Like many radically new businesses, those who met a growing need, and got in early, made fortunes. That is what Fish and Grinnell did, even if they started out fourth in the race.

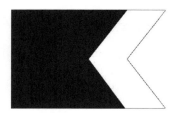

Blue Swallowtail – The House Flag of Grinnell, Minturn & Company
FOTW *Flags Of The World*
http://flagspot.net/flags/

Fish and Grinnell's first line of monthly packets was its Blue Swallowtail Line (1822-1880). It derived its name from its distinctive blue and white swallow-tailed "house flag." The company also became known as the "Fourth Line of Liverpool Packets." So successful was the firm that only one year later they built and purchased additional vessels and started a New York-to-London line, the Red Swallowtail Line (1823-1880). In 1825, Preserved Fish retired—thus depriving New Yorkers of numerous belly laughs at the sound of his name. Joseph Grinnell's brothers Henry and Moses then joined the firm, and it was renamed Fish, Grinnell & Co. In 1829, Joseph Grinnell retired. He was already a wealthy man at thirty-nine.

The life of Robert Bowne Minturn appears at first glance to be a classic rags-to-riches story, but family money and family connections underlay his success. Still, he was a self-starter. Leaving school at fourteen when his father died, Minturn became a counting-house clerk for a small New York City shipper. He proved to be so valuable to the owner that he was made a partner at age twenty. His sister's marriage into the Grinnell family served as an entrée to the upper echelons of that family's business. Minturn

---

[4] The name, Preserved, refers to being "preserved from sin." The name is pronounced with three syllables. The family name, Fish, is well-known in New York for producing a governor, a senator, congressmen, and diplomats.

joined Fish, Grinnell & Co. and, in 1832, he became a partner in the firm. The company was renamed Grinnell, Minturn & Company.

Robert Minturn and the Grinnell brothers not only built an immensely profitable merchant shipping firm, they were forward thinkers as well. For example, they acquired the newly-built *Flying Cloud*, America's greatest clipper ship, and one of the fastest clipper ships ever launched. At 1,782 tons, she was also the largest merchant sailing ship then afloat. The family succeeded as good citizens as well. Both Joseph Grinnell and Moses Hicks Grinnell became congressmen from New York. Moses also was the New York City Commissioner of Charities. Henry Grinnell financed several expeditions, including two in search of the missing arctic explorer, Sir John Franklin. He was also an advocate for the interests of sailors. Joseph Grinnell was the first president of the American Geographical Society and a founder of St. Luke's Hospital. Robert Minturn became an advocate for emigrant rights and helped advance a fresh idea of his wife, Anna Mary Wendell, to create a central park in New York City. Moses Grinnell served as a member of the original Central Park Commission.

"Packet Row" on South Street – 1828
From John and Alice Durant's
Pictorial History of Ships on the High Seas and Inland Waters (1953)

Grinnell, Minturn & Company was justifiably proud of its fleet's speed records in the mid 1830s. Their Swallowtail Line of Packets had record-breaking and near-record-breaking transatlantic times each month for a twelve-month period in 1835-36. The firm prominently displayed these crossing times in the Liverpool and New York newspapers. The fastest crossing eastbound to Liverpool was made by the *Independence*, which left New York on April 8, 1836, and completed her voyage to Liverpool in the spectacular time of fourteen-and-a-half days. The average for the line was under three weeks. For the same period, their competitor, the Black Ball Line, had average times one day longer to Liverpool, and two days longer to New York. Grinnell, Minturn & Company wanted to keep their lead.

Grinnell, Minturn & Co.'s
Swallowtail Line of Packets Transatlantic Times
Liverpool Albion, 1836

Eastbound, New York-to-Liverpool

Ship	Left New York	Days in Passage
Geo. Washington	Oct. 8	18
Napoleon	Nov. 10	20
Independence	Dec. 9	20
Roscoe	Jan. 10	17
Geo. Washington	Feb. 9	22
Napoleon	March 9	18
Independence	April 8	14 ½
Roscoe	May 9	26
Geo. Washington	June 8	17
Pennsylvania	July 8	21
Independence	Aug. 8	22
Roscoe	Sept. 9	19
Average Crossing		**20**

Westbound, Liverpool-to-New York

Ship	Left Liverpool	Days in Passage
Roscoe	Oct. 25	31
Geo. Washington	Nov. 25	36
Napoleon	Dec. 24	42
Independence	Feb. 5	23
Roscoe	Feb. 26	32
Geo. Washington	March 28	33
Napoleon	April 30	28
Independence	May 24	21
Roscoe	June 27	36
Geo. Washington	July 24	30
Pennsylvania	Aug. 24	28
Independence	Sept. 26	36
Average Crossing		**33**

For competitive reasons, the firm could not allow a slower ship, even a relatively new one such as the *Bristol*, to jeopardize its industry-leading North Atlantic crossing times, so the *Bristol* was placed under a separate partnership—Woodhull, Minturn & Company. The tactic of concealing underperformers has stood the test of time, and is no stranger to today's mutual funds, airlines, government bureaucracies, auto companies, unions, and school districts. Concealing an underperformer was one thing, but witnessing a huge loss of life was another matter. Thus, after the wreck of the *Bristol*, Woodhull, Minturn & Company transformed itself into a high-quality packet line, so that it could offer a safer mode of freight transport and passenger travel. The firm prospered and eventually merged into Grinnell, Minturn & Company.

However, in October 1836, when the *Bristol* set sail on her final voyage, the firm of Woodhull, Minturn & Company was still blind to the risk of placing one hundred passengers below decks on a slow-moving cargo ship. With steep exit ladders, no life jackets, and an insufficient number of lifeboats aboard, it was simply a matter of time before a calamity occurred on one of its cargo ships. And so the story of the wreck of the *Bristol* begins, innocently enough, and with high spirits, at the Prince's Dock in Liverpool, England.

Grinnell, Minturn & Company's Cape-Horner Clipper, the *Flying Cloud*, in 1851.

Built by Donald McKay of East Boston, Massachusetts, and sold to Grinnell, Minturn & Company, of New York, the Cape-Horner *Flying Cloud* was one of the fastest—if not the fastest—clipper ships ever launched. She completed the New-York-to-San-Francisco run in a record 89 days. For a short time, she was the largest merchant sailing ship afloat, at 1,782 tons.

Liverpool, October 1836

On Sunday morning, October 15, 1836, hundreds of tall, graceful, one-, two-, and three-masted wooden ships were tied up at the Prince's Dock in Liverpool. Among them were the American ships *Bristol* and *Mexico*, by coincidence berthed together. It was late in the year for a North Atlantic crossing, especially with over one hundred passengers scheduled to sail aboard each of the two ships; but at least the cool, clear, autumn weather was promising. The almost-new, 450-ton *Bristol* was preparing to leave that very day on the outgoing tide of the Mersey River for the month-long return leg of this, her third voyage out of her home port of New York. The *Mexico*, also out of New York, was smaller, at 279 tons, and ten years older, but she had a coppered and copper-fastened bottom and at least *looked* sea-worthy, even though she was not. The barque, owned by Samuel Broom of New York, was also bound for New York Harbor, about a week after the *Bristol*.

Although the two ships lay close together at the Prince's Dock, their berths back home in New York were at opposite ends of the maritime pecking-order. The *Bristol's* berth was a prime, company-owned East River pier, whereas the *Mexico* tied up at rented space on the North River (as the lower Hudson was then called), alongside riverboats, steam tugs, transient ships, and coastal sloops.

It was the custom for American captains to dine together when berthed in foreign ports, so it is likely that Captain Alexander McKown of the *Bristol* and Captain Charles Winslow of the *Mexico* did so as a courtesy to each other and to discuss the practical issues of their late-season return voyages to New York. Status was important, so McKown, with the larger ship, more polished crew, and more distinguished ownership, would have sent his cabin boy over to invite Winslow to dinner ashore. Captains never entertained one another at their captains' tables because cooking-fires were prohibited at the Prince's Dock. Hundreds of wooden ships, all crowded together, created a potential tinderbox.

Captains McKown and Winslow surely had much to discuss: mutual acquaintances, foreign ports, technically complex square-riggers, and problems related to the onset of the winter storm season. Indeed, winter changed every calculation for a ship's captain. In early summer, a westbound voyage to New York could be a one-month pleasure cruise. In winter, it could be two months of constant beating into the wind and waves. Some captains and shipowners even refused to sail this late in the year. As a result, dozens of ships at the Prince's Dock were being prepared for over-wintering at Liverpool.

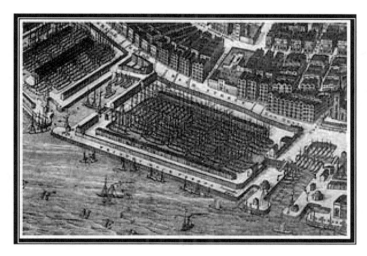

The Prince's Dock, Liverpool

1840s

Merseyside Maritime Museum Research Library

Because Winslow was a Philadelphian newly based out of New York, he may have wanted to discuss certain sailing issues with McKown, an experienced New York captain. There was, for example, the final approach into the New York Bight to consider. The Bight was the dangerously narrowing "V" of ocean between the coast of New Jersey and the South Shore of Long Island. There were also shoals, currents, and counter-currents near the harbor entrance to be concerned about.

For the *Bristol*, the time for planning was over. Captain McKown had his entire sixteen-man crew on deck before sunrise, tending to the sails and rigging. As McKown later testified at an official inquiry, the ship was fully ready to sail.

> On the fifteenth day of October last, having on board a cargo consisting of railroad iron, wheat, steel, copper, hardware and other merchandise, bound for the port of New York; that said vessel [the *Bristol*] was then tight-staunch, and strong, as well above and below;

well manned, and victualled, tackled, and appareled; fit for merchant service, and had her cargo properly stowed and secured.

— Pennington, Wm., Hormblower, Jos. C., Darcy, John S., and Gifford, Archer. *A Statement of the Facts and Circumstances Relative to the Operation of the Pilot Laws of New York (1840).*

Most of the *Bristol's* passengers had arrived the day before, and had spent the night aboard ship. This allowed them time to stow their baggage, set up their sleeping areas, familiarize themselves with the vessel, and settle in for the long voyage ahead. As late-arriving emigrants scurried up the gangway that morning, they were greeted by the sound of dancing feet and music from below decks. As was true for almost every emigrant ship to leave Liverpool, lively melodies played on bagpipes, violins, flutes, or hornpipes, signaled to all that this was a time of great excitement and joy.[5]

A commotion arose as a large carriage pulled up at dockside, loaded with passengers and their numerous trunks. As the fashionably-dressed occupants descended from the vehicle and approached the ship, a steward and two servant girls rushed down the gangway to assist them. The leader of the group was a sixty-five-year-old woman, Mrs. Frances Hogan, the widow of Michael Hogan, Esq., the former American consul to Chile.

Mrs. Hogan might have been expected to return to New York on one of the faster packet ships, but the *Bristol* better fit her needs. She had lived on four different continents, and had sailed most of the oceans of the world. She and her husband had been merchant shippers before their retirement, and she "knew the ropes." To her, a few extra days at sea were something to be enjoyed. There was also a more practical reason. The lower price of a first-cabin ticket on the *Bristol*, as compared to the packets, undoubtedly influenced her choice. Mrs. Hogan's wealth had been considerably diminished from the fabulous levels of earlier years.

This world traveler also knew how to judge sailing ships. After all, she and her husband had owned several merchant ships, each one solidly built. The *Bristol's* recent construction, highly regarded captain, spacious staterooms, and first-class service undoubtedly attracted her. These advantages were especially important to her because she had several members of her family along on this voyage: her daughters Frances (Fanny) Hogan and Sophia Donnelly, her son-in-law Arthur Donnelly, and the Donnellys' two children. She had even arranged for a nurse to accompany the children on this trip. As the most-traveled individual of this well-traveled

---

[5] *The London Illustrated News* of July 6, 1850, provides an excellent account of affairs at the Prince's Dock in the mid 1800s.

family group, Frances Hogan undoubtedly had a strong sense of responsibility for their welfare. Six weeks into the voyage, when the lives of all aboard the ship were threatened, Mrs. Hogan's decisions would help save all but one of her family.

Frances Hogan was born in 1771, in Bombay, India. Her father was an English merchant and sea captain based there, and her mother was a relatively dark-skinned Indian Parsee or Portuguese—accounts differ. Years later, after moving to New York, Frances would be referred to as a "dark Indian princess." When she was quite young, her parents sent her to England, on the first of her many ocean voyages, to receive "the best English education." On her return to Bombay as a teenager, she met a dashing, Irish-born merchant shipper, Michael Hogan, six years her senior. Hogan's humble, non-English origins proved to be no barrier to courting Frances, and they were married as soon as she reached the age of eighteen. Thus began the couple's incredible life's journey, one that could fill a book. In fact it has. A descendant, Michael Stykes, has written *Captain Hogan—Sailor, Merchant, Diplomat on Six Continents*, a volume about the lives of Michael and Frances Hogan.

Captain Michael Hogan
Michael H. Stykes,
Captain Hogan

The Hogans' first big step after their marriage was to build a ship, in Calcutta—the three-masted, 654-ton *Marquis Cornwallis*—using borrowed money. In 1792, Frances and Michael sailed the *Cornwallis* to London, carrying East Indian products to market. Frances proved that she was an intrepid sailor when she gave birth to their first child, William, just days after the completion of the nearly four-month voyage.

Leaving Frances and the baby in London, Michael continued in the business of shipping trade-goods between England, India, and the Far East, but he was not satisfied with his modest profits, which were not at all commensurate with his long absences and the risks. Sadly, the methods Michael Hogan used to improve his situation were immoral. The best that can be said about his activities in the 1790s and early 1800s is that most of what he did was within the law. But that does not quite tell the story, because he simply bribed the necessary officials as needed. Various historians have called Michael Hogan "notorious," "infamous," "duplicitous," "a hypocrite," "a bare-faced smuggler," and a "practitioner of tricks and deceits."

In 1795, on the first of many voyages into the darkest corners of merchant shipping, Michael Hogan filled unused space in the cargo hold of the *Marquis Cornwallis* by transporting 241 Irish prisoners to exile in Australia. Many of these men and women were common criminals, but as many as one hundred of them were radical-separatist "Irish Defenders." Just before the ship set sail from Cork, an Irish-born member of the military guard refused to be involved in the transport of men he believed were Irish patriots. He asked to be relieved of duty. Hogan, who was born in Ireland's County Clare, and thus might have been expected to be lenient, ordered that the soldier be given one hundred fifty lashes with a knotted rope.

After a month at sea, word reached Captain Hogan that there was a mutinous plot among the prisoners—and that it involved some Irish soldiers. He struck quickly, personally leading the charge below decks with his pistol blazing and his whip flying. When the smoke cleared, seven men lay dead. Another thirty-five prisoners lay wounded, flayed, and bleeding on the prison-deck. Hogan's shameful conduct knew no bounds. A year into the same voyage, a female prisoner gave birth to a baby girl. When the woman reached Australia, she listed the child's name as Mary Hogan on birth documents, and named Michael Hogan as the father.

Michael Hogan's two-year, round-trip voyage to Australia was far less profitable than he had anticipated. He needed to find a different business-model. On returning to London, he presented his plan to Frances, one that would mean moving to yet another continent, Africa, and which would require even lower morals than whipping and shooting his fellow Irishmen. He promised Frances that this time they would have more time together, and earn huge profits—from slave trading out of Cape Town. And so, in 1798, the Hogans, their five-year-old son William, and two-year-old daughter Fanny sailed to their new home on the tip of Africa.

Although slave trading was an old, established business, Michael Hogan had discovered a fresh source of "supply," one that he had come across on his trips around the Cape to India. It was Mozambique. From there he began to transport men and women to Cape Town by the hundreds, for sale to Cape farmers and for transshipment to Brazil. Britain had declared slavery illegal in the home country in the early 1790s. However, it did not prohibit the international slave trade until 1808, so Hogan's business was technically "legal."

Frances Hogan's European-born neighbors in Cape Town had ambiguous feelings toward her. They accepted her into their social circle, yet referred to her as "a woman of color." Frances, despite the darkness of her own skin, was able to discriminate against people darker than she, and use them to her advantage. If her Irish husband had no qualms about using a knotted rope on Irish prisoners, Frances had none about personally owning dozens of "colored" slaves. In an 1800 census, the Hogans listed thirty-one slaves as their personal property, along with a fine house, and several horses and oxen. This was an extraordinary number of slaves for people living in a city. One possible explanation is that Frances took on the task of grooming handpicked slaves for sale as trained household servants.

By 1804, when Michael Hogan was thirty-eight and Frances thirty-two, they were wealthy beyond their wildest dreams. They had accumulated the equivalent of six million dollars today by buying and selling human beings. Perhaps they tired of the awful business; but more likely, they worried about having narrowly escaped various bribery and other charges in Cape Town—charges that could easily be reinstated. In any event, they decided to move to, of all places, New York City.

When they got to New York, the Hogans' blood-stained slate was wiped clean. As is still the case in the "Big Apple," money counted more than anything, and past misdeeds were ignored. The Hogans built a mansion on an elegant estate that extended from 119th Street to 125th Street between Amsterdam Avenue and the Hudson River. Today, this includes much of what is now Riverside Park, Riverside Church, Grant's Tomb, Union Theological Seminary, and Columbia's Teachers College. Michael called the estate Claremont, a name derived from his birthplace in County Clare. So eager were the Hogans to achieve acceptance among wealthy, Protestant, New Yorkers that they abandoned their Roman Catholic origins and became Episcopalians. They even imported a two-horse curricle (carriage) from England.

The leading citizens of New York City paid lavish attention to the Hogans—and even more attention to their riches. The Hogans had rarely before invested in the business ventures of others; indeed, they had been highly successful entrepreneurs, albeit in the slave trade. Their new American "friends" persuaded them to put large amounts of money into shipping and land-purchase schemes, always promoted by New York's "best" people. The Hogans were gulled, snookered, bamboozled, and deceived. Within ten years, they were stripped of all but a fraction of the enormous wealth they had brought from Cape Town. They even lost the Claremont estate. The only thing Michael Hogan got from his powerful New York City connections was an appointment as U.S. Consul in remote Valparaiso, Chile. Considering how the Hogans had acquired their riches in the first place, it is difficult to be sympathetic.

33

The Hogans received three minor legacies from their friends in New York. The first was the name Claremont Avenue, in Manhattan, which still runs through the heart of what once was the Hogans' estate. They also had a village in upstate New York, Hogansburg, named after them—a reminder of the various, failed, land schemes they entered into near there. Finally, another upstate village, Bombay, got its name in recognition of Frances' birthplace in India. These names, which still exist today, recall the sad and remarkable history of the merchant shippers and slavers, Michael and Frances Hogan.

When Michael died in 1833, Frances began the difficult process of liquidating their far-flung holdings in places as distant as Australia and Africa. The autumn of 1836 found her in Liverpool, returning to New York City from one of these asset-gathering trips, accompanied by her two daughters, her son-in-law, her two granddaughters, and Vinissa.

Vinissa—no last name is recorded—had once been Frances Hogan's personal slave and the nursemaid to her children. She had been purchased more than thirty years before in Cape Town. In 1804, on the eve of the Hogans' permanent departure from Cape Town to New York, Frances had given Vinissa a choice: sign an indenture binding herself to the Hogan family for the next fourteen years as a freed "apprentice," or be sold to a new master in Cape Town. To a young African woman, the fear of being brutalized by a new master was quite real. There was effectively no choice for Vinissa. She affixed her "X" to the agreement. Now, more than three decades later, Vinissa was aboard the *Bristol*, employed by Mrs. Hogan as a nursemaid to her granddaughters.

Three other people occupied private staterooms in the *Bristol's* first cabin, rounding out the first-cabin passenger list at ten. One was a lawyer, Francis Burtsall, Esq., whose city or even country of residence is not known. The other two were businessmen, James Hale Charlton and Edward Ash Charlton. They were originally from Bristol, England, but now resided in Charleston, South Carolina. The Carolinas were still a large supplier to Britain of rice, cotton, and live oak timbers for shipbuilding, so these men may have been involved in one of those businesses.

Second cabin on the *Bristol* had none of the luxuries of first cabin. Instead of staterooms there were double-decked berths separated by partitions. This arrangement at least provided a reasonable amount of privacy for families and for women traveling alone. In the center of the second-cabin space, tables and benches were fastened to the deck as a place for relaxation and for taking meals. There was also a separate storage space for trunks. Spartan as this was, it was superior to steerage, with its long rows of dormitory-style bunks running the length of the deck, and with trunks stacked in the middle.

The *Bristol's* first cabin, second cabin, and steerage reflected the economic class separations of early nineteenth-century England, Ireland, Scotland, Wales, and the United States. Well-off passengers such as the Hogans, the Donnellys, Mr. Burtsall, and James and Edward Charlton, were not upper-class. If they were, they would be on a packet, and not aboard a second-tier vessel such as this; but they still stood apart on the *Bristol*. Tradespeople and medical doctors occupied second cabin. Farmhands and laborers traveled in steerage.

The tailors, shoemakers, doctors, and dressmakers in the *Bristol's* second cabin reflected the middle class of Great Britain and Ireland, small as that group was. In 1836, a physician's status was not much above a barber. At least one of the doctors was aboard to satisfy the newly-passed *British Passengers Act of 1835*. That legislation required vessels with more than one hundred passengers to have a doctor aboard to serve the medical needs of the passengers, and the *Bristol* had 127 passengers. It is possible that the shipowner, Woodhull & Minturn, provided a higher level of service than the law required. Indeed, there is evidence that the *Bristol's* owners were not just interested in maximizing profits, as so many other shipowners were. For example, the ship sailed from Liverpool with only half the maximum number of passengers she could legally have carried based on her tonnage, thus allowing relatively spacious accommodations for all.

Even so, conditions aboard the *Bristol*, especially in second cabin and steerage, were basic at best. The claustrophobic spaces of second cabin and steerage were filled with the stench of unwashed bodies—and smells even worse than that—creating conditions difficult to imagine today. The passenger areas were lighted by thirteen whale-oil lamps and by the small amount of natural light that shone through thick, glass "bull's-eyes" built into the ship's deck and sides. The only well-lit and ventilated areas below decks were the windowed stern cabins occupied by the first-cabin passengers, the captain, and the two ship's officers.

First-cabin passengers on the *Bristol* had an important amenity for their exclusive use—a deck cabin situated just aft of the mizzenmast. It was called the round-house, because one could walk completely 'round the outside of it. Although this strongly constructed cabin was built to withstand the force of waves washing over the deck, it would later fail when severely tested. If not for the round-house, however, most of the first-cabin passengers would have drowned in the wreck of the *Bristol*.

The round-house had glazed ports, a skylight, benches, and a table. First-cabin passengers could take their meals and afternoon tea there if they wished. Steerage passengers were not only denied access to the round-house, they could not even walk freely about the deck. A white line was drawn across the deck, amidships, rail to rail. First-cabin and second-cabin passengers could cross this line to the steerage side, but steerage passengers could not cross to the cabin side.

All of the *Bristol's* first-cabin passengers, even the Donnelly children, had been on long ocean voyages before. However, few of the second-cabin or steerage passengers—the majority of whom were women and children—had made journeys beyond their just-completed day-sails to Liverpool. These short trips were made on the many paddlewheel steamboats that shuttled people and freight from Dublin, Belfast, Holyhead, and Dumfries to Liverpool. For most of these people this was the trip of a lifetime, across the vast North Atlantic Ocean, to a new life in a new land.

After settling themselves in the dimly-lit space that would confine them for the next month or so, passengers came up on deck to watch the sailors and dockworkers complete final preparations as the *Bristol* was readied for departure from the Prince's Dock. Liverpool's Prince's Dock was constructed in 1821 to handle the tremendous increase in shipping to and from North America. The dock had a fortress-like appearance, surrounded as it was by a massive "Boundary Wall" one mile and three-quarters in length. The wall's purpose was to control access to the piers, and thus prevent pilferage. Parts of the dock can still be seen today along the Mersey River.

The Prince's Dock, Liverpool

As it appeared in 1835

<http://www.bwpics.co.uk/gallery/princes.html>

Moving a ship out of the dock was not a simple task. So many tall ships were in the Prince's Dock in 1836 that some sorting out had to be done. A dockmaster standing high on the poop deck of a nearby vessel used a megaphone to hail a ship blocking the *Bristol's* exit: "Ahoy, *Mexico*! Get out a stern line and sheer alongside *Highlander*." Sailors pulled on lines to nudge the vessels into place. After this slow-motion ballet of giants was concluded and the *Bristol* was clear, a command by the dockmaster sent electricity through everyone aboard the *Bristol*: "*Bristol* ahoy! *Bristol* ahoy! Take aboard line and prepare to depart." With an outburst of shouts, bells, and whistles, dock lines were untied and taken aboard, while other lines were tossed to the opposite dock so that the ship could be pulled out to the Mersey River. The dockmaster now commanded, "*Bristol* away!" The men on the opposite dock leaned into their lines and pulled the tall ship toward the massive entry gates opening onto the Mersey River. An American flag flew proudly from the varnished staff at the stern of the almost new, mint-condition ship.[6]

Brick se faisant haler hors le Port
From *Recueil de Petites Marines* By Jean Baugean (1817)
Men hauling a vessel from dockside.

Arms waved aboard the *Bristol* and were answered by dockworkers and by Liverpudlian[7] onlookers who routinely gathered near the entry-gates to watch the tall ships pass. Some of the passengers aboard the departing *Bristol* and some of the *Mexico's* early-arriving passengers at the Prince's

---

[6] The dockmaster commands are from Herman Melville's description of ship maneuvers at the Prince's Dock, in *Redburn, His First Voyage* (1849).
[7] The appellation "Liverpudlian" was used as early as 1833 in the English *New Sporting Magazine*. Residents of Liverpool were also called "scousers," in reference to the nineteenth-century sailors' stew of potatoes, onions, flour, and salt meat.

Dock may have wondered whether they might meet each other someday on the other side of the Atlantic. Little could any of them know that within three months, eight out of ten of the passengers and crew of both ships, 215 people in all, would be dead—half of them by drowning in an instant aboard the *Bristol*, the others by slowly freezing to death aboard the *Mexico*. Nor could 139 of their number know that they would end up lying shoulder to shoulder in a mass grave on Long Island.

Down the Mersey

As the gates of the Prince's Dock yawned wide, a paddlewheel steam tug approached the *Bristol* and attached a towline. The steamboat's engine increased its beat, tightened the tow rope, and gradually pulled the great ship out of the dock and into the Mersey River. As the *Bristol* moved downstream, the emigrants experienced inevitable feelings of separation and loss. Like those before them, and like so many more after them, they were overwhelmed with conflicting emotions: the sad recollection of privation and the lack of opportunity at home, the sense of adventure and great hope for the future, and the uncertainty and pain of leaving behind the place of their birth. This intense mixture of sadness and joy brought tears to all but the most stoic among them. Gathered at the dock-gates with hats raised and handkerchiefs waving were clusters of family, friends, and Liverpudlian onlookers, sharing for just a moment the emigrants' fear, joy, regret, and hope.

A poem from *The Illustrated London News* (July 6, 1850) highlights the conflicting feelings that not only the English, but also the Irish, Welsh, and Scottish emigrants experienced as they sailed from the port of Liverpool:

> Farewell, England!
> Blessings on thee –
> Stern and niggard as thou art.
> Harshly mother, thou hast used me,
> And my bread thou hast refused me:
> But 'tis agony to depart.

As the steam tug pulled the *Bristol* the twenty or so miles down the Mersey past coaling docks, storehouses, villages, and farmhouses to the open sea, far-off thoughts of past and future were harshly interrupted by two unpleasant ceremonies—the *Roll-call of the Passengers* and the *Search for*

Stowaways. So desperate were some impoverished people to emigrate that they were willing to risk their lives as stowaways. Five pounds passage seems a small sum today, but allowing for inflation and changes in exchange rates, it was equivalent to over five hundred dollars, a difficult sum for an unemployed farmer or factory worker to raise.

**A three-masted, square-rigged ship at the Mersey Docks,
across the river from the Prince's Dock**
Untitled, Maritime Museum of Liverpool, unknown artist.

Stowaways used various unscrupulous means to gain access to ships sailing to America. Some men concealed themselves in crates with air holes drilled through the wood. Others came aboard inside barrels, covered up to the chin with hard biscuits. But most stowaways simply sneaked aboard in the dead of night or during the confusion of loading, hoping to remain inconspicuous among the paying passengers, or by hiding themselves in a convenient dark corner of the cargo hold. These men were not afraid of being discovered far out at sea, since the captain would not then turn back on account of a stowaway. Thus, the first formal on-board procedure was the *Search for Stowaways*—while there was still time and opportunity to locate them, seize them, and unceremoniously dump them onto the deck of the steam tug, to be taken back to a magistrate in Liverpool for prosecution and punishment for the crime of fraud. To a fair-minded and competent captain such as Alexander McKown, stowaways were thieves who deserved severe punishment.

The on-board search was brutally conducted. All passengers were ordered to come up on deck. Then a ship's officer, accompanied by a few muscular crewmen, headed below holding lanterns, pikes, and hammers. The pikes were fitted with sharp nails at the end and were used to probe into dark corners and under bunks. The hammers were used to pound suspiciously lumpy bedding. Barrels and large chests were turned upside down on the assumption that any stowaway who abruptly found himself head-downward, would be so severely discomfited, not to mention terrified that his escape was now blocked, that he would cry out for mercy. The simple announcement by the ship's officer that hammer-pounding, nail-pike-probing, and barrel-turning were about to begin was enough to persuade most stowaways to reveal themselves with an immediate cry for mercy. Captured stowaways were placed under guard until the ship reached the steam tug's departure point, at which time they were summarily off-loaded to the tug in as rough-handed a manner as the sailors could manage.

Despite the intensive search, some stowaways managed to remain concealed. Those who were caught too far at sea to be returned to Liverpool were dealt with severely. At a minimum, they were required to work for their passage, performing such tasks as cleaning chamber pots, dumping slop buckets, and holystoning the decks with blocks of soft sandstone. Sometimes their treatment was far worse, including tar-and-feathering and forced marches on the open deck in the cold and rain.

While the *Search for Stowaways* was being aggressively prosecuted below decks, the *Roll-call of the Passengers* was proceeding on the main deck. The task was meticulously performed by another ship's officer, accompanied by a representative from William and James Brown and Co., the *Bristol's* passenger broker in Liverpool. The broker began the roll-call by climbing up on the ship's rail and barking out instructions. He held onto the ship's rigging with one hand and clutched a passenger list in the other, as he arranged the passengers by ticket class. The ten first-cabin passengers were permitted to retire to the round-house, where they could observe the roll-call through the portholes. The forty-nine second-cabin passengers were then organized aft of the white line drawn across the deck. The sixty-eight steerage passengers were organized on the forward side of the line.

The broker began collecting paid-passage documents from each passenger. Any passenger lacking proof of payment was placed under guard, joining the stowaways already caught. As the officer moved through the assembled passengers, he was on the alert for over-age children. Suckling infants could travel for free, so mothers were known to hold four- or five-year-olds against their breast in a desperate attempt to conceal the true size of their "infant" under a heavy wool coat. The broker was also on the alert for youths older than the half-price-fare-limit of twelve years of age. Discovery of any of these frauds led to the usual plea for mercy along with a request for a reduced fare or even free passage because of poverty. Only one thing could persuade the ticket broker to allow a non-ticketed or improperly-ticketed person to stay on board: that was the sudden, miraculous appearance of gold or silver coins that had been sewn into the lining of a coat, and "discovered" just before the person was placed under guard.

Shortly after the conclusion of the *Roll-call* and the *Search for Stowaways*, the *Bristol* reached the mouth of the Mersey River, still under tow. The tug picked its way through the shoals to the open sea and then backed down to allow the 450-ton ship to glide slowly to a stop. The tug then circled back alongside her to take off the passenger broker, the stowaways, and any passengers lacking proper tickets. They would all be returned to Liverpool as soon as the steam tug could engage an inbound vessel desiring a tow up the Mersey. The wait could be overnight.

Captain McKown and his sixteen-man crew could now address the main business at hand—sailing the *Bristol* to New York with her 127 passengers and 300 tons of cargo. As they set out on their 3,400-mile voyage, the passengers and crew undoubtedly had great faith in both their captain and his ship. Benjamin Thompson wrote the following in *The History of Long Island* (1843):

> The *Bristol* was an American ship, nearly new, this being her second voyage, and commanded by Captain McKown, a gentleman long and favorably known as an able, prudent and experienced shipmaster.[8]

As the *Bristol* proceeded on her journey across the North Atlantic toward her awful fate, these complimentary words about her captain would prove to be more than justified by his actions. The ship, too, would prove to be worthy, but not against the awesome power of the sea.

For the moment, first-time passengers were undoubtedly surprised that a stationary, 450-ton ship with 300 tons of railroad iron and coal in her belly could pitch and roll in a moderate sea. Passengers leaning over the rail could see the *Bristol's* oxidizing copper bottom alternately exposed and covered as the tall ship dipped and rose, with streams of seawater flowing

---

[8] Sailing notices in various New York newspapers, and records in the U.S. National Archive prove it was the *Bristol's* third voyage. Thompson errs in saying it was her second voyage (2: pg. 268).

down her sides. Then the order came for all passengers to clear the deck, so that the sails could be hoisted. This was a grand sight even in the Age of Sail, because square-rigged, three-masted ships had the largest spread of canvas for their size of any vessel afloat.

Charles Dickens' first sighting of an American tall ship was from an approaching steamboat. He was preparing to board her as a passenger. It was an unforgettable sight:

> The ship which yesterday had been in such a crowded dock that she might have retired from trade for good-and-all, for any chance she seemed to have to going to sea, was now full sixteen miles away. A gallant sight she was, when we, fast gaining on her in a steamboat, saw her in the distance riding at anchor: her tall masts pointing up in graceful lines against the sky, and every rope and spar expressed in delicate threadlike outline: gallant too when we being all aboard, the anchor came up to the sturdy chorus "Cheerily men, oh cheerily!" and she followed proudly in the towing steamboat's wake. . . but bravest and most gallant of all, when the tow rope being cast adrift the canvas fluttered from her masts, and spreading her white wings she soared away upon her free and solitary course.
>
> — Chapter 16, *American Notes,* 1842.

First-cabin passengers were permitted to remain inside the round-house so they could observe the sights through the skylights. At the cry of "All hands! Set sail! Ahoy!" the crew began their well-rehearsed ballet of climbing the masts to the yardarms, loosening the sails, and bracing the yards. Even the most experienced travelers sitting in the round-house, including former shipowner Frances Hogan, were thrilled by a sight that has inspired men and women for centuries—a square-rigged ship setting sail. Below decks, the steerage and second-cabin passengers could hear the burst of unintelligible orders from the mates, the hurrying about on deck, and the squeal of block and tackle. The thick, glass bull's-eyes in the deck gave, at best, an out-of-focus view, quite unlike what could be seen from the skylights in the round-house.

All hands were on duty, as was the case anytime a ship set sail, neared port, or required a sail change in suddenly adverse weather conditions. According to the custom aboard merchant ships, Captain McKown divided his crew of sixteen—fourteen sailors plus his two officers—into two watches of eight men each, the starboard watch and the port (or larboard) watch. As tradition decreed, the first watch went to the first mate, William Tapscott.

Two-Watch System in 1836

Middle Watch	Midnight to 4 AM	(0000 - 0400)
Morning Watch	4 AM to 8 AM	(0400 - 0800)
Forenoon Watch	8 AM to Noon	(0800 - 1200)
Afternoon Watch	Noon to 4 PM	(1200 - 1600)
First Dog Watch	4 PM to 6 PM	(1600 - 1800)
Second Dog Watch	6 PM to 8 PM	(1800 - 2000)
First Watch	8 PM to Midnight	(2000 - 0000)

Every sailor was "on watch," sailing the ship, in four-hour and two-hour intervals for an average of twelve hours per day on watch.[9] This meant that sailors never got more than four continuous hours of sleep. A pair of two-hour watches, called the dog-watches, served to rotate the watch hours so that the men did not have to serve the same watches day after day. From 8 AM to 4 PM, the men "off watch" generally had to work on ship's maintenance while those "on watch" sailed the ship. The sailors' full workday was therefore often sixteen hours a day, except on Sunday, when it was only twelve hours long. The workweek aboard ship was longer and more closely-supervised than that of state prison convicts of the day. A one-month crossing earned the *Bristol's* sailors twelve dollars. Because the *Bristol's* departure was on a Sunday, and all the crew had to work the entire day searching for stowaways and setting sail, they had great hope that they would be given a few hours free time later in the week as compensation. But that would happen only at the pleasure of the captain and the mates.

On hearing the command to set sail, the two watches separated and raced each other climbing their assigned mainmast and foremast to spread their respective sails. They descended and divided once again, with one watch hoisting the mizzenmast's sails and the other setting the jibs and the staysails. Once all the sails were set, the *Bristol* surged ahead to the south and west, out into the great Atlantic. They were under full sail, with royals and top gallants flying, jibs and staysails running fore and aft, and stunsails extended from the booms. As Captain McKown later reported, the return trip to New York began "auspiciously, under clear skies and with a fair breeze." ("Two Late Awful Shipwrecks Near Sandy Hook," *New York Sun*, January 12, 1837, Supplement.)

---

[9] Aboard today's merchant ships there are *three* watches, resulting in an average of eight hours a day on watch.

Even below decks, the passengers could sense the wind catching the sails. The side-to-side rolling of the stationary *Bristol* now became a steady heeling to leeward. The irregular slap of choppy waves was replaced by the powerful sound and rhythm of the bow meeting and rising through each wave, then dropping into the trough behind it. These were sensations that would persist for the next thirty-five days. A different rhythm was created by the crew, as they chanted various accompaniments to group efforts such as hoisting sails or holystoning the deck:

> We're outward bound this very day,
> Good-bye, fare you well,
> Good-bye, fare you well.
> We're outward bound this very day,
> Hurrah, my boys, we're outward bound.
> —Early Nineteenth-Century Sea Chant.

Every U.S. registered ship was required by law to carry a certified crew list when entering or leaving a domestic port. When the *Bristol* left the Prince's Dock on her final voyage to New York, a crew list was validated by the United States consul in Liverpool and stowed in Captain McKown's cabin, but that list was lost when the ship was destroyed five weeks later.

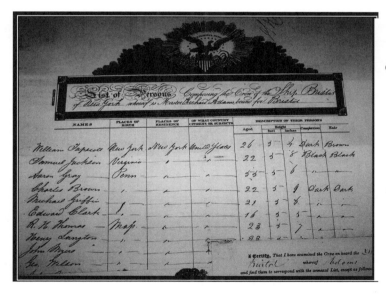

List of Persons Composing the Crew of the Ship Bristol
Certified at the Port of New York, August 5, 1835.

U.S. National Archives Record Administration, New York City Office.

(The full list is transcribed on page 46.)

An earlier crew list, seen here, covered the *Bristol's* maiden voyage. It has been preserved at the U.S. National Archives and Records Administration, in New York City. That voyage, from New York to Bristol, England and back, was begun in August 1835, and completed in January

1836. Richard Adams was the captain on that voyage, not Alexander McKown. As was common on merchant ships of the day, many of the crew from the first voyage left for berths on other ships, and were replaced by new men. Even with those changes, the earlier list suggests a great deal about the *Bristol's* crew on her final voyage.

List of Persons Composing the Crew of the Ship Bristol
(On her maiden voyage)
Certified at the Port of New York, August 5, 1835
U.S. National Archives Record Administration, New York City Office

Names	Place of Birth	Place of Residence	Citizen of	Age	Ht	Complexion	Hair
William Tapscott	New York	New York	United States	26	5' 4"	Dark	Brown
Samuel Jackson	Virginia	"	"	22	5' 8"	Black	Black
Aaron Gray	Pennsylvania	"	"	55	5' 6"	"	"
Charles Brown	"	"	"	22	5' 9"	Dark	Brown
Michael Griffin	"	"	"	21	5' 6"	"	"
Edward Clark	"	"	"	16	5' 5"	"	"
R.H. Thomas	Mass.	"	"	23	5' 7"	"	"
Henry Langston	"	"	"	23	5' 7"	"	"
John Meyers	"	"	"	21	5' 7"	"	"
George Wilson	"	"	"	21	5' 3"	"	"
John Miller	Louisiana	"	"	23	5' 7"	"	"
Charles Steadman	New York	"	"	17	5' 3"	"	"
Samuel Denson	"	"	"	22	5' 3"	"	"
Antem Tyson	Maine	"	"	22	5' 8"	"	"
John Freeman	New York	"	"	20	5' 6"	"	"
Phineas Davis	"	"	"	27	5' 9"	"	"

The sixteen sailors aboard the *Bristol* on her maiden voyage averaged 24 years of age—22 years without considering 55-year-old Aaron Gray. The young age of the crew reflects the tremendous physical demands placed on these men, including lifting and hauling heavy cargo and climbing sixty-foot-high masts. Their average height was five feet six inches. The 16-year-old and 17-year-old crewmembers on the list are a reminder that at 22 years of age, most sailors had already been at sea for five or more years.

As was typical of American ships at the time, all the crewmen were U.S. citizens, in this case hailing from six states. The presence of a small complement of black sailors—two on the *Bristol*—was also typical. A random sample of National Archives crew lists from 1836 reveals that of thirty ships sailing from New York Harbor that year, fifteen had one black crewman aboard—sometimes identified as the cook—five others had two or three black sailors aboard, and ten ships had no black sailors at all.

There is no additional, detailed information about the crew of the *Bristol* on her final voyage beyond the testimony the captain gave much later. (Pennington, et. al., *A Statement of the Facts : Pilot Laws*, 1840, "Appendix," pg. 4.) That statement lists William Tapscott—the first mate on the maiden voyage—as still on the ship, along with a new second mate, James Malone. Five other crew members, all replacement seamen, are identified: William Alfred Baker, James Braddock, Henry Owens, Samuel Kilburn, and John Bacon.

Leaving the steam tug behind, the *Bristol* and her sixteen-man crew left the Mersey River estuary, sailed briskly south through the Irish Sea, and rounded the coast of Ireland. Favorable winds and sunny autumn days provided easy sailing for the crew, and allowed the passengers frequent opportunities to come up on deck. This was a fine beginning to what the captain later said was a "pleasant and prosperous voyage" across the Atlantic (*Sunday Morning News*, November 27, 1836). His description was valid only to a point, for he used those words just one day before the journey's tragic ending. The *Bristol's* captain, two mates, and fourteen sailors were a well-trained, well-led, finely-tuned team sailing an almost-new ship across the North Atlantic. The failure of just one crewmember to perform his assigned task should not have led to a disaster, and yet it did.

The *Bristol* at Sea

The *Bristol* did not run on a schedule, nor was she large enough or fast enough to be classified as a packet, but she provided a level of service well above transient vessels such as the *Mexico*. The transients sailed at a snail's pace, changed itineraries at the captain's whim, and provided virtually nothing for their passengers beyond a supply of fresh water flavored by the previous contents of the barrel, food barely fit for consumption, waste buckets, a mop, and rows of bunk beds, often shared. Passengers on transient ships were sometimes ordered to disembark at a port where they had no intention of ending their voyage. The *Bristol's* passengers expected much better service, and they got it.

Mrs. Hogan and the other first-cabin passengers had paid about twenty-five guineas each—nine-month's wages for a laborer—an amount out of the reach of all but a few well-off travelers. They got private staterooms, took their meals at the captain's table or in the round-house, and were waited on by servant girls—Elizabeth Dairy, from Derry, and Catharine Mooney, from Kings County, Ireland. The two young women were steerage passengers working their way across the Atlantic. They worked with the ship's two stewards, a cabin boy, and the cook in catering to the first-cabin passengers' needs, including meal service, afternoon tea, washing clothes, preparing baths, and emptying chamber pots. The menu in first cabin featured fresh-baked bread, vegetables, eggs, cheese, salted and smoked meats, smoked fish, tea, coffee, beer, and wine. Animals housed in pens on deck—chickens, lambs, ducks, geese, and pigs—were slaughtered to provide fresh meat a thousand miles out at sea.

Second cabin aboard the *Bristol*, at around £7, offered a service level well below that of first cabin. The forty-nine passengers in second cabin, many of them tradesmen and professionals, were better able to afford a few amenities than were the laborers and farm workers in steerage. Second cabin got a cold breakfast and one simple hot meal a day—generally boiled salt beef or salt pork, with potatoes or beans. They also had a steward who provided minimal services such as mopping the deck once a day.

Each of the sixty-eight passengers in steerage paid about £5 for passage. They slept in curtained cabinets stacked two high, and received a plentiful, daily allotment of oatmeal, bread, hard biscuits, potatoes, salt beef, and salt pork. They had to cook this food themselves on coal stoves on deck, or eat it cold. As unappealing as the *Bristol's* food-service appears, it was a substantial step above steerage class on ships such as the *Mexico*, where the passengers had to store and ration a food supply for the entire voyage.

The weather was good for the *Bristol's* Atlantic crossing, so male passengers were permitted to come up on deck to bathe at announced times. The few men who took advantage of this used ropes to haul up buckets of cold North Atlantic seawater, then doused each other. Anyone else in second cabin and steerage wishing to bathe had to carry pails of seawater below decks, and wash with a sponge and soap.

All in all, conditions aboard the *Bristol*, although they appear to have been impossibly harsh by today's standards, were what the passengers expected . . . or perhaps better. As Francis Burtsall, a surviving first-cabin passenger and experienced traveler wrote:

> I consider it my duty to state the entire satisfaction manifested by both the cabin and steerage passengers during the whole voyage.
> —*Morning Courier & New York Express*, November 25, 1836.

Montauk Lighthouse

In use since 1792. One of four U.S. lighthouses sighted from the *Bristol*.

Photo by Arthur S. Mattson (2006)

Near dawn on November 19, a Saturday morning, after thirty-four pleasant days at sea, the ship passed the Montauk Lighthouse several miles off the starboard bow. The lighthouse, which was authorized in 1792 by the Second Congress under George Washington, and completed in 1796, was the first of four lighthouses that marked the final stages of the *Bristol's* voyage. The one-hundred-foot-tall Montauk Lighthouse tower has been part of Long Island's land and seascape for over two centuries. It still serves as an active aid to navigation as it did in 1836, when the *Bristol's* passengers and crew sailed past in eager anticipation of their arrival in New York.

As the ship cruised all day and the next night along the 118-mile length of Long Island's South Shore, the helmsman gave a wide berth to the island's low-lying barrier beaches and shifting sandbars. The rustic fishermen's shacks that dotted the shore could not be seen from miles out at sea, and there were few landmarks on which to gauge progress. There was, however, a second lighthouse, the Fire Island Light. That seventy-four-foot-high, cream-colored, octagonal building of Connecticut River blue split stone was completed in 1826. It was never truly effective because of its lack of height, and was torn down and rebuilt in 1858. Captain McKown knew the South Shore of Long Island well, and he probably used the Fire Island Light to mark the half-way point of the *Bristol's* progress from Montauk Point to New York Harbor.

The Fire Island Light, Built in 1826 and Rebuilt in 1858
Shown here in the early twentieth century.
American Environmental Photographs Collection, University of Chicago Library

On Sunday, November 20, the passengers were awake at sunrise, knowing that their destination was soon at hand. They were greeted by the mate's announcement that the entrance to New York Harbor was only a few hours away. Excitement aboard the ship was as great as it had been when the *Bristol* left the Prince's Dock in Liverpool. Captain McKown later described the weather that Sunday morning as "remarkably pleasant and clear with a fine breeze from the southeast, and smooth water" (*Long Island Democrat*, December 21, 1836). He advised the passengers that if the breeze held, there was some chance they would arrive off Sandy Hook well before noon. He even speculated that the ship, with luck, might be tied up at Woodhull & Minturn's Dover Street dock in time for the passengers to attend Sunday evening church services ashore.

That morning, Captain McKown presided over a Sunday worship service, a "thanksgiving service," on the main deck. He offered praise to God, to the nodding approval of the assembled passengers. The *Long Island Democrat* newspaper recounted the captain's words, based on a survivor's recollection:

> We have seen the works of the Lord in the mighty deep. Let us praise the Lord for his goodness and for his wonderful works to the children of men. We have reached our desired haven.
>
> —*Long Island Democrat*, December 21, 1836.

So pleased were the passengers with the entire voyage that they presented a letter to the captain, one they had composed for the occasion entitled "A Return of Thanks." It was signed by every passenger. Smiles were radiant throughout the ship. The festivities were dampened only slightly when the breeze lessened, slowing the ship. Stunsails were set at the ends of the yards to pick up the light wind. Two landmarks on Long Island's South Shore, called out from the lookout's perch, provided clear evidence that the *Bristol* was nearing New York Harbor. The first was the Old Sand Hole Methodist Church, a plain two-and-a half-story building on a thirty-foot rise, a few miles inland at Near Rockaway. The second was the Marine Pavilion, an elegant two-story hotel and resort a few hundred yards from the beach at Far Rockaway.

As his ship passed these familiar landmarks, Captain McKown could never have guessed that these same structures would later mark the tragic end of his voyage. Indeed, the *Long Island Democrat* reported that as the *Bristol* cruised along this very portion of the Long Island coast, Captain McKown told a group of passengers that he "cared not for, nor feared Rockaway or the Rockaway shoals," because he "knew the coast too well." These words would come back to haunt him when the *Bristol* was wrecked on those very shoals, when dozens upon dozens of her dead passengers were stacked in a barn behind the Marine Pavilion, and when seventy-seven unclaimed bodies were interred at the Mariners Burying Ground at the Old Sand Hole Church.

The passengers, too, had no thought whatsoever for the horrors they would face in just a few hours. Many clung to the rapidly-fading hope of a Sunday evening arrival, and refused to change out of the Sunday-best clothing they had dressed their children and themselves in—as the *Long Island Democrat* reported—"for so delightful an occasion." Sadly, for most of them, these Sunday-best clothes would become their funeral garb.

The slow cruise along the last few miles of Long Island's coast was now under such a light, constant breeze that little work was required to handle the sails, so the off-watch crew joined in the festivities. November 20 was the crew's "day off," because it was a Sunday. As a result, only half the crew had to stand watches during the day. The rest of the men had their own celebrations on the foredeck, singing ballads and sea chanties—and in the forecastle, drinking rum. As subsequent events suggest, they may have celebrated too much.

This was a slow, gentle finish to a fine voyage, but Captain McKown would have preferred a stiffer breeze and an earlier arrival at New York Harbor, not just because of the expectations he had given his passengers, but because he undoubtedly knew that every additional hour at sea is an hour of potential danger. At half-past eight on Sunday evening, there was at least the comfort of seeing the Navesink Lighthouse with its twin-lights burning brightly atop the Atlantic Highlands of New Jersey, four miles south of New York Harbor. Coming next into view was the Sandy Hook Light at the very entrance to New York Harbor. An hour later, McKown ordered his crew to round-to off the Hook and told the first mate to sound the ship's bell and raise lantern signals as a call for a pilot boat to approach. The *Bristol* was almost home.

The Entrance to New York Harbor

The entrance to New York Harbor had been a navigation nightmare for ship captains since 1609, when Henry Hudson complained about a "very shoal'd barre." Little had changed by 1836, when the *Bristol* arrived off Sandy Hook. The entrance was still dotted with shifting sandbars, uncharted shoals, and wrecks; and there were still no channel markers. Once a vessel made it past the Hook, there was a tortuous, twenty-five mile journey before reaching the East River docks. As a result, all but the most experienced captains depended on harbor pilots to conduct safe passage, especially at night.

The area's navigation difficulties have their origin in the geological history of the area. New York Harbor, the Hudson River, and Long Island were all formed 20,000 years ago when the Wisconsinan glaciation sent a thousand-foot-thick sheet of ice across Canada and the northern part of the United States as far south as Manhattan and Long Island. So much water was stored in the glacier that the sea level dropped by over three hundred feet, leaving Manhattan and Long Island one hundred fifty miles inland, landlocked by a vast glacial outwash plain fanning out to the southeast. When the glacier melted, it sent a roaring river down what is now the Hudson River Valley. That glacial river flowed through the outwash plain, carving a deep valley extending hundreds of miles out into what is today the ocean floor. This underwater feature, called the Hudson River Canyon, runs through the heart of the New York Bight. When the glacier melted and released the water it had withheld from the sea, the outwash plain was drowned by the rising ocean, and silt began to fill both the lower Hudson River and the entrance to New York Harbor.

New York's Lower Bay opens to the Atlantic Ocean in a broad expanse of water. A seven-mile-long, unimpeded line can be drawn across the harbor entrance from Coney Island, New York to Sandy Hook, New Jersey. The opening suggests a wide shipping lane, but looks are deceiving; the usable channel is less than a half mile wide. Before there was regular dredging, a vessel's route into the Lower Bay required sharp maneuvering through "The Elbow," as the passage around the East Bank Shoals was called.

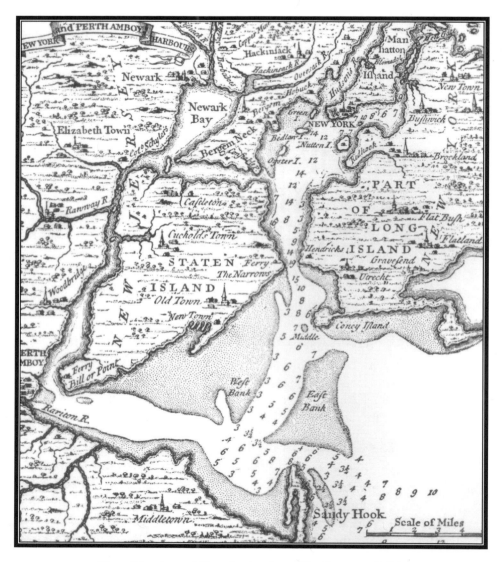

New York and Perth Amboy Harbours, 1733
(Depth in fathoms – one fathom equals six feet)
New York Public Library

The glacially-deposited shoals in and around New York Harbor are continually moved about by the south-flowing Hudson River and by incoming Atlantic Ocean swells. The westward drift of Long Island beach sand and the northward drift of New Jersey sand add to the problem. The following drawing shows how all these damaging forces focus themselves at the Atlantic Ocean entrance to New York Harbor and along the coasts of New Jersey and Long Island.

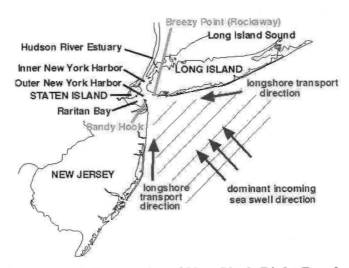

Geology and Geography of New York Bight Beaches
From "Sedimentology of Beaches and Barrier Islands"
Phil Stoffer and Paula Messina.

The constricted, usable entrance to New York Harbor, combined with the drifting shoals at its mouth, had a devastating effect on shipping, especially when New York began to grow into an important seaport. During the colonial period, so many ships were wrecked and cargos lost on the shoals of New Jersey, Rockaway, and New York Harbor that New York City's merchants organized two prize drawings to fund the construction of a wooden lighthouse at Sandy Hook. On June 4, 1764, the new lighthouse's whale oil lamps were first lit. Five years later, the structure was rebuilt in white stone and brick. The Sandy Hook Lighthouse was there when the *Bristol* arrived in 1836, and it is still in operation today as the oldest lighthouse in continuous service in the United States.

The Sandy Hook Lighthouse

Still operating after almost 250 years of service.

Photo by Arthur S. Mattson 2006

The Sandy Hook Lighthouse was not the only navigation aid implemented to reduce New York's shipping losses. Because the light was deemed to be too low-lying to be effective at long range, two matching octagonal-shaped lighthouses were constructed at Navesink, New Jersey in 1828. The twin lights were placed atop the Atlantic Highlands, four miles to the south of the Hook. On a clear night, the twin lights were visible twenty-one miles away, compared to sixteen miles for the Sandy Hook Light.

The Navesink Twin Lighthouse, built 1828.
Diorama presented by the Twinlight Historical Society, Navesink, New Jersey.
Photo by Arthur S. Mattson, 2006.

In 1841, the Navesink Lights were the first in the United States to employ the powerful, beam-directing Fresnel lens. However, this was too late by five years to have helped the *Bristol* and the *Mexico*, each of which was wrecked near the outer range of the older-style lights. In 1862, the twin lighthouses at Navesink were rebuilt in brownstone, in the conjoined configuration seen in a recent photo below:

The Navesink Twin Lighthouse Today
Built in 1828, reconstructed in 1862.
Photo by Arthur S. Mattson, 2006.

In 1823, the first Sandy Hook Lightship, the *V-V*, was anchored on station twelve miles off the Hook, well out in the New York Bight, "in the chops of the channel." However, in 1829, after a series of shipwrecks at the Delaware Capes, the lightship was relocated there, and she remained at the Capes until 1838. Had this lightship been anchored in the New York Bight in the fall and winter of 1836-37, she would have provided a nighttime point of reference—she had a light and a bell—for both the *Bristol* and the *Mexico*, as their captains attempted to stay offshore while still remaining close to Sandy Hook. The wrecks of the two ships soon brought a lightship back to the Bight.

In 1835, Navy Lt. Cdr. Thomas R. Gedney was directed to take a series of soundings off Sandy Hook using a lead-weighted line. By this process he identified a new and safer channel, one even the harbor pilots did not know of. However, Gedney's recommendations were not published in time to have been in the hands of the captains of the *Bristol* and the *Mexico* when they left on their final voyages. Thus, they remained dependent on the New York pilots.

Despite the eventual addition of navigation aids such as Fresnel lenses, the Ambrose Lightship, accurate charts, and navigation buoys, the harbor entrance plagued mariners until 1907, when a proper channel, the Ambrose Channel, was finally dredged past the Hook and across the "elbow" at the entrance to New York's Lower Bay. Today the channel is a comfortable two thousand feet wide and forty feet deep.

New York's Lower Bay—Looking South to the Atlantic Ocean
Clockwise from upper right corner: Sandy Hook, a line of ships in the Ambrose Ship Channel, the Verrazano Narrows Bridge connecting Staten Island on the right to Brooklyn's Fort Hamilton on the left, Coney Island, and Breezy Point at the upper left.
http://www.geo.hunter.cuny.edu/bight/index.html

When the *Bristol* finally arrived off Sandy Hook on the night of November 20, 1836, Captain McKown sounded the ship's bell and hoisted lanterns, as signals for a pilot to come out and guide him into New York Harbor. This failed to bring a pilot boat out from their sheltered anchorage inside Sandy Hook Harbor. McKown ordered his crew to fire Roman candles into the sky. Still there was no response. His displeasure increasing by the minute, the captain ordered that the ship's gun be fired. Again there was no response. In violation of informal harbor rules—there were no *written rules*—the pilots had inexplicably abandoned their twenty-four-hour-a-day posts, and no one answered the *Bristol's* signals.[10]

Reluctantly, Captain McKown ordered his crew to prepare to spend the night off the Hook. A bow anchor was set in the eight fathoms (forty-eight feet) of water, and additional oil lamps were hung from the masts. The twin flames of the Navesink Light, easily visible four miles to the south, and the even closer Sandy Hook Light would help them maintain their position even if the anchor failed to hold in the strong currents.

For the passengers, these last few hours of waiting were frustrating, but it was still a time for celebration. The captain instructed his officers to allow the passengers to come on deck to observe the Navesink and Sandy Hook Lights. The lights gleamed through the starlit, moonless night, and served to remind many of the passengers that they had families and friends on shore, waiting for word that they had landed. The *New York Herald* quoted a surviving passenger, Michael McGintry:

> On Sunday night we all rejoiced. The evening was very beautiful, the land was before us and the wind was favourable. We retired to rest in the full assurance of landing the next day at New York.
> —*New York Herald*, November 29, 1836.

---

[10] A full discussion of the involvement of the New York harbor pilots in the wrecks of the *Bristol* and the *Mexico* can be found in Part III, page 213, in a chapter entitled, "The Condemnation of the New York Pilots."

The Wreck of the *Bristol*

Around midnight, the wind began to blow fresh from the southeast, and the weather changed rapidly for the worse, "thick and rainy, and wind increasing," was how one passenger described it (*Morning Courier* – November 24, 1836). An hour later it was blowing so hard that Captain McKown feared the anchor would drag and that the *Bristol* would be driven onto the harbor's East Bank Shoals. He ordered the crew to weigh anchor and move offshore. The captain wanted to get clear of the coasts of New Jersey and Long Island for the duration of the storm, and yet maintain a position allowing an easy return to Sandy Hook in the morning. Because the Ambrose Lightship had been removed seven years before from its station twelve miles out in the New York Bight, and because the Fire Island Light was too far away, he had only the Navesink and Sandy Hook lighthouses available as nighttime navigation reference points. Thus, he had to stay closer in-shore than he might have wished.

After making some calculations, McKown ordered the first mate, William Tapscott, to set sail under three double-reefed topsails, furled fore and main spencers, and the jib. The fore-and-aft-rigged spencers and the jib would help the ship sail close to the wind as the ship tacked back and forth out into the Bight. On the homeward sail, the topsail reefs could be let out for a speedy run back to the Hook.

Sometime after 1 AM, the captain ordered Tapscott to take two tacks of two hours each. The first tack was in an east by northeast direction angled toward the South Shore of Long Island, short of the Rockaway Shoals, the very place that the captain earlier had remarked to a passenger that he "cared not for, nor feared." This maneuver was to be followed by a second, longer tack to the south, keeping well off the New Jersey coast. After these first two maneuvers, the order was to bring the ship about, bearing to the northwest, and return to Sandy Hook before dawn. As an extra precaution, he ordered continual soundings with a lead-line throughout the night, and directed that a log of those soundings be kept. The captain went to bed, still annoyed with the harbor pilots' failure to be on station, but unconcerned, as the orders he had given to the first mate were clear, logical, and unambiguous.

Other captains had a different view of the risk of maneuvering anywhere near the Rockaway Shoals while waiting for delinquent harbor pilots to appear. Captain John Earl wrote the following about the danger:

> [P]ilots were never to be found beyond the Bar [meaning Sandy Hook]; and vessels must run the hazard of seeking them there. If our pilots were bound to cruise on a line with Fire Inlet and Barnegat, they would seldom be out of sight of the Highlands in clear weather, and it would then be the practice of all strangers [i.e., ships needing a pilot] to lie by for a pilot, instead of running into an "eel-pot," for such, in effect, is the approach to Sandy Hook. By the time a ship comes up with the Bar, she is perfectly embayed, and with the wind S. E. cannot clear on either tack; nor is it perhaps generally known that on the flood tide, the in-draught at Rockaway Inlet is such as to render it impossible, on the starboard tack, to depend on the course steered, and but little is known by sounding.
> —Pennington, et. al., *Statement of the Facts : Pilot Laws* (1840).

Had Captain McKown or his officers been aware of Captain Earl's fears, they may have steered clear of the Rockaway Shoals and the Rockaway Inlet. As it was, things went terribly wrong. At 1:30 AM, the first mate, William Tapscott, needed to get some sleep because he was assigned the next watch, beginning at 4 AM. He transmitted the captain's sailing orders to the second mate, James Malone, and retired to his cabin. It is not known whether Tapscott misunderstood the captain's order, or if Malone misunderstood the first mate. Perhaps some of the blame could even be placed on the currents of Rockaway Inlet. However, so egregious was the resulting sailing error that it may well have been that too many cups of grog had been drawn from the ship's stores in the arrival celebration several hours earlier.

At 3 AM, the lead sounded at twelve fathoms (72 feet deep); at 3:30 AM the depth was ten-and-a-half fathoms (63 feet deep); at 3:40 AM it was ten fathoms (60 feet deep). No one seemed to be concerned that the ship was gradually entering shallower water. At this point, the *Bristol* had traveled almost twenty miles northeast, in a straight line from below Sandy Hook. She was off Rockaway Beach, closing in on the Rockaway Shoals. The ship should have turned to the south forty minutes earlier, as the captain had ordered. She should have been well off the coasts of Long Island and New Jersey.

The sailing error would not have been critical far out in the Atlantic where over-running a tack would require a routine, compensating adjustment to get back on course—along with a stiff punishment administered to the offender. But here, in the "V" formed by the Long Island and New Jersey coasts, here in the "eel pot" of the New York Bight, on a black stormy night, it was a disaster.

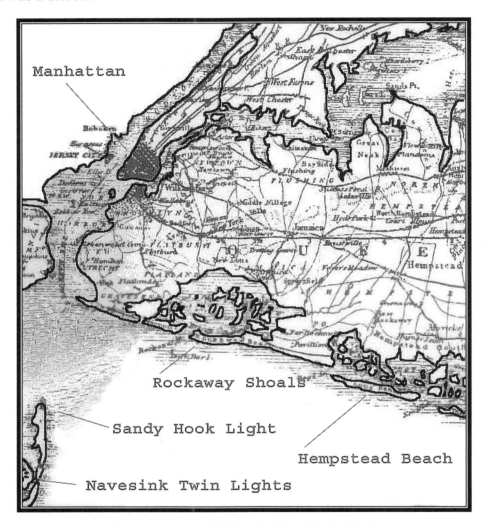

The Dangerous "V" of the New York Bight
Between the Coasts of New Jersey and Long Island
Detail is from the *Travelers Map of Long Island*, J.H.Colton (1848).

The Marine Pavilion at Far Rockaway, ca. 1836
NOAA Archive

In 1836, the Atlantic beaches of New York's Queens County were undeveloped except for a single location on the Rockaway Peninsula, about twenty-five miles by dirt road from New York City.[11] This remote place, called the Marine Pavilion, was a fashionable resort. Ironically, disease was the reason for its creation. In the summer of 1832, a cholera epidemic killed 3,513 people in New York City, leaving coffin makers unable to keep up with the demand. Half the city's 200,000 residents fled, but they found few places where they could go. As a result, a splendid, 160-room seaside hotel was built as a summer retreat for those who could afford to escape the hot, fetid city and its contagions. It was completed in 1834. Historian Benjamin Thompson wrote in 1839 that the pavilion was "a large and splendid edifice, standing upon the margin of the Atlantic; and has hitherto been kept in a style not excelled by any hotel in the Union."

By day the tall, 235-foot wide Marine Pavilion, with its Ionic colonnades and 75-foot and 45-foot wings, was a landmark easily identifiable from the sea. At night, in season, oil lamps lighted the 80-foot-long dining hall and the ocean-front piazza. But on this dark night in late November the summer guests were gone, and the unlit hotel was not visible to the crew of the *Bristol* as the ship approached—if indeed the watch was even awake.

---

[11] In 1836, Queens County included all of today's Nassau and Queens Counties. Nassau County was created in 1899, by act of the New York State Legislature.

As the tall ship continued on her ruinous course shoreward, the crew remained oblivious to the sound of waves hitting the beach at Rockaway.[12] A crewman continued throwing the lead. At 3:45 AM, just as the next watch was coming on deck, the crewman screamed out, "Five fathoms! Five fathoms!" (thirty feet).

Pandemonium ensued. Instantly, the helm was ordered to be put hard over, to bring the ship about, but with three hundred tons of iron and coal in her belly, the *Bristol* could not turn in time, and glided softly to a stop on a sandy shoal just four hundred yards off the beach. She had grounded on the Rockaway Shoals, five miles west of the Marine Pavilion, her bow angled toward the shore, probably near today's Jacob Riis Park.[13]

The shouts of the crew brought Captain McKown out on deck wearing no jacket or shoes, dressed in the clothes he had been sleeping in—his vest and pantaloons. The captain did not need to be told what had happened. He felt the absence of the ship's motion; he heard the nearby surf; and he felt the breeze coming from the stern quarter. After asking the time, he realized that a tack had not been executed, that his ship was aground off Long Island. Looking southwest, he saw the Sandy Hook and Navesink Lights off in the distance. It was now perfectly clear where the *Bristol* lay—Rockaway.

Several attempts to move the ship off the shoals failed. The captain's concern then shifted to the safety of his passengers. McKown wanted to get his passengers ashore as soon as possible, but the presence of so many women and children on the *Bristol* surely influenced his next decision. He could have begun shuttling passengers ashore in the ship's boats that night. However, the seas were rough, and it seemed safer to wait until daylight.

McKown was familiar with Long Island's South Shore and knew he could expect no immediate help from land. But there were baymen's cottages

---

[12]   The name *Rockaway* has nothing to do with rocks; it relates to the Lenape Algonquin Indian name for sand. The Lenapes who lived near the ocean barrier beaches of southwestern Long Island called their home "Rechqua-Akie," which means "Sandy Place." The name refers to the sand dumped on Long Island when a series of glaciers, the last of which retreated 15,000 years ago, formed the island. The thousand-mile-wide, thousand-foot-high ice-flows that scraped out the Finger Lakes of New York and shaped the river valleys of New England, also ground stone into sand and pushed it south like a giant plow. When the glaciers reached their farthest extent, they piled-up a ribbon of sand extending from Long Island to Cape Cod, including Block Island, Martha's Vineyard, and Nantucket in between. In the 1640s, when the English and Dutch arrived, the Lenape place name was corrupted to "Rockaway."

[13]   Some early accounts reported the location of the wreck as five miles *east* of the Marine Pavilion, not west, which puts the location of the wreck in some doubt. However, the consensus of reports has the wreck to the west of the Pavilion.

nearby, and inland hamlets, and perhaps even a winter caretaker at the Marine Pavilion. It was important to get assistance as soon as possible. So he instructed the first mate to fire the ship's signal gun and rockets.

Today on Long Island, noise pollution abounds even in "the still of the night"—from an airplane fifteen thousand feet overhead, a parkway five miles away, an electric transformer down the street, a furnace in the basement, a refrigerator in the kitchen, and a clock on the nightstand. Long-time Long Island resident Whittaker Chambers wrote in his book *Witness* (1952) that in the 1910s, before all the noise of the modern era, he could clearly hear from his home in Lynbrook the crash of ocean waves on the shore at Long Beach, over five miles away as the crow flies. On the stormy night of November 21, 1836, the sound of the *Bristol's* wreck gun carried many miles inland, and attracted the attention of local citizens. Help would soon be on the way.

The mates informed the passengers that they should expect to be taken ashore in the ship's boats at first light, and that they should prepare small parcels, including their valuables. Their trunks and other possessions would be carried ashore later by the crew and delivered to the offices of Woodhull & Minturn in New York City. The captain insisted that the decks remain clear so that his crew could prepare the small boats for launching at first light. First-cabin passengers could stay in the round-house if they wished, but all steerage and second-cabin passengers had to go below. As logical and conservative as it was to keep the passengers below decks and wait for first light, the result was calamitous.

Captain McKown still had hope for a successful conclusion to the voyage by re-floating his ship. The ship had struck the bar softly, and there appeared to be no damage to her hull. So there was the distinct possibility that a combination of a rising tide and a favorable wind might carry the ship off the shoal once the storm subsided. If that lucky chance did not ensue, there was another way to save the ship. Woodhull & Minturn, the ship's owners, could arrange for assistance from a man most captains knew, but never wanted to actually do business with. He was Henry F. Schenck, captain of the rescue and salvage lighter *Walter R. Jones*.

McKown could envision how the salvage operation would play out. Schenck would sail his shallow-drafted rescue schooner out from her berth in New York Harbor to Rockaway Beach, where the *Bristol* lay. He would nose the *Walter R. Jones* beside the *Bristol*, drop anchor, and tightly secure the two vessels beam-to-beam. Then Schenck's crew and McKown's crew would off-load to the *Jones* enough of the *Bristol's* cargo of iron bars to lighten the ship and allow her to be "kedged" off the bar using carried-out anchors, winches, and windlasses.

Captain McKown's decision to wait the storm out was a reasonable strategy, but at sea there is an immense variable in all equations—the weather. Just before daybreak, the storm took a dramatic turn for the worse. Gale winds roared in from the southeast, from the open sea, and began to push a tremendous tidal surge into the "V" of the New York Bight and up against the Long Island coast. McKown, concerned now about the rapid deterioration of the weather, ordered his first mate to inform the steerage and second-cabin passengers that they absolutely must remain below for their own protection, and that the deck hatches would be tightly secured until the storm passed. The first-cabin passengers were given the option of remaining inside the round-house, but it was suggested they, too, go below. Some elected to stay in the round-house.

Ever more powerful waves began to strike the *Bristol*, nudging the stern around until the ship was taking the brunt of the storm amidships. There she stayed. Despite the rising tide and pounding waves, the vessel did not move. The dead weight of hundreds of tons of iron rails and bar-iron lying deep in her hold held the ship broadside, up against a sandbar. The *Bristol* was now an anvil, receiving blow after blow from the hammering waves.

Captain McKown's earlier reluctance to launch the ship's boats at night had now put his passengers in greater peril, albeit unintentionally. They sat below decks and in the round-house, paralyzed with fear as the ship's timbers shuddered with the booming impact of each wave. Launching a small boat was now impossible because of the intensity of the storm.

It was mayhem on deck as waves surged over the ship, pulling loose the ship's rigging and tearing away the bulwarks. The crew had secured the hatches to protect the cargo and passengers, but the sailors were now in danger of being washed overboard themselves. So they climbed onto the masts and rigging. Despite the dire circumstances, McKown was fully prepared to ride out the storm. After all, the *Bristol* was just three years old and tightly-built. He had every reason to expect that the hull would remain intact even with the violent pounding and the damage to the ship's rigging and bulwarks. Keeping the passengers below under secure hatches still seemed to be the best way to protect them, and to save his ship.

Even Captain McKown, with all his maritime experience, must have been shocked at the destructive power that the sea now turned against his ship. For millennia, sailors have whispered about "rogue waves" and "monster waves" that are much larger than any surrounding waves, and which sometimes are powerful enough to severely damage or even sink ships at sea. Mariners who encountered them described "walls of water" with a "pyramid shape," a characteristic that immediately distinguishes them from ordinary waves. Twentieth-century oceanographers had no proof of such waves, but they allowed for the possibility that such monster waves caused the sudden, inexplicable disappearance of ocean-going vessels. They even went so far as to create a technical definition and a name for these storied, but scientifically unobserved waves: "Rogue waves, also known as freak waves . . . are more than double the significant wave height (SWH), which is itself defined as the mean of the largest third of waves in a wave record" (www. sciencedaily.com).

The first scientific measurement of a freak wave took place unexpectedly during a winter storm in the North Sea, when a huge wave hit Norway's Draupner oil platform on New Year's Day, 1995. A laser-based wave-monitor mounted on the underside of the oil rig recorded that a freak wave swept under the platform, doing minor damage in the process.

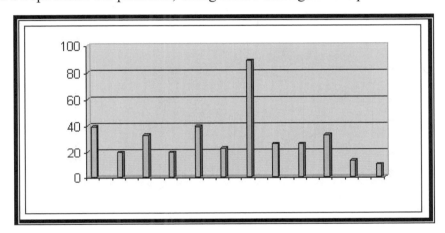

**Freak Wave Sequence from the Draupner Oil Platform,
January 1, 1995**

Vertical axis is the height of a series of waves in feet.
The graph is based on data from *Freak Wave Event at Draupner Jacket*, by Sverre Haver.

The wave was measured at eighty-five feet above sea level, while the "mean of the largest third of waves in the wave record" was a mere forty feet. This wave, which easily met scientists' definition of a freak wave, became known as "The New Year's Wave." In 2002, in a follow-up study named *Project MaxWave*, researchers from the German Coastal Research Centre (GKSS) used data collected by satellite to identify a large number of radar signatures that appeared to show freak waves in the open ocean, mostly off the coast of southern Africa. More recently, buoys moored in the Gulf of Mexico at the time of Hurricane Katrina indicated the existence of such large waves during that storm.

Scientists believe that events similar to the open-ocean freak wave, but on a smaller scale, can impact the shoreline, particularly when large storm waves approach shallower waters and are refracted and diffracted, as shown in the following aerial photograph.

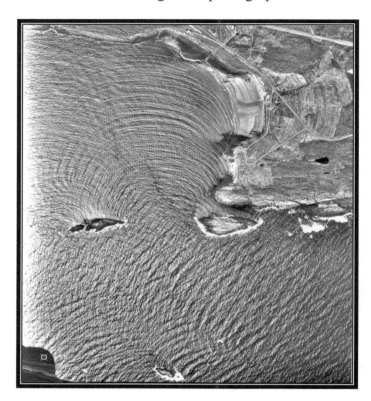

Refraction and Diffraction of Shore Waves at Finnmark

Photograph by Fjellanger Widerøe

"Freak Waves, Rogue Waves, Extreme Waves and Ocean Wave Climate."

<www.math.uio.no/~ka rstent/seminarV05/Have r2004.pdf>

Disproportionately large coastal waves are called sneaker waves, because they appear in a wave train without warning. The South Shore of Long Island, with its exposure to the open ocean, strong currents, and its shifting offshore sandbars, is a candidate for such a rare and unexpected wave event. Indeed, waves of fifty feet have been recorded in the New York Bight at the Ambrose Light. Just such a wave appears to have struck the *Bristol* at Rockaway Shoals.

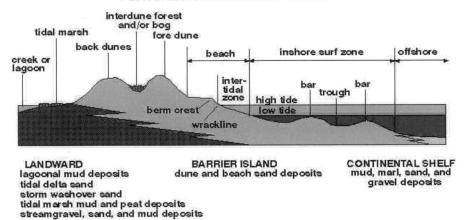

FEATURES OF A BARRIER ISLAND

**This cross-section of a Long Island barrier beach shows
offshore sandbars and troughs like those the *Bristol* was stranded on.**
"Dynamics of Beaches and Barrier Islands"
Phil Stoffer and Paula Messina

Long before the *Bristol* grounded there, Rockaway Shoals had earned the name "Ship Shoals," because it was the scene of so many shipwrecks. But in the fall and winter of 1836, Rockaway Shoals became a veritable graveyard for ships. On October 10, 1836, just six days before the *Bristol* set sail from Liverpool, the *New York Herald* reported three wrecks within ten miles of the spot where the *Bristol* later went aground. Captain McKown was certainly not aware of these wrecks, because he was out at sea. Had he known about them, he might not have treated Rockaway Shoals with such apparent indifference. The following are the wreck reports:

- The schooner *Purdy*, [Captain] Briggs, from New York bound for Baltimore was wrecked on Long Beach on Tuesday evening at 9 o'clock.

- The schooner *Franklin*, [Captain] Shelly, from York River, went ashore on Hempstead Beach on Wednesday evening. The captain and one hand were drowned. Was bound for Portland.

- *Norfolk*, bound for Providence, Rhode Island, went ashore the same night on the Ship Shoals between Charles and Hog Island.

This concentration of wrecks at such a small part of Long Island suggests that some unusual riptides or wave action was taking place in conjunction with some truly extreme weather. These violent storms appear to have travelled across the North Atlantic and pummeled Europe as well. Robert Hendrickson's *Ocean Almanac* (1984) described what happened:

> During a severe storm on December 25, 1836, stones forming part of the breakwater at Cherbourg, France, and weighing nearly 7,000 pounds each, were thrown over a wall 20 feet high, which surmounts the stone embankment. . . A block of concrete 2,500 cubic feet in volume and weighing 125 tons was shifted more than three feet from its original position.

The account from Cherbourg is analogous to what happened at Rockaway Beach. An unnamed crewman's account published in the *New York Herald* (November 25, 1836) told of a "tremendous wave" engulfing the *Bristol* as she sat stranded on the sandbar. Another report in the *Long Island Democrat* (November 30, 1836) indicated that the wave hit the ship broadsides and moved the 450-ton vessel rapidly shoreward, knocking passengers off their feet. Those asleep found themselves thrown from their bunks onto the deck. The first-class passengers in the round-house must have been terrified as the massive wall of water completely covered the structure and nearly swept it away. Indeed, a later wave did just that.

The damage to the ship was devastating. Everything on deck was carried off except the masts, the taffrail, and the round-house. Worst of all, the wave tore off the hatches. This left the forecastle, the cargo hold, the cabins, and the steerage deck open to the sea. One hundred people—ninety-five passengers and five crewmen—were about to die.

Death in Steerage

The Wreck of the *Bristol*
1830s - Unknown Artist.
From *Perils of the Port of New York* by Jeanette Rattray.

> Not a sound, a moan, was heard. The work of death was instantaneous. Sixty persons were hurried, unwarned and unprepared, into eternity.
>
> —*Hempstead Inquirer,* November 30, 1836.

One hundred and twenty-seven passengers were trapped inside the *Bristol* when the immense wave struck at Rockaway Beach. Sixty-eight were in steerage, forty-nine in second cabin, and ten in the round-house. Most of their names, both survivors and the dead, are known from lists that were published in New York City newspapers. These lists, arranged by passenger class, are transcribed later in this chapter, and in the next two chapters. They suggest much about the men, women, and children who suddenly found themselves in terrifying mortal danger in the hold of the ship.

A large majority of the steerage passengers aboard the *Bristol* were Irish. Of the nineteen steerage passengers that did survive, eighteen were identified as having come from Ireland, from places ranging from Londonderry in the north, to Dublin in the east, to Derry in the southwest. Although no hometowns and counties were reported for the forty-nine steerage passengers who drowned, most had Irish surnames. It may seem odd that such a large proportion of Irish should be emigrating nine years before the Great Famine began in 1845, but it is not at all strange. In the thirty years before the famine, well over one million people left Ireland for England, North America, and Australia.

There are several reasons for the pre-famine emigration. As Frank Welsh writes in *The Four Nations, a History of the United Kingdom* (2003), poverty and prosperity existed side by side in Ireland in the 1830s, and provided contrasting motives for the Irish to leave. Some people fled after repeated joblessness and local famines, while other emigrants, as Welsh writes, "were more than usually enterprising, and prosperous enough." Indeed, many of the steerage passengers on the *Bristol* were not at all impoverished. When their bodies washed ashore on Rockaway Beach, the numerous gold coins found sewn into their coat-linings reveal that some of these people were not being forced out of Ireland at all, but were consciously transferring their skills, their energy, and their limited family wealth to America. Moreover, the sixty-eight people in steerage had booked passage on Woodhull & Minturn's well-outfitted and relatively-spacious ship *Bristol*. The cost of their passage was about one-third higher than the far less-reputable *Mexico*, with her overcrowded steerage deck and minimal services. The desperately poor aboard that vessel are a far different case, and will be discussed in Part II.

Some of the steerage passengers on the *Bristol* had experience in trades or in service positions. They were seeking opportunities in America, where their capital, their skills, and their effort could earn a far greater return than in Ireland. Among those with skills were John Finnigan, a wheelwright, and John Paisley, a butcher.

The lists of the *Bristol's* steerage passengers reflect an emigration strategy that is still used today in many lands, including the United States. Vigorous men went over first, to work, send money back home, and, after establishing themselves, to send for their families or return home to bring them over. Indeed, thirty of the sixty-eight steerage passengers (44 percent) were men traveling to New York with no women or children accompanying them. Almost all of the survivors from steerage would come from this group of unaccompanied men—because of the difficulty of the escape from steerage.

There were only six women and children (9 percent of the total in steerage) who were not accompanied by men. They were Mrs. O'Nealy and her three children, Mrs. Bennett, and Rosy McDonald. None of them would survive.

Most of the women and children in steerage had a man in their party. There were thirty-two such passengers (47 percent), including thirteen children, in these family groups. The only people from these families that would survive were the two servant girls and their brothers. When Elizabeth Dairy and Catharine Mooney gained employment aboard the *Bristol* as servants for the wealthy passengers in first cabin, their initiative not only earned them free passage to America, it saved their lives. When the sneaker wave struck, the two girls and their brothers, William Dairy and Michael Mooney, were the only steerage passengers who were not trapped below decks. They were in the round-house.[14]

As was typical of merchant ships in 1836, The *Bristol* had no emergency exits, no crewmen assigned to assist the passengers, no lifeboat drills, and no life jackets. The dozens of steerage passengers huddled below decks simply relied on the captain's statement that the *Bristol* was new and strong, and that she would withstand the fury of the storm. In the dim light of a single oil lamp, passengers sat clutching their shore-parcels and fingering their concealed gold coins. They all expected to be taken ashore in the ship's boats at daybreak. Many of the children remained dressed in the Sunday-best clothing they had put on the previous day when the ship stood off Sandy Hook. Their parents soothed them to sleep, singing and praying over the deafening noise of the rising storm.

Then the sneaker wave struck. In an instant, the butcher, the wheelwright, the parents, and the children were confronted by the greatest physical challenge of their lives, one that only a few had any hope of surviving. An unnamed steerage passenger who eventually made it to shore said the wave was so powerful that it threw him hard to the deck. After recovering his footing, he found water surging down the hatchway at a formidable rate. The *Bristol* had been driven off the sandbar that had held it so firmly, and now wallowed deep into a trough behind it. As water rushed

---

[14] It is not known whether the two Mooneys and the two Dairys were siblings or married couples. Because the two women were referred to in the newspapers without the customary "Mrs." for married women, they will be referred to here as brothers and sisters.

down into the hold the ship began to lie so low that each succeeding wave, coming only seconds apart, dumped ever greater quantities of seawater down the hatches.

The steerage passengers had barely recovered from the shock of being thrown off their feet and out of their bunks when they were confronted by a wall of water surging toward them, quenching the oil lamp as it splashed by. With the lamp now extinguished, the water could no longer be seen in the blackness; it could only be felt, rising about their legs. The sound of the rushing water was exceeded by the panicky screams of children for their parents, parents for their children, and friends for friends.

Thousands of gallons of seawater spread out across the steerage deck, carrying everything that was movable—bedding, shore-parcels, trunks, food, chamber pots, and violins. There was one hope in each person's mind: somehow to gather family and friends, get to the ladder, and climb up and out the steerage hatchway, which was the only exit to the main deck. But the rush of seawater was a powerful impediment. Escape was possible only for the strongest among them, and for those who through luck or foresight were close to the ladder when the wave struck. Even those few were in grave danger, as new waves crashed onto the main deck and poured cascades of black seawater down from the darkness above. The survivors clawed their way up the ladder between surges, using brute strength against the force of the down-rushing water.

Most of the passengers could not accomplish such a feat. Mr. and Mrs. Mackenott collected their three daughters and their son and waded in the darkness toward where they thought the ladder was. Mrs. O'Nealy with her two daughters and a son, the Whites and their three children, and the Buchannans and their three children, all pushed against the water's flow toward the unseen ladder. Stronger people, mostly men, pushed roughly past them. As the families picked their way forward, water kept flowing relentlessly toward them, restricting their progress. It rose about their bodies in alarming surges. Soon the water was at chest level, and progress was almost impossible. The water kept rising.

Sebastian Junger describes in *The Perfect Storm* (1997) the silent "work of death" by drowning when the ship *Andrea Gail*, a Massachusetts fishing boat, disappeared off the Georges Bank in a gale, with the loss of all hands. There were no survivors to tell the story, but even if there had been, there would, of course, still be no one able to relate the experiences of the drowned men. So Junger presented scientific evidence along with a "lived-to-tell-about-it" story from a man who had nearly drowned. He was John Lawson, a Scottish ship's doctor, who wrote in the *Edinburgh Medical Journal* about his near-death experience.

Lawson was a passenger on a voyage to Ceylon, in 1892, when his ship went down unexpectedly in a typhoon. As the ship was sinking to the bottom, Lawson managed to put on a life vest and claw his way out of the hold, but found that he and the ship were already underwater. He wrote:

> The ship was going down rapidly, and I was pulled down with her, struggling to extricate myself.
> I got clear, under water, and immediately struck out to reach the surface, only to go further down. This exertion was a waste of breath, and after ten or fifteen seconds, the effort of inspiration could no longer be sustained. It seemed that I was held in a vice which was gradually being screwed up tight until it felt as if the sternum and spinal column must break. Many years ago, my old teacher used to describe how painless and easy a death by drowning was – "like falling about in a green field in early summer" – and this flashed across my brain at the time. The "gulping" efforts became less frequent, and the pressure seemed unbearable, but gradually the pain began to ease up. I appeared to be in a pleasant dream, although I had enough will power to think of friends at home and the sight of the Grampian [mountains], familiar to me as a boy, that was brought into my view. Before losing consciousness, the chest pain had completely disappeared and the sensation was actually pleasant.
> When consciousness returned, I found myself on the surface, and managed to get a few dozen good inspirations. [15]

A reading of Dr. Lawson's account might lead one to speculate that the dozens of men, women, and children who drowned in the wreck of the *Bristol* had a peaceful ending. They did not. Their deaths were agonizing. [16]

For those passengers who were too distant from the ladder or not strong enough, there were moments of horror to be endured before the end. The cold water relentlessly rose in the claustrophobic blackness. Children were held higher and higher in their parents' arms. Some may have climbed onto upper bunks or grabbed onto floating trunks. But once the water reached the overhead, at six or so feet, there was nowhere to go, and no air left to breathe. And so the trapped passengers experienced the sequence of physical effects described by Dr. Lawson: painful constriction in their air-starved lungs, dry gulps (laryngospasms), wet gulps of seawater, semi-conscious paroxysm, stillness, and death.

---

[15] Lawson uses a physiological term, "inspiration," meaning the drawing of air into the lungs.
[16] See the Preface of this book for more on this topic.

For the many children on the *Bristol* who drowned, their last terrifying moments may have been more drawn-out than for their parents. Children can maintain some consciousness underwater for as long as a minute after all oxygen is gone from the lungs, and can have a heartbeat for up to five minutes. The chill of seawater in late November would have slowed their metabolism and extended those times even further.

Of the sixty-eight people in steerage, forty-nine drowned, and only nineteen got out alive. That not one of the fifteen children or eight women below decks survived is stark testimony to the difficulty of the escape. But there is something else about the deaths of the children that is truly remarkable. In a clear demonstration of the powerful bond that exists between parent and child, *not one of the ten parents of these fifteen children got out alive.* The families perished together, as the mothers and fathers struggled desperately to extricate their entire family from the flooded hold of the *Bristol*. The familial bond was stronger than the instinct for self-preservation. These parents would rather die than leave their children behind.

Forty-Nine Steerage Passengers Who Drowned in the Wreck of the *Bristol*

(From the memory of Captain McKown.
He provided no additional information about these passengers.)

Sources: The *New York Sun*, January 12, 1837, and
The *New York Herald,* November 11, 1836.

Name
Mrs. Bennett
Mr. Braham
Wm. Buchannan
His wife
Their oldest child
Their middle child
Their youngest child
A person with last name Deary
U. Deavy
Deavy's sister
T. Delany
P. Diagin
His wife
E. Dorey
Andrew Doyle
A person with last name Garshney
Pat Handerhand

(Continued on the next page)

Steerage Deaths (Continued)

T. Hundlin
A person with last name Kearney
Patrick Lamb
A person with last name Larry
Mr. Mackenott (or Macaumont or Mackeonott)
His wife
Their oldest daughter
Their middle daughter
Their youngest daughter
Their son
Richard Markey
Rosy McDonald
A person with last name Onders
Mrs. O'Nealy
Her daughter
Her older son
Her younger son
Mr. Phinegan
His wife
Mr. Peaseley
His wife
Their child
Wm. Quigley
A person with last name Quinn
A person with last name Scott
A person with last name Smith
A child with last name Smith
T. White
His wife
Their oldest child
Their middle child
Their youngest child

The few men who struggled out onto the main deck now faced a fresh danger—being washed overboard. The crewmembers up on the masts and out on the bowsprit pulled to safety as many passengers as they could, but some were washed overboard.

A forty-year-old man from Londonderry, Northern Ireland, identified only by his first name, Michael, was one of the steerage passengers who made it up out of the death trap and onto the mast. He was reported as being "entirely deaf and dumb," and in the company of friends and family. When the sneaker wave struck, knocking passengers off their feet and dousing the oil lamp in steerage, Michael was immediately separated from his party—

none of whom survived. It is difficult to comprehend just how precarious and terrifying a position he was in. As a deaf mute, Michael could not cry out to his family and friends or hear their cries. He could not hear the shouts of those near the hatch, calling to others to come that way as the only means of escape. In the night's blackness, with the oil lamp extinguished, he was sightless, too. There was only one way to survive: use his sense of touch. Striking out on his own, and feeling his way in the darkness, Michael fought his way, always against the flow of water, toward the ladder. Then he climbed up and out through the hatchway. Michael showed incredible courage, perseverance, and strength to survive such difficult circumstances. The news reports written about him give a hint of how traumatic the ordeal was, and how difficult his remaining life's journey would be:

> *A pitiable object* – Yesterday, a gentleman driving across Long Island to this city [New York City] in his wagon, overtook a man who was both deaf and dumb, [walking] in company with others, whom he ascertained were among the number of those who had escaped from the wreck of the ship *Bristol* on Rockaway Beach. He was induced to take the poor mute into his wagon and bring him to this city, as he was informed that in addition to being cast away, he had been taken from the wreck in a state of nudity except for his shirt, with the loss of a chest and all his effects, except what he could carry in his hand. He was clad in the clothes of a drowned sailor.
>
> He was brought by the gentleman to the alms-house office to be taken care of and protected. On examining him there, there were found four gold sovereigns, two dollars, and some small change, which together with a few papers not revealing his name, were all he had saved from the wreck. As he could not speak nor read or write and as his manual conversation [sign language] was unintelligible to the officers, and to all except the reporter of one of the small papers, the latter alone was able to communicate with him and to ascertain that he had been possessed of more money, that he was an Englishman, that his name was Michael, but that his head was too much disordered to give further information. He was detained and comfortably provided for.
>
> —*Morning Courier*, November 25, 1836.

A report in the *New York Commercial Advertiser* of November 24, 1836, stated that the *Bristol's* owners, Woodhull & Minturn, were generously making arrangements to send Michael back to Liverpool. This act was less charitable than it seems. Under New York State law, the shipowner was required to reimburse the almshouse up to $300 of support money expended for any emigrant they brought to the United States who became a ward of the state. By shipping Michael back to Liverpool—in steerage class, of course—they avoided this payment.

Nineteen Steerage Passengers Saved from the *Bristol*
(From the memory of Captain McKown)

Sources: The *New York Sun*, January 12, 1837;
The *New York Herald,* November 25, 1836;
The *New York Commercial Advertiser,* November 28, 1836; and
The *Morning Courier*, November 25, 1836.

Name	Other Information
John Carr	Kildare
William Dairy	Derry, laborer
Elizabeth Dairy	Derry, first-cabin servant girl
Richard Faulkner	County Louth
John Finnigan	Dublin, wheelwright
James Gaffney	County Cavan
Patrick Lamb	Dublin, laborer
Peter Markey	County Louth, currier
Michael McGintry	Dublin
Patrick O'Mealy	Kings County
Thomas O'Mealy	Kings County
Michael Mooney	Kings County, laborer
Catharine Mooney	Kings County, first-cabin servant girl
John Paisley	England, butcher
John Roach	Limerick
Mr. Warren	County Wicklow
Samuel Warren	County Wicklow
James Warren	County Wicklow
Michael (no last name given)	Deaf and dumb man from Londonderry, about 40 years old

Death in Second Cabin

In the 1830s, Ireland had few people who could be called middle class. Indeed, the vast majority of Irishmen were hardscrabble farmers who grew potatoes on an acre or two that they rented from well-to-do landlords. A talented, hard-working tenant farmer had little incentive to improve his situation because, if he built a new barn, for example, he would lose it at the expiration of his lease, at which time the landlord would become the owner of the improvement. A big attraction in the United States was that a farmer could own his land and own his barn.

Indeed, America was a land of opportunity, and not just for farmers. The second-cabin passengers on the *Bristol* were economic opportunists engaged in a variety of occupations. Unfortunately, little is known about them beyond the lists of victims and survivors printed in the newspapers of the day, along with a few spare descriptions. But those lists reveal a lot about this diverse group of men and women. For example, while steerage passengers were almost exclusively Irish, second cabin included at least one Welshman, three Scots, four New Yorkers, and five Englishmen, along with nineteen Irishmen.

Some in second cabin had occupations much in demand in New York. For example, John Dunn, a Dubliner, was a shoemaker, and S. Thomas was a tailor. Others on the ship had already found success in the United States, and were now returning from visits to their former residences in Ireland and England. Two unnamed women, one of whom was a dressmaker, were returning to New York. Another transplanted Irishman, Christopher Shields, had been visiting family in Ireland, and was returning home to Brooklyn, where he lived with his wife and children. Mr. Graham had emigrated from England sixteen years before. He was now accompanying his nephew to New York.

In addition to the fact that the travelers in second cabin were willing to pay more for their accommodations than those in steerage, there are other clues as to their higher economic status. The *Bristol* was legally required to have just one doctor aboard to serve her 127 passengers, yet two doctors, Dr. McMullin and Dr. Aiken, both from Northern Ireland, were listed in second cabin. It is likely that at least one of these physicians was traveling not just for the meager pay offered to a ship's doctor, or for the adventure, but to establish himself in the United States. When the body of one of the doctors—the corpse was not further identified—washed up on Rockaway Beach, gold coins equivalent to ten thousand dollars today were found sewn into the linings of his coat.

Second cabin was more elaborately constructed in comparison to the long, straight rows of bunks on the steerage deck. It had partitions separating the sleeping quarters from the dining and socializing space. In the sleeping area, partitions set groups of bunks apart to afford some minimal privacy for family groups and for women traveling alone. Unfortunately, these enhancements, as desirable as they were, may have blocked the passengers' path to the ladder. As a result, the survival rate in second cabin was far lower than in steerage. Only six passengers of forty-nine managed to escape.

When the powerful waves had begun to boom against the side of the ship, sending vibrations through the decks and the bulkheads, the passengers in second cabin, like those in steerage, had lain in their bunks in fear. Then the unimaginable happened. The sneaker wave roared down the open hatchway and hurled its cold, black mass of seawater out across the cabin, around the partitions, and into the lower bunks. Everyone—the laborers, tailors, doctors, and dressmakers—reacted immediately, but most had no possibility of escape. One of the few survivors from second cabin, Michael McGintry, described his fellow passengers' futile attempts:

> Then came the shock, and the rush of waters—the force of the waters sweeping down the hatchway prevented almost anyone from escaping. Those who essayed were driven back to death.[17] With much difficulty, much bruised, by the mercy of God, I escaped, and from that part of the vessel five more only lived.
> —The *New York Herald*, November 29, 1836.

Although passenger McGintry reported that there were five other survivors from second cabin, none of the five were named in the newspapers. But they are known, thanks to a family history that has been preserved. It is

---

[17] In nineteenth-century usage, to "essay" meant to try to accomplish something.

the oral and written history of the Horan family of upstate New York, as passed down through the decades. It reveals that the unnamed survivors from second cabin were probably Michael Horan and as many as four of his sons. Horan, from Gillen Parish in Kings County, Ireland, had relatives living in upstate New York, and his destination was the Troy, New York area.

While the facts are not perfectly clear, Horan, the father of seven children—six boys and a girl—appears to have made a cautious determination not to place his entire family at risk aboard one ship. He may have brought only his middle sons with him, leaving his wife Mary, a daughter, and probably his eldest and youngest sons behind. The plan was to send for them later. Separating the family was a fortunate decision. The boys who accompanied him were strong and agile enough to work together as a group in overcoming incredible odds. The details of the Horans' escape were not recorded, but it must have been no easy matter, particularly for the younger boys. A news account describes the trials of an unnamed survivor and his son—possibly Michael Horan and his young son, Kyran.

> We have conversed with one of the passengers wrecked in the *Bristol*, who describes the scene as most appalling. He himself clung to the wreck for many hours, holding his son in his lap.
> —*The Times of London*, December 20, 1836.
> (Reprinted from an unnamed New York newspaper)

Mary Horan and the other children were able to emigrate to New York later, uniting the family once again. Michael and Mary Horan's numerous descendants still reside in upstate New York, many of them in the Troy and Albany areas. Among the Horans' descendants are businesspeople, professionals, writers, and a senior New York State Assemblyman. The success of these heirs provides some indication of the tremendous loss in potentially productive citizens when one hundred emigrants died in the wreck of the *Bristol*.

Six Passengers in Second Cabin
Who Survived the Wreck of the *Bristol*

Sources: *New York Herald*, November 29, 1836.
McEneny Family History. [18]

Name	Other Information
Michael McGintry (or McGinty)	None
Michael Horan	Gillen Parish in Kings County, Ireland. Settled in Troy, New York.
(?)Thomas, his second son	"
(?)John, his third son	"
(?)James, his fourth son	"
(?)Kyran, his fifth son	"

Forty-Three Passengers in Second Cabin
Who Perished in the Wreck of the *Bristol*
Primarily from the recollection of Captain McKown

Sources: *New York Sun*, January 12, 1837.
New York Herald, November 25, 1836.
Morning Courier & New York Express, various dates.
New York Commercial Advertiser, November 24, 1836.

Name	Other Information
Dr. Aiken	North of Ireland, Medical Doctor
Mrs. Andrews	Derry (She was listed as steerage in the *New York Commercial Advertiser*)
Her eldest daughter	Derry
Her middle daughter	Derry
Her youngest daughter	Derry
Her son	Derry
Mr. Bailiff	Dumfries, Scotland
Thomas Black	Scotland
Mr. Burke	Tipperary
His sister	Tipperary
Jno. Cod	Dublin
Andrew Doyle	Donoghue, Ireland
John Dunn	Dublin, Shoemaker

(Continued on the next page)

---

[18] The details of the McEneny Family History are imprecise as to specifically which of Michael Horan's children traveled with him on the *Bristol*.

Second Cabin Deaths (Continued)

D. Evans	None
Mr. Stephen Graham	Manchester, England
His nephew, initials "N.T."	None
S. Graham	Tailor
Mr. Graham	Lived in America for sixteen years. Went back to England to bring his nephew over.
His nephew, Thomas G. Graham	England
T. Horton	None
Mr. Lacey	None
Mrs. Lacey	None
Mrs. Lucy	Dublin
Mr. McDermott	Donoghue, Ireland
A person with the last name McFacters	None
Dr. McMullin	North of Ireland, Medical Doctor
A person with the last name O'Reilly	Dublin
A person with the last name Reilly (or Reily)	None
Christopher Shields	Brooklyn (died on shore)
J. Thomas	None
Lewis Thomas	Wales
Thomas Thomas	Wales
Mr. Warren	None
His elder son	None
His younger son	None
James Will	Scotland
Mr. Wise	None
His cousin, Georgia Wise	None
Mrs. Wolfe	England
Her niece	England
Unidentified woman	New York, Dressmaker
Unidentified woman	New York
Unidentified man	None

Escape from First Cabin

Ten people occupied staterooms in first cabin: Mrs. Frances Hogan; her two daughters, Fanny Hogan and Sophia Donnelly; her son-in-law, Arthur Donnelly; the Donnellys' two children; the children's nurse, Vinissa; and three businessmen, Francis Burtsall, Esq., James Hale Charlton, and Edward Ash Charlton. As the *Bristol* glided to a stop onto the Rockaway Shoals, the commotion on deck roused them from their comfortable beds. After repeated attempts failed to move the ship out to deeper water, Captain McKown, instructed all passengers—first cabin included—to prepare shore-parcels and to get ready for the ship's boats to take them ashore in the morning. When he ordered the hatches to be secured, there was no choice for the steerage and second cabin passengers; they had to stay below. However, Mrs. Hogan, Mr. Donnelly, and the others in first cabin were given an option: they could remain below decks under a secured hatch cover, or they could take their shore-parcels up to the round-house, and wait there. Whatever their choice, they would be the first to leave the ship. Once on shore they could hire a carriage to take them to Manhattan by evening.

The decision was not at all clear. With the storm worsening by the moment, the staterooms below decks offered better protection, but the solidly-built round-house had the distinct advantage of a quick exit. Frances Hogan and her son-in-law, Arthur Donnelly, were well equipped to make this decision. After all, Donnelly was a merchant shipper himself, and Mrs. Hogan probably had more sailing experience than any other passenger aboard the *Bristol*—other than her son-in-law—and she had most likely spent more time at sea than many of the younger sailors. Moreover, she had faced critical situations before.

In the 1820s, the Hogans lived in Valparaiso, Chile, where Frances' husband Michael was the U.S. consul. Valparaiso was then virtually a "Wild

85

West" town. When armed bandits simultaneously attacked the American and French consulate compounds, Frances learned the value of being prepared for the worst. Her household was armed with rifles and pistols, which they used to drive off the attackers. The nearby French consulate had made no such contingency, and was sacked.

A few years later, a devastating earthquake struck Valparaiso and destroyed most of its buildings. The Hogans again were prepared for the worst. As soon as the tremors began, they immediately ran from the house and headed for the harbor by a pre-planned route. As they ran, they heard the sound of buildings crumbling behind them. Upon reaching the shore, they commandeered a yawl and rowed it to the safety of an anchored ship. The Hogans' house and its furniture were destroyed by the earthquake. Twelve foreigners died. Not one person in the Hogan household was even injured.

Now, aboard the *Bristol*, Frances Hogan did what her life-experiences taught her. She had spent literally years at sea, and knew its awesome power from first-hand observation. She and her family members went up into the round-house with their shore-parcels and jewelry chests. Vinissa and the two servant girls, Elizabeth Dairy and Catharine Mooney, came with them. Francis Burtsall, Esq. and the two other passengers from first cabin, James Hale Charlton and Edward Ash Charlton, did not join them and stayed below.

The women and children were not safe with only Mr. Donnelly in the round-house to assist them in an emergency. Thus, before the steerage hatch was secured, she arranged for the servant girls' brothers, William Dairy and Michael Mooney, to be sent for. The two young Irishmen were laborers. They had the strength to assist the women and children in the event of a crisis. Frances had acquired her "insurance policy." And it paid off.

When the giant sneaker wave exploded against the side of the *Bristol* and tore across the deck, it surged up, over, and around the round-house, terrifying the people inside. As seawater swirled inside the damaged structure, the occupants knew they had to get out immediately. The men inside got the women and children out on deck, and with the help of the crew, quickly hoisted them up into the mizzenmast rigging. It was fortunate that everyone moved fast, because a following wave swept the weakened round-house completely off the deck.

All the women and girls in steerage and second cabin—two dozen of them—died. However, in first cabin, a sixty-five-year-old grandmother, her two daughters, her two grandchildren, their nursemaid, and two servant girls all survived—thanks to luck, good decisions, strong men to help them, and the privilege of wealth and position.

Mr. Burtsall and the two Messers Charlton managed to escape from their cabins and climb the mast. Two of them would later drown.

Ten Passengers in First Cabin on the *Bristol*
(A list from the memory of Captain McKown)
(See the Steerage List for the four others who were in the round-house)

Sources:
New York Sun, January 12, 1837.
LI Democrat, December 7, 1836.

Name	Other Information	Survival
Mrs. Frances Hogan (65)	Widow of Michael Hogan, Esq., of New York City, the U.S. consul at Valparaiso, Chile.	Survived the wreck.
Miss Frances ("Fanny") Hogan (41)	Daughter of Mrs. Hogan, resident of New York City	Survived the wreck.
Mrs. Sophia Donnelly (34)	Daughter of Mrs. Hogan, traveling from India to NYC via England with her husband and two children.	Survived the wreck.
Mr. Arthur Donnelly	Husband of Sophia Donnelly, an English merchant of Irish descent, emigrating to NYC with his family.	Escaped from the cabin, but drowned later.
The Donnellys' elder daughter, a child	Born in Calcutta, India.	Survived the wreck.
The Donnellys' younger daughter, a child	Born in Calcutta, India.	Survived the wreck.
Vinissa, nursemaid to the Donnellys' children	Of New York City. Previously Mrs. Hogan's slave in Cape Town, Africa. Freed in 1804 and indentured to the Hogans until 1828.	Survived the wreck.
Francis Burtsall, Esq.	None	Survived the wreck.
James Hale Carleton	Originally from Bristol, England.	Escaped from the cabin, but drowned later.
Edward Ash Carleton	Originally from Bristol, England.	Escaped from the cabin, but drowned later.

Rescue

Survivors continued to fight their way up the ladders, through the open hatches, and out into the black night. They were now confronted by a new terror—powerful waves surging across the ship's deck. Several passengers were immediately washed overboard and drowned. Others, on hearing shouts from the crewmembers up on the masts and in the rigging, climbed up or were pulled up. Ninety or so passengers had already drowned, but about thirty others made it to relative safety by clinging for dear life to whatever they could hold onto. A Long Island newspaper described the chaos:

> The scene that now presented itself on deck, beggars description. . .
> Every spot that could afford shelter from the sea was filled by some
> of the survivors, who lashed themselves to the sails, the rigging, and
> the masts.
>
> —*Hempstead Inquirer,* November 30, 1836.

It is difficult to imagine the survivors' shock and despair. Their possessions had been washed away in a matter of seconds, and their lives were still in peril despite having narrowly escaped drowning just moments before. The greatest anxiety was, of course, felt by those who had been separated from family members or friends. Their eyes madly scanned the darkness as they screamed the names of the missing, hoping for a familiar shout from below, or a sudden outcry from higher in the rigging. But no new voices were heard. There was only the sound of wind and waves. The almost-new, proud, American ship *Bristol* was now a watery tomb.

When the sneaker wave crashed into the *Bristol*, it took with it Captain McKown's last hope to save his ship. His only goal now was to save his remaining passengers and crew. However, nothing could be done until daylight—except pray. The ship's boats had been swept away, so his best hope was that someone on land had heard or seen his wreck signals, and would mount a rescue. From the sound of waves breaking on the dark, unseen shore, the ship lay only a few hundred yards from land. However, any attempt to swim through these violent seas, or even to drift ashore by holding onto a broken spar, was far riskier than clinging to the stricken ship. Hopes soon rose when lanterns were seen moving on the beach.

Two local fishermen, Oliver Cornell and Stephen Watts, lived in cottages on Rockaway Beach. They had heard the ship's wreck gun and had seen the rockets in the night sky. Cornell and Watts ran more than five miles inland to the home of Stephen Rider, a well-to-do squire, to report the wreck. Rider had heard the guns, too, and had already dispatched servants to call out the residents of the tiny hamlet of Rockaway, Long Island.

As word spread around the Rockaway Peninsula, fishermen and farmers began to gather on the beach opposite the wreck. At around 7 AM, they could begin to see the wreck through the murky dawn and the sea spray. Then they spotted passengers and crewmen clinging to the masts, spars, bowsprit, and rigging of the stricken vessel. They also saw waves washing over the deck of the stranded ship. The surf ran so high that no one on shore was willing to launch a rescue boat. Skilled help, however, was on the way. Stephen Rider's servants were bringing wreck-master David T. Jennings to the beach.

The waters off Long Island's South Shore from Montauk Point to Coney Island are known to wreck divers as "Shipwreck Valley." Over four hundred shipwrecks have been documented there, from the *Prins Maurits* in 1657 to the *Gwendoline Steers* in 1962—victims of riptides, onshore winds, shifting sandbars, and shoals. In 1787, just months before the U.S. Constitution was drafted, New York State passed a law calling for the governor to appoint a wreck-master for each county bordering the sea. The state's wreck-master system remained in place for over one hundred years, until the statute was finally taken off the books in 1890.

Before the wreck-master law was passed, it was common for the entire population of a village to descend on a shipwreck and seize whatever they could lay their hands on. Long Island's South Shore provided numerous such opportunities. New York State's wreck-master legislation was designed to control this lawlessness. Wreck-masters had to be leading citizens of their communities. It was their job to see that nothing was removed from a wreck or from the beach until the shipowners or insurers could transport or sell-on-the-spot any of the wreck's cargo, spars, anchors, ropes, or other items of value. Wreck-masters were also charged with organizing and directing volunteer rescue efforts and identifying and burying the dead.

Wreck-master Jennings took charge immediately upon his arrival at Rockaway Beach. At his direction a surfboat was hauled out to the beach, but conditions were too hazardous to attempt a rescue. By 11 AM, it was clear that the storm was not abating. Jennings, a skilled boatman, chose three local fishermen—George Combs and two men named Oliver Cornell, possibly father and son—to help him effect a rescue, despite the risks. No one on the Rockaway Peninsula was better equipped than they. Although the boat was small for the task, the men's long experience as fishermen in the open ocean had frequently required them to skillfully handle small boats in heavy seas and surf—though never so heavy as this.

On stormy November days, Rockaway fishermen generally remained inside their cottages repairing nets, not launching boats. But the sight of women and children clinging to the *Bristol's* rigging, and the distant sound of their screams, brought out the best in these men. They were ready to risk their lives for total strangers.

After repositioning the boat to a point well east of the *Bristol*, to allow for the ocean current's westerly pull, they assayed their chances. From their intimate knowledge of local tides, they knew that although the storm surge had brought the sea to an apparent flood level, it was in fact low tide. They had to act now, before things got worse.

A Three-man Surfboat Challenges the Elements
<www.mollymookseaspray.com.au/location.html>

The four men climbed into the boat, with oars held at the ready. Other men held tightly to the gunwales, and waited for a "smooth chance"—a fisherman's name for a momentary lull in a violent sea. With a shout, the men at the gunwales powerfully ran the boat out and over a smaller incoming wave. They kept pushing until the water was too deep. The four oarsmen pulled on their oars with all their strength as the first large wave met the bow, raised it almost vertically, and then dropped it with a force almost great enough to stave in her bottom. All four oarsmen now rowed straight out, allowing the cross-current to pull them west toward the ship. Their target was the lee side of the *Bristol,* where the grounded hulk of the ship would serve as a breakwater against the worst of the oncoming seas.

A long coil of rope lay on the beach, with one end of it attached to the stern of the rescue boat. As the four boatmen rowed away, the line was played out from shore. The plan was for the rowers to pull the line out to the *Bristol* and attach it to the ship. Then they would pull a second line back from the ship to the shore. The two lines would then be used to haul the surfboat back and forth like a ferry. Sadly, the plan went quickly awry. The east-to-west current dragged so viciously at the trailing rope that Jennings and his crew could not maintain their heading to the wreck. They were forced back to the beach.

Meanwhile, the situation was rapidly deteriorating aboard the *Bristol.* The masts, especially the mainmast, were shaking so violently with the impact of each wave that they threatened to lever the ship over onto her side, throwing passengers and crew into the sea. Captain McKown told everyone who was in the mainmast to go up into the foremast. He then ordered the crew to cut down the main. After the huge timber fell crashing into the sea, the ship lay easier. The measure was effective, but the captain had merely bought time.

Back on shore, Jennings, Combs, and the two Cornells had not given up, but they needed to change their plan of attack. With the tide now rising, their boat was too small for the task, so they launched a larger boat, this time without employing a drag line. Progress was better, but when they reached the *Bristol's* lee they feared approaching too close. There was the risk of entanglement in the recently-fallen mainmast. The mast was hanging off the lee side with spars and rigging still attached.

The desperate passengers and crew screamed to be saved, but the rescuers stood off, pointing at the obstruction. One young woman refused to passively look on while the rescuers were so tantalizingly close. She was Elizabeth Dairy or Catharine Mooney—the news reports did not say who she was, only that she was a servant girl. She had avoided death in steerage when the sneaker wave struck, because she was in the round-house with the first-cabin passengers. She had been pulled up along with the others onto the mizzenmast.

It is difficult to understand what motivated her to do what she did next. She may in fact have misunderstood the rescuers' pointing at the fallen mast as being an indication of where the rescue would be made. Perhaps it was a compulsive panic. Regardless, the young woman had a desperate wish to get off the ship. Undeterred by the impossibly dangerous situation before her, she climbed down from the mizzenmast, waded through the surf washing over the deck, and climbed out onto the fallen mainmast where it stretched shoreward. She then picked her way through the shattered rigging, out toward the rescue boat, as waves rose and fell about her body. Jennings and his men must have been astonished at the sight, but they approached close enough for her to leap off the mast and swim for the boat. Just moments after she was hauled into the surfboat, a huge wave swept over the ship, submerged the fallen mast, and nearly swamped the boat. The boatmen retreated to shore with just that one remarkable passenger, and waited for the mainmast's obstructions to be cleared.

The rescuers had to acknowledge that with the tide continuing to rise, even this boat was too small. They obtained a third, larger boat, pushed it through the surf, and again rowed out to the ship. Meanwhile, Captain McKown had been busy. He ordered the obstructing spars and rigging to be cut away from the fallen mainmast. As the surfboat approached once again, McKown was faced with a critical decision, one that was not at all obvious in the year 1836: who should go first into the rescue boat? But he already knew what he must do.

Women and Children First

The maritime tradition of "women and children first" is many centuries old, but in the early nineteenth century the idea was more lip-service than moral duty. Often as not, the rule was "crewmen first and passengers be damned." Captain Alexander McKown of the *Bristol* honored the moral duty of a ship's master to the letter. In contrast, Captain Charles Winslow of the *Mexico* chose self preservation, as did many other captains and crews of that era.

The Wreck of the William Brown: A True Tale of Overcrowded Lifeboats and Murder at Sea, by Tom Koch, is a harrowing account of the emigrant ship *William Brown*, which sank far from land about five years after the wrecks of the *Bristol* and the *Mexico*, in 1841. The *Brown*'s crewmen, in order to lighten their lifeboat when a storm threatened, tossed sixteen male and female passengers out of the boat to their deaths. But was this a crime? It took a federal court case against one of the crewmen—in *United States vs. Alexander Holmes*—to establish that in the event of "extreme danger," captains and crews are compelled to "sacrifice their lives" for the benefit of the passengers.

This verdict did little to influence actual conduct at sea. After all, the black-robed judges were sitting high and dry at their benches while the situation they were ruling on called for captains and crewmen to sacrifice their own lives to save a stranger's—and they must do this while exposed to "extreme danger" at sea. Indeed, it took much more than judicial rulings to firmly establish the maritime traditions we have today.

Authoritative sources (see, for example the website, *Historic-UK.com*) cite the wreck of the H.M.S. *Birkenhead* in 1852, as the inspiring example for the modern tradition of "women and children first." The *Birkenhead* was a paddlewheel steamer, packed with British soldiers on their way to South

Africa. Their mission was to remove the native Xhosa people from their land. Fifty-four women and children—the families of officers aboard—were among the 643 people on the ship. When the steamer struck a reef near Cape Town and began to sink into shark-infested waters, the steamer's captain gave the order to launch the vessel's lifeboats. Because of poor maintenance, only three boats could be launched; so he ordered that the women and children be placed into the first boat, a large cutter. He then filled a second cutter and a smaller gig with about one hundred soldiers and sailors.

Wreck of *Birkenhead*, 1852
CW Briggs lantern slides - George Eastman House
Still Photograph Archive - collodion on glass.

Almost five hundred soldiers were still on deck, with no useable lifeboats remaining. The men began to edge toward the rail of the listing ship in the direction of the cutter that held the women and children. Army Major Alexander Seaton held his sword high and said, "The cutter with the women and children will be swamped. I implore you not to do this thing, and I ask you to stand fast." Although the deck continued to tilt, the men stood fast in orderly rows. The two cutters and the gig moved away, and the *Birkenhead* slid slowly beneath the sea. Hundreds of soldiers drowned. Most of those who tried to swim the two miles to shore were killed by great white sharks.

The steadfastness of these men inspired writers and poets, including Rudyard Kipling, who wrote about the *Birkenhead* in "Soldier an' Sailor Too":

> To stand and be still
> to the Birken'ead Drill
> is a damn tough bullet to chew.

Mariners of the time were less impressed with the discipline of the troops than were the poets. They were acutely aware that the army officers on the *Birkenhead* would have *shot* any man threatening to swamp the cutter. After all, the cutter was carrying the officers' wives and children.

The Wreck of the U.S. Steamship *Arctic* off Newfoundland in 1854.
Published by N. Currier, drawn by J. E. Buttersworth, 1854.

Word of the *Birkenhead* tragedy and its heroism reached the United States, but the moral suasion of the idea of "women and children first" was slow to take hold. In 1854, the American luxury steamboat *Arctic,* a side-wheeler, collided with the fishing tender *Vesta* off Newfoundland. When the *Arctic* began taking on water, the crew and the male passengers forced their way into the few available lifeboats, shoving women and children to the deck, and even pushing some of them into the sea. As David W. Shaw writes in *The Sea Shall Embrace Them* (2002), several crewmen and an officer escaped in a lifeboat filled to half its capacity—but loaded with provisions, including cigars. The officer and crewmen raised their pistols and threatened to shoot anyone who came near their boat. Of the 408 crewmen and passengers on board the *Arctic*, only 86 survived. Most of them were crewmen. All of them were men. Every single one of the 90 or so women and children aboard the ship drowned. At least one maritime tradition *was* observed aboard the *Arctic*: Captain James C. Luce went down with his ship, as he stood on her deck holding his young son in his arms. Miraculously, Luce's life preserver pulled him back to the surface, where he clung to a wooden box and was saved. His son, however, drowned.

By the time the *Titanic* sank in 1912, a convergence of both maritime law and maritime practice had finally developed such that women and children were given priority in a life-threatening situation. Lamentably, it also took the *Titanic's* sinking to finally bring about regulations requiring sufficient lifeboats for the full number of passengers and crew aboard a ship.

The wreck of the *Bristol* does not include acts of murder as in the sinking of the *William Brown* in 1841, or the drama of hundreds of British soldiers standing fast in ranks as the *Birkenhead* went down in 1852. Nor does it have the inhumanity exhibited when the *Arctic* sank in 1854, or the scale of the *Titanic's* fatalities in 1912. But the tragic deaths of one hundred people on the *Bristol*—the largest accidental mass death in the history of the United States to that point—along with the heroism of the Rockaway boatmen and of Captain Alexander McKown, must rank it with the great events of American maritime history.

Captain McKown had made his moral decision long before the rescue boat headed out from shore on the third rescue attempt. It was that the women and children aboard the *Bristol* must be the first to leave the ship— and that he would be the last man to go ashore. It is remarkable that he took this principled stance seventeen years before the heralded example of the *Birkenhead*.

McKown knew that not everyone aboard the *Bristol* might agree with his principles, so he made careful preparations. Although a servant girl had climbed out along the fallen mainmast and was taken ashore in the surfboat, the idea of maneuvering a grandmother and small children out along the half-submerged mast was unworkable. He had to find another way. Once the entangling spars and rigging had been cut free from the fallen mast, the rescue boat could now approach the ship's stern quarter. McKown repositioned the mizzenmast's lowest spar so that it extended shoreward, out over the water, and rigged safety lines along its length. Then he gathered the women and children along this spar to await the rescue. Most of the crew and the male passengers were now in the foremast or out on the bowsprit. Thus, they were separated from the mizzenmast by the open space amidships—where the main mast used to be—and by the waves continually surging over the deck. The captain was ready.

When the surfboat drew near, McKown hailed the rescuers, and directed them to approach the ship at the carefully repositioned mizzenmast spar. He then ordered that the women and children be taken off first—and buttressed all the men's courage by declaring that *he* would not leave the *Bristol* until everyone, including the crew, was rescued.

The example that the captain set was critical. After all, it was far from certain that there would be any more rescue attempts. The storm surge was rising about the ship, putting her decks farther underwater and threatening to drop the two remaining masts—the foremast and the mizzen—and break up the ship. The later tragedies of the *Arctic* and the *William Brown* are proof that, under extreme circumstances, this was still very much the age of "every man for himself." Indeed, in a later chapter about the wreck of the *Mexico*, we will see the "every man for himself" rule carried out to the full. However, Captain McKown's forceful command presence and his careful preparation for the rescue carried the day. His leadership by example overcame the baser instincts that his crew and the male passengers might otherwise have followed.

Jennings' rescue boat approached the mizzen spar and he began taking off the women and children, including all the female members of the Donnelly party. There was room for two more people. The captain, seeing no other women and children nearby—he may not have been aware that Michael Horan was clinging to the foremast with his young son in his lap—instructed Mrs. Hogan's son-in-law, Arthur Donnelly, to join his family in the boat. He also told the first mate, William Tapscott, to get in to help handle the boat.

As Donnelly was about to step in, he paused and looked back over his shoulder, perhaps feeling guilty at receiving preference merely for being a first-cabin passenger. Moreover, he probably knew that the second servant girl must still be aboard the ship. Looking up, he saw her high in the rigging, clinging to the mizzen top. Donnelly pointed to the girl, but Captain McKown yelled down to Donnelly to "save yourself if at all possible." Donnelly refused. In a remarkably selfless act, he insisted on giving up his seat to the servant girl, and rejoined the captain in the mizzen rigging as she climbed down and entered the rescue boat. Arthur Donnelly would never see his family again.

When the rescuers neared the shore, a huge comber too large to be managed by the boatmen rose up from behind. It lifted the stern so high that the oars were useless. The bow was thrust forward and downward, submerging it. The boat then "pitch-poled," with the stern tossed up and over the bow, spilling boatmen and passengers into the water, and leaving the surfboat upside down. Men on shore rushed out to drag the sputtering men, women, and children ashore. All were saved.

The boat was dragged ashore, but because of the still-rising seas, the boatmen requested an even larger boat before they would go out again. A suitable one had been dragged to the beach by a team of horses, but its owner, a fisherman, having just watched the near-destruction of the last boat, was unwilling to risk losing the source of his livelihood in such awful surf. He refused. After waiting for another boat to be brought out, the Rockaway boatmen rowed a fourth time to the *Bristol*, this time taking off eight or nine male passengers and crewmen. By the time they returned to the beach, the seas had risen to such heights that further attempts were impossible.

The Rockaway boatmen—Jennings, Combs, and the two Cornells— had braved the elements for four hours, making four rescue attempts with four different surfboats. They had taken off no one in the first attempt, a servant girl in the second try, eight women and children and the first mate in the third effort, and eight or nine male passengers and crew in the fourth attempt. It was now evening. Storm clouds obscured the setting autumn sun. Not only was the flood-tide near its height and the sea at its worst, the boatmen were exhausted. They decided to wait for the storm to subside, for the flood-tide to retreat, and for daylight.

Aboard the *Bristol* there was no rest from the storm, as it raged with renewed fury. As night fell, the ship began to go to pieces. A huge wave hit the ship with such force that it toppled the weakened foremast and dropped it shoreward. As the mast tumbled into the sea, it pried open a large hole in the foredeck, and almost split the ship in two. There were sixteen men clinging to the foremast when it went down. All were tossed into the sea. Several of them, including first-cabin passengers James and Edward Charlton, had tied themselves to the mast. They drowned immediately. Others, suddenly finding themselves in the water, faced an awful decision—for the few that could swim—whether to strike out for shore four hundred yards away in the darkness, or to swim back to the sinking ship against the wind, the waves, and the current. Of those who attempted to swim to shore, none made it. A steward, a cabin boy, and two sailors struggled to swim back to the ship, and they also drowned.

Those who survived the falling foremast did so largely through luck. First-cabin passenger Francis Burtsall fell into the sea but managed to grab a floating bobstay—a rope attached to the bowsprit. He hauled himself back to the bow and was pulled up. Another man, a sailor, managed to grab a floating line and pull himself to the *Bristol's* jib boom. He, too, was hauled back on board.

Both the mainmast and the foremast were now gone, and most of the foredeck was in splinters. The only portions of the ship still above water were the bowsprit, the mizzenmast, and the taffrail, which was the carved, ornamental, raised deck and railing running around the stern. Captain McKown and Mr. Donnelly were the only ones left in the mizzen rigging. The other passengers and crewmen were out on the bowsprit. When the captain was later asked by a reporter from the *Long Island Democrat* what his thoughts were as he clung to the shaking mizzenmast of his broken ship, he replied:

> I thought that I was undone forever and would never be able to obtain command of another vessel. Mr. Donnelly tried to cheer me up, and told me that so much confidence had he in my conduct and capability, that if I could not procure a vessel, he would give me one himself.
>
> —*Long Island Democrat*, November 30, 1836.

Arthur Donnelly was not making a promise he could not keep. An Englishman of Irish extraction, Donnelly had engaged in the merchant shipping business all his adult life. It was while transacting shipping business in Valparaiso, Chile that he met Michael and Frances Hogan and married their daughter, Sophia. Mrs. Hogan had recently persuaded him to move to New York and establish a shipping business there. His wife could thereby be reunited with her brother, sisters, and mother already living in New York. Arthur Donnelly's plans were about to be cut short.

The high tide continued to magnify the power of the waves. The only mast still standing, though just barely, was the mizzenmast where the captain and Mr. Donnelly were sitting. It was shaking violently and showed signs of coming down. Even at such a desperate time, McKown kept his hopes alive, and laid plans for preserving, for a time at least, Donnelly's life and his own. The bowsprit offered the best and most elevated protection, but because the sea had now claimed everything between the mizzen and the bow, there was simply no way to get there. There was, however, some small protection aft, at the taffrail. If the two men could tie themselves to the taffrail, there was some chance of holding on. The question was whether they could reach it at all.

Leading the way in the darkness, McKown climbed down from the shaking mast. The waves that surged around the base of the mizzenmast were barely visible, so the captain had to calculate the rise and fall of the surf mostly by sound. When the moment came, he jumped down from the mast, ran for the taffrail through knee-high rushing water, and grabbed a length of rope that was tied there. Before securing himself to the taffrail, the captain called back to Donnelly and told him that he was tossing the end of the line to help him get across the slippery deck. McKown threw the line, but it fell short. Donnelly jumped down from the mast to grab the line, but this was a fatal mistake. He should have allowed the captain to retrieve it, re-coil it, and throw it again. As Donnelly reached for the line, a wave hit and washed him overboard. This unselfish man, this hero who had given his place in the rescue boat to a servant girl, was swept away and drowned. As the *Long Island Democrat* of November 30, 1836, reported, "He was drowned, and fell a victim to his own philanthropy."

As Captain McKown had predicted it would, the mizzenmast fell. All three masts were now gone, and Rockaway Beach was strewn for miles with spars, rigging, torn sails, planks, bodies, and all manner of debris. Although those standing on shore could not see the wreck in the darkness, or even hear any shouts over the wind noise, they knew from what they saw wash up on the beach that further calamity had struck the *Bristol*. The consensus of opinion was that the ship had been destroyed, and that all were drowned. The four rescuers went off to get some sleep.

At around eleven or twelve o'clock Monday night, faint cries could be heard over the slightly lessened noise of wind and surf. With the tide now back near its ebb, some boatmen on the beach debated whether to attempt a nighttime rescue. They feared there would be no one left to rescue by the next ebb tide, eleven hours later.

John Abrams, Hiram Abrams, Gilbert Craft, Thomas Combs, and Oliver Cornell—he may have been one of the two Oliver Cornells who made the earlier rescues—manned the four oars and tiller of the largest boat available. In three nighttime trips, made with great difficulty, they succeeded in taking off the rest of the men. Captain McKown, as he had promised, was the last person taken into the rescue boat, a testament to his bravery.

In all, thirty-two passengers and twelve crewmen, including the captain, were saved on the stormy day and night of November 21, 1836. Ninety-five passengers and five crewmen drowned. Surely, any list of the bravest men in maritime history must include those who risked their lives that day:

Alexander McKown, Captain
Arthur Donnelly, Passenger
David T. Jennings, Wreck-Master
John Abrams, Boatman
Hiram Abrams, Boatman
George Combs, Boatman
Thomas Combs, Boatman
Oliver Cornell, Boatman

Oliver Cornell, Boatman
Gilbert Craft, Boatman

When Captain McKown came ashore in the last rescue boat, he was seriously ill. From the moment his ship slid to a stop on a sandbar at Rockaway Shoals until he came ashore almost twenty-four hours later, the captain had remained on deck dressed in the same vest and pantaloons he had slept in. He had suffered from exposure to wind, water, and cold, and was so badly bruised and injured by the washing of the waves, especially during the hours he was lashed to the taffrail, that he was unable to walk. He was carried by wagon seven miles to wreck-master Jennings's house, to recuperate.

Because so many survivors were in poor physical condition, and because the night was windy, cold, and wet, shelter had to be found quickly. The luxurious Marine Pavilion was nearby, five miles toward the mainland, but its owners refused to open its doors to poor emigrants and sailors. Long Island fishermen again came to the rescue. Men described as "poor, but worthy men, living on the beach" gave the survivors "such hospitality as they could offer." They were Rodin Rider, a Mr. Foster, and Oliver Cornell—probably one of the rescuers. Other survivors were put up at the homes of wreck-master Jennings and coroner Daniel Mott.

The following day, representatives of the shipowner and the insurance underwriters came out to Rockaway Beach to inspect the wreck, to salvage what they could, and to offer assistance to the passengers and crew. Trunks, boxes, and twenty-four puncheons of whiskey—casks of 70-135 gallons each—were strewn along the beach as far as seven miles to the west. This small but valuable portion of the cargo was recovered for the owners. Altogether these items were worth $5,590.

Items Salvaged from the *Bristol*
New York Commercial Advertiser, November 28, 1836.

24 puncheons (70-135 gallon casks) of whiskey	$3,836
2 bales of carpeting	1,435
5 crates of earthenware	245
2 chests	15
Lot of trunks	25
Box of cloth	10
Lot of yarn	21
Mahogany box	3
Total	**$5,590**

The insurance brokers also arranged for Captain Schenck to come out from New York Harbor to conduct a salvage operation. He arrived with the schooner *Walter R. Jones* and the rescue lighters *William McNeil* and *Mary Alma* for the purpose of recovering spars, masts, ropes, anchors, fittings, planks, and as much sunken cargo as could be raised. He enlisted sixteen local fishermen to aid him, but little of salvageable value could be recovered. Seven weeks later, Schenk would be called upon to salvage the cargo of the *Mexico*, when she was wrecked off Long Beach. He would die there when the shears, an apparatus rigged for raising and moving heavy weights, collapsed on the icy deck of the *Walter R. Jones*.

The *New York Gazette* of November 23, 1836, reported that on the *Bristol's* final voyage, she carried a cargo weighing well over three hundred tons. This included an unknown number of crates and barrels containing manufactured goods—including silk, yarn, hose, ribbons, and muslin—and a much heavier cargo of iron, coal and wheat.

Cargo – Bristol's Last Voyage
250 Tons of railroad iron
50 Tons of coal
9,000 Bushels of wheat
Manufactured goods of unknown quantity

The *Bristol's* cargo assignees on her final voyage are known from a listing in the *New York Sun*, January 12, 1837, but it was not reported which cargo went to which assignee.

Cargo Assignees – Bristol's Last Voyage
Woodhull & Minturn (the owners)
Edward Field & Co.
M. Spies
E.W. Roberts
Delavan & Brothers
E. P. & W. Heyer
Willis & Brothers
Thompson & Co.
J. J. Kissam
Russel, Mattison & Co., and others

The complete cargo manifest from the *Bristol's* final voyage was lost in the wreck, but a corresponding list from the return trip of her maiden voyage to England in the winter of 1835-36 survives, and provides a good idea of the kinds of manufactured goods the ship may have carried on her final voyage:

The *Bristol's* Cargo – Maiden Voyage Homebound from Liverpool
Morning Courier & New York Express, January 4, 1836.

Quantity	Description	Consignee
15,000	Fire bricks	W.F. Jaques
112	Jars of orchil[19]	"
125	Crates mdze	"
30	Bdls iron	"
1,400	Boxes tobacco pipes	"
22	Cases port wine	"
1	Case mdze	"
20 tons	Barilla[20]	"
30	Bkts glass bottles	"
10,258	Bars iron	"
491	Bolts	"
18	Boxes tin plates	Williams & Roberts
8	Cases	"
17	Boxes	W. W. Chester
1	Bale	G. Meyer
12	Tcs	"
1	Bale	G. Lovel
31 dozen	Mdze	D. Scott
1 dozen	Mdze	A.G. & M.S. Thorpe
1 dozen	Mdze	A. Gracie
556	Boxes tin plates	Williams & Roberts
91	Bdls sheet iron	"
93	Cases copper	J. Maney
900	Boxes copper	S. Hicks & Sons
100	Iron moulds	E. Gee & Co.
37	Cases tin plates	S. Whale
550	Boxes glass	H.S. Leverleh
20	Cks brass manufactory	Phelps Dodge & Co.
829	Boxes tin plates	"
1	Bbl tin plates	S. Waite
80	Cases mdze	"
2	Cks mdze	R. Evans & Co.
1	Box mdze	J. Keat
1	Bbl mdze	E. Bevan

(continued on the next page)

---

[19] **Orchil** (also archil). A purple dye extracted from lichen. Known as "the poor man's purple," its use dates to Greek antiquity.

[20] **Barilla.** A bushy plant of Old World salt marshes and sea beaches, it has prickly leaves that are burned to produce a crude soda ash. The alkali produced from the plant, an impure carbonate of soda, is used for making soap and glass, and for bleaching purposes.

The *Bristol's* Cargo (Continued)

Quantity	Description	Consignee
2	Boxes mdze	Masters & Markoe
1	Truss	J. Cheslett
1	Hamper	S. Hartford
12	Bales	To Order
15	Boxes tin plates	"
10	Hampers bottles	"
100	Rings wire	Phelps Dodge & Co.

The fact that the *Bristol* was carrying nine thousand bushels of wheat to the United States on its final voyage seems surprising when one considers that by 1836 domestic wheat shipments by way of the Erie Canal had significantly lowered the price in New York. But England, with a vast supply of exploitable labor in Ireland, along with a well-developed canal, steamboat, and railway system, was able to compete. Tragically, English merchants were shipping wheat to New York at a time when famine was already on the rise in Ireland and Scotland. Over the next ten years such practices would lead to starvation on a massive scale.

For the most part, the *Bristol's* cargo of wheat, crates, barrels, and coal ended up either ruined by seawater or was so widely distributed across the Rockaway Shoals that it could not be recovered. It is not known why the railroad iron could not have been grappled from the sea-bottom. Perhaps it was recovered, and the news report was incomplete. The ship itself was insured by unnamed New York City insurers for $27,000—a half million dollars today—and the cargo was insured at a value of $4,000—seventy-five thousand dollars today. The Board of Insurance Brokers voted a total of $200 "for the relief of the sufferers of the wreck who are in distress." If each of the twenty-five survivors from steerage and second cabin got an equal share of this relief payment, the amount would be less than $150 per person today, a pitiful sum considering the possessions they lost and the terrible ordeal they experienced.

Although the *Bristol* disaster brought out the very best in Long Islanders, particularly in the actions of the rescuers and of the men and women who took in the survivors, as news of the wreck rapidly spread across the Rockaway Peninsula and beyond, it also brought out the very worst in people. The shipowner and the insurers were not the only ones who had their eyes on any valuables that might wash ashore. The "harpies," "monsters," "men-vultures," "land pirates," and "fiends" of Long Island were also out on Rockaway Beach. Stealthily they walked among the sand dunes, watching and waiting for prey.

Fiends in Human Form

Is not there some chosen curse,
Some secret thunderstorm in heaven,
Red with uncommon wrath,
To blast such uncommon iniquity?
—*New York Gazette*, November 24, 1836.
Regarding the Rockaway corpse robbers.

Waves pounded the remains of the *Bristol* for days, smashing her to pieces. The in-and-out surge of seawater worked bodies loose from where they were trapped below decks in second cabin and steerage, and sent them floating away westward on the crosscurrent. Ashen-faced corpses washed ashore for miles along deserted Rockaway Beach, and were collected for the coroner, Daniel Mott. Because Mott was not equipped to handle so many bodies, his processing of the corpses was hastily done. He received strong criticism from the *New York Commercial Advertiser* of November 26, 1836, which reported that the bodies of fifty-two men, women, and children were lying "in a promiscuous heap in a barn near the beach." Mott had to use the barn because the owners of the Marine Pavilion refused to allow the dead emigrants and sailors to be placed on their elegant premises.

Coroner Mott found substantial sums of money in the clothing of the first few bodies that were recovered. Ninety-six English sovereigns—gold coins worth over ten thousand dollars today—were discovered sewn into the lining of the greatcoat of one of the two physicians aboard the *Bristol*. That victim, who was only identified as "a doctor," was either Dr. McMullin or Dr. Aiken from Northern Ireland, each of whom was traveling in second cabin. The weight of the gold in the doctor's coat would have made his escape from below decks difficult. Another sixteen sovereigns were found in the pockets of a victim identified only as a "red-haired man, about five feet high, not recognized."

Word of these finds spread like wildfire. News reporters on the scene described the awful events that soon took place:

> From the great length of the beach on which the bodies are washed, it is impossible to keep any guard, and consequently the corpses are immediately stripped of everything valuable about them. The beach is filled with wagons coming from a distance of twenty or thirty miles, and the people in them are watching like cormorants for their prey. Our Reporter, in riding along, saw a body come ashore, and the first thing on which these harpies placed their hands, were the pockets.
> —*New York Commercial Advertiser,* November 24, 1836.

> About 20 bodies floated ashore, and we are pained to add that the first movement of many on the beach was to search and strip them of everything available. Great numbers of monsters, in the shape of men, on hearing of the disaster, hurried to the scene; some from a distance of twenty miles, not for the humane purpose of assisting their fellow creatures in distress, but to rob them and plunder them. Everything that came ashore was seized by them, and at once carried beyond the reach of the rightful owners.
> —*New York Sunday Morning News*
> [As later reported in the *Long Island Democrat*, November 30, 1836.]

> Of the inhuman conduct of the harpies—the men-vultures—who thronged the coast to prey upon the dead, indignation wants words to express its horror.
> —*New York Herald,* November 24, 1836.

> [They are] fiends in human form.
> —*New York Gazette,* November 26, 1836.

It was even worse than the contemporaneous accounts describe. Apparently, the newspapers of the 1830s were restrained by a sensibility that has been lost. Indeed, it took almost sixty years for the full story to come out, when the *New York Times* (February 4, 1895) printed the following ghoulish account: "Many of the bodies were without fingers and ears, thieves having cut them off to get jewelry." Thievery on the beach was not confined to the plunder of the dead:

And to those whom the waves and the mercy of God had spared, what was the conduct of their brother man? Their persons, their trunks, were searched and robbed by the fiends that gathered around the wreck. One hapless being, thrown senseless but yet alive on the shore, and having about him his all—ten sovereigns—was plundered of them.

> — John Warner Barber and Henry Howe.
> *Historical Collections of the State of New York* (1842).

Mrs. Donnelly, among other articles, lost a valuable case of jewels, and soon after, one of these land pirates was seen parading these.

> —*New York Sunday Morning News*
> [Reprinted in the *Long Island Democrat*, November 30, 1836.]

Mrs. Hogan's daughter, Mrs. Sophia Donnelly, had carried her jewel case from first cabin and still had it with her when her rescue boat approached Rockaway Beach. But when the boat flipped over, she was surrounded by "helping" hands, and the jewelry case disappeared.

Early nineteenth-century residents of Long Island, like people who have lived on coastlines around the world, believed in the rule of "Findin's Keepin." This meant it was acceptable to walk off with valuable items from a shipwreck—cargo, masts, clothing, or anything else that washed up on shore—though not to the extreme of cutting off fingers and earlobes, or swiping jewelry cases. The Reverend Nathaniel Prime wrote in his *History of Long Island* (1845):

> [T]here are men [on Long Island] who would scorn the imputation of taking the most trifling article of their neighbor's property, who would not hesitate, under a mistaken notion of right, to appropriate to their own use, whatever they might find on the shore, without making the least effort to discover the rightful owner. . . A strange impression exists that whatever is driven up by the waves, is the legitimate prey of the finder.

Neither the jewel-case-thief nor the body-robbers were caught, but some of those who seized other valuable items on the beach soon found out that following the local rule of "Findin's Keepin" was not only a crime, it was a federal crime. Within a few days of the wreck, five men—Daniel Smith, George Combs, Lawrence Coombs, John Welling, and Peter Wycoff—were accused of walking off with various goods that washed ashore, though not of robbing bodies. All five men were arrested by U.S. marshals, charged, and put behind bars on the basis that, unless these items had been completely abandoned by their owners, seizing them was a violation of federal law.

It would be a sad irony if the George Combs who was arrested was the same brave fisherman of that name who participated in the rescue. But that cannot be concluded from the name alone, because there were more Combs, Coombs, Coombes, and Combes on Long Island at the time than one could shake a clam rake at. Moreover, some of the men who were arrested appear not to have been poor Long Island farmers or fishermen at all, but well-off opportunists who later made bail ranging from $1,000 to $2,000, a huge sum of money at the time. The five men were indicted in federal court under the ninth section of the *Congressional Act of 1825*, Chapter 276. (See Part III, pages 250-253 for details of the case, *U.S. v. Coombs, 37 U.S. 72 January Term, 1838*.)

Although *U.S. v. Coombs* was the only court case to have arisen from the *Bristol* and the *Mexico* disasters, anyone looking back from the vantage point of the twenty-first century could find potential civil or even criminal misconduct in the actions (and inactions) of the harbor pilots, shipowners, passenger brokers, crews, and captains—misconduct sufficient to be tried in courts of law. But this was the 1830s, a time when 215 people could die just a few hundred yards from shore in the two wrecks, and yet *no one* was held legally responsible.

New York's newspapermen, on the other hand, were beginning to look at things in a different way than anyone had ever done before. In the process, their reporting of the *Bristol* and the *Mexico* disasters became important early steps in the development of modern investigative journalism. They also delivered an unfamiliar jolt to the people of Long Island and the City of New York.

New York Newspapers Cover the Wreck

In the 1830s, copies of New York City newspapers were regularly carried by stagecoach to nearby communities such as Hempstead, New Haven, and Trenton, and by coastal packet and steamboat to more distant places such as Boston, Charleston, and New Orleans. Packet ships carried the newspapers across the Atlantic to London and Liverpool. However, shipwrecks were so commonplace that newspapers such as the *Boston Daily Advertiser, Liverpool Mercury, Dublin Evening Post*, and *The Times of London* simply repeated a few facts straight out of the New York papers: ship's name, owner's name, captain, home port, destination, wreck location, tonnage, cargo, amount of insurance, and number of deaths. Not only were these newspapers ploddingly dull to begin with, there were social class barriers at work in Europe and the United States, so the deaths of ninety-five steerage and second-cabin emigrants aboard the *Bristol*, most of whom were from Ireland, England, Scotland, and Wales, were simply not important news. Nor was there any reporting of the dramatic events of the wreck itself, or the New York pilots' absence from their posts. This kind of in-depth investigative reporting was unknown at the time—except in New York City.

In New York City the *Bristol* shipwreck story and the soon-to-follow *Mexico* story took on lives of their own. After all, the ships, owners, harbor pilots, insurers, land-pirates, and one of the captains were from New York. Several of the victims, too, were New Yorkers or were related to New Yorkers, and almost all the passengers on both ships had New York State as their final destination. And so, New York City's newspapers went beyond the customary listings of names and numbers. For one of the very first times in newspaper history, they investigated and reported on items of popular interest.

In 1836, James Gordon Bennett (1795-1872), a Scottish emigrant, was the publisher, editor, typesetter, and chief reporter of the one-year-old penny paper, the *New York Herald*, with offices in a Wall Street cellar. Although he sat behind a desk made from two barrels and a plank, Bennett's credo was not the least bit humble:

> A newspaper can send more souls to heaven and save more souls from hell, than all of the churches or chapels in New York— besides making money at the same time. Let it be tried. . . I am determined to make the *Herald* the greatest paper that ever appeared in the world. . . I have infused life, glowing eloquence, philosophy, taste, sentiment, wit and humor into the daily newspaper. . . Shakespeare is the great genius of the drama . . . and I mean to be the genius of the daily newspaper press. (1835)

James Gordon Bennett, Publisher of the *New York Herald*
Studio of Matthew Brady
Library of Congress

Bennett printed the usual statistics about the wreck of the *Bristol* and the *Mexico*, along with some gripping details, which in itself was bold. But he went much further than the other New York publishers when he passionately chased down leads. For example, he personally interviewed survivors in the hospital, and went so far as to challenge a harbor pilot right on the streets of New York about his comrades' dereliction of duty. The pilot's response was to throw a punch in the direction of Bennett's prodigious nose. Another publisher, one not interested in such confrontational reporting, wondered how the pilot could have missed.

A story Bennett wrote about the burial of a *Bristol* victim is illustrative of his colorful style, and it reveals one of the strangest episodes connected to the wreck. Christopher Shields, an Irishman by birth, had left his pregnant wife and children at home in Williamsburgh, Brooklyn so that he could visit his family in Ireland. Shields was a vigorous young man, one of just a few second-cabin passengers who managed to escape the down-rushing flood of seawater. On reaching the deck, he climbed a mast and waited for the women and children to depart before entering a rescue boat. The *Herald* reported what happened next:

> No sooner had [Shields'] feet touched the land—which he had never more expected to reach—than his joy at his deliverance, and the thoughts of seeing his wife and relatives again, caused a violent hysterical affection of laughter, in which he dropped down dead upon the beach.
>
> —*New York Herald*, November 29, 1836.

For other publishers this would have been the end of the Shields' story. However, Bennett followed it a few steps further. Shields was a Catholic, so coroner Daniel Mott proposed that he be buried in a Catholic burying ground. A priest—the Rev. Mr. Walsh—was sent for, but Walsh refused to inter Shields, "in consequence of his having married a Protestant." The Rev. Walsh even prohibited his church sexton from preparing an unsanctified grave, for the additional reason that "Shields had not received the sacrament of Extreme Unction and that he should not therefore be buried in sacred ground." A Protestant clergyman was sent for, and Shields was given a decent burial in the presence of his wife, his children, and his friends.

After relating the chaotic events surrounding Shields' interment, Bennett, a Catholic himself, issued a personal cry of protest when he wrote the following about the Rev. Mr. Walsh:

> Let this priest recollect that we both breathe in a land of liberty and of law and that, instead of kneeling to *him* in his confessional, we call upon him to get down upon his knees at once, in the great confessional of public opinion, to say the truth in the same breath with *mea culpa, mea culpa, mea maxima culpa*.
>
> —*New York Herald*, December 2, 1836.

A fresh, news sensation arrived six weeks later, in January 1837, with the loss of the *Mexico*, which occurred under remarkably similar, yet even more painful circumstances. Bennett's chief rival, Benjamin H. Day, publisher of the *New York Sun*, grabbed hold of the *Mexico* story. For weeks the two publishers gave riveting attention to the wreck, and other newspapers followed their lead. The days of uninspired news-reporting were over.

Bennett's lively, investigative, confrontational style found an admiring, newly-discovered audience—the public—not just the elites and the mercantile class of advertisers. His presses could barely keep up with the demand. By mid-1837, his circulation multiplied to twenty thousand copies a day (from zero in 1835), and he doubled his price to two cents. The *Herald* eventually outstripped even Horace Greeley's *New York Tribune*, and became New York City's leading paper.

Thanks to the efforts—and, at times, the hubris—of pioneering publishers such as James Gordon Bennett and Benjamin H. Day, a remarkable amount of information about the wrecks of the *Bristol* and the *Mexico* was recorded. But investigative journalism was still in its infancy, and the news reports were far from complete. To more fully understand the depths of these twin tragedies, it is necessary to examine sources that reveal the dark side of American merchant shipping in 1836, including the appalling trade in "white cargo," the pernicious practice of racism, and the almost criminal dereliction of duty of the New York harbor pilots.

We now turn to the voyage of the barque *Mexico*. If the wreck of the *Bristol* is tragic, the wreck of the *Mexico* is horrible beyond words. This is true not only because of how the victims died—by freezing—but because of the despicable actions and inactions of those around them. Men of wealth, privilege, and power were so corrupted by deeply-ingrained motives of profit, pride, and self-preservation, that they lost all sense of responsibility for the 115 people in their care.

Part II

The Wreck of the *Mexico*

Voyage to Sicily

A 317-ton Barque, the *Anna Robertson*, Built in 1842.
The barque had two boats and a cookhouse on the main deck, as did the *Mexico.*
Artist: Nicholas Camilieri

The year 1835 was filled with big decisions for Samuel Broom, a Pennsylvania dealer in sugar and confectionery products. He had always used shipping companies to move raw materials and finished products between distant ports and his Philadelphia factory and warehouse; but from now on he would be a merchant shipper himself, transporting goods for his own account and for others. Early nineteenth century shipowners generally worked in partnership with ship captains, and shared the venture's profits with them. Thus Broom's first step was to hire an experienced ship's master. He chose a fellow Philadelphian, forty-six-year-old Charles Winslow, to help carry out his plan.

While little is known about Samuel Broom, much is known about Captain Charles Winslow. Winslow lived in Philadelphia with his wife Elizabeth and daughter Martha—that is for the few weeks each year that he was on shore. He was a fifth-generation American, a direct descendant of Kenelm Winslow. (Kenelm was the brother of Edward Winslow, the Governor of the Plymouth Colony.) Charles was born in Maine, on May 30, 1789, the son of Carpenter Winslow and Betsey Colburn. Carpenter had worked with Betsey's father, Major Reuben Colburn, in building two hundred flat-bottomed riverboats for Benedict Arnold's attack on Quebec. They completed the job in just two weeks. Thus, Captain Charles Winslow was descended from heroes of the American Revolution on both sides of his family line.

Winslow's parents lived in Pittstown (now Pittston), Maine, where they raised nine sons. In 1815, the family moved to Punxsutawney, Pennsylvania in search of inexpensive land and a climate better suited to farming. But Western Pennsylvania was a rough wilderness, and the family had to live on game until they could clear enough land to farm.

Five of the sons chose to remain on the land; four others went to sea. The four seagoing brothers all rose through the ranks to become ships' captains, and all but one of them would die on voyages. Charles, the oldest of the nine sons, commanded various ships in the Mediterranean, Caribbean, U.S. East Coast, and North Atlantic trades before taking command of the *Mexico*. George, the second oldest of the four seagoing brothers, made the best choice by commanding ships in the China trade. By 1830, at age thirty-nine, George's percentage interests allowed him to retire a wealthy man. David, the next oldest, made the worst choice when he followed a sordid path he hoped would lead quickly to wealth. In 1816, at age twenty-two, he took command of a slave ship out of Havana. His intention was to buy slaves in Africa and sell them in Cuba at a sale price equal to ten times their purchase price. His first and only slave voyage ended in disaster. D. P. Holton's *Winslow Memorial – Family Records Vol. II* (1888) summarily relates David Winslow's ending: "Went to Africa and was captured while ashore, nothing being known concerning his fate. He was unmarried."

The last of the Winslow boys to go to sea was Caleb-Smith Winslow. As the *Winslow Memorial* tells it:

> He was a sea-captain; in 1844 left Pittsburgh for New Orleans, and when last heard from was on the Mississippi River. It is supposed that he was lost many years ago in a steamer on that river.

In 1835, the year that Samuel Broom was looking for an experienced business partner, one who could sail a tall ship, Charles Winslow's younger brother George had retired five years earlier. Charles' decision to join Broom in this start-up venture was a gamble, but it also was an opportunity to make up for lost time. While his proportional share in the profit of the venture is not known, in all likelihood it was higher than the usual 1/16th.

Winslow recommended that Broom purchase an eleven-year-old, three-masted barque, the *Mexico*, a ship that Enoch Train, a New England merchant, had put up for sale. Broom bought the barque and insured her for the purchase price of $8,000 (about $200,000 today). Winslow then hired three Philadelphians to work as first mate and senior crewmen.

Broom opened a merchant shipping office in New York City, because that was where the action was, where big money could be made, and made quickly. Records from the U.S. National Archives and from the "Marine Intelligence" columns of the *Morning Courier and New York Express* newspaper show that in 1835, Broom and Winslow began to use the *Mexico* as a transient, what we would call a "tramp steamer" today, i.e., a ship not operating on a fixed schedule, but adjusting its itinerary as dictated by trade opportunities. Unfortunately, Winslow's first important voyage with the *Mexico* was a 12,000-mile odyssey of financial failure, and it would eventually lead to ruinous decisions.

The *Mexico* left the Port of New York on that voyage in September 1835, setting sail for the English Channel with a crew of eleven men. There is no record of the cargo, but in all likelihood the barque carried American products such as lumber, furs, and hides, along with Samuel Broom's confectionery goods: candied fruits, jellies, and sugar-coated nuts. The initial destination on this voyage was the port of Cowes, on the Isle of Wight. Cowes (or Cowes-and-a-Market as it was then called) was a duty-free *entrepot*, which meant that international trade goods could be imported and re-exported there without paying duties. Cowes had risen to prominence in the late 1700s, in response to the increased European demand for American tobacco and Carolina rice. The port's merchants acted as indispensable middlemen in redirecting these American cargos to traders in countries such as France and Holland, and in moving European products such as French wines and Dutch pottery to America. Even though the rice and tobacco transshipment business had fallen on hard times by the mid-1830s, transient vessels such as the *Mexico* could still find buyers for their cargos and obtain fresh cargos to bring back home, by going to nearby ports to which the Cowes merchants might direct them.

When Winslow reached Cowes, he found slim pickings. The best he could do was to acquire the rights to goods in far off Messina, Sicily. Foreign currencies and exchange rates meant little to merchant sea captains. A bag of owner Samuel Broom's silver and gold coins, kept in a locked chest in the captain's cabin, was all Winslow needed to make a transaction happen. After entering the Mediterranean Sea and picking up the Sicilian cargo, Winslow sailed the *Mexico* back to New York. She arrived in April 1836. The 12,000-mile voyage had taken eight months.

In the *Mexico's* hold, as reported in the *Morning Courier and New York Express* of April 8, 1836, was the following cargo:

The *Mexico's* Sicilian Cargo – 1835-36 Voyage.

905	Cantars of sulfur
100	Bales of rags
240	Bags of sumac
150	Bags of filberts
1,400	Boxes of lemons
318	Boxes of oranges
36	Cases of merchandise to Samuel Broom

- **Cantars of sulfur**. From the late 1700s to the late 1800s, 95 percent of the world's industrial need for sulfur was met by mined Sicilian sulfur deposits. Sulfur was an important component of black gunpowder and matches in the 1830s. The word cantar is the English spelling for the Arab quintal, a metric unit equal to 110 pounds.

- **Rags**. Until 1878, almost all newsprint was created from linen and rags, which were bought in bulk and treated in chemical baths before being pressed and rolled into paper.

- **Sumac.** This ground, Mediterranean seed has a sour, tart, and salty taste. It was used as a seasoning on rice, in marinades, and as a rub for meat and poultry. Ground and dried sumac leaves were also used in tanning and dyeing.

- **Filberts**. Ninety percent of the world production of filbert nuts, a cousin to the hazelnut, still comes from the Mediterranean—principally Turkey, Greece, and Italy. In 1835, it was closer to one hundred percent. The filbert bush blooms in February near St. Filbert's day; thus, the name of the plant and later the nut.

The *Mexico's* original, signed crew list is preserved in the U.S. National Archives Record Administration in New York. It identifies, by name, the eleven men that sailed on the voyage to Sicily, including the captain, first mate, and the nine other crewmen. It is reproduced on the following page, with a transcription.

List of Persons Composing the Crew of the Barque *Mexico*
On her return from Cowes and a Market (April 8, 1836)
U.S. National Archives Record Administration, New York City Office.

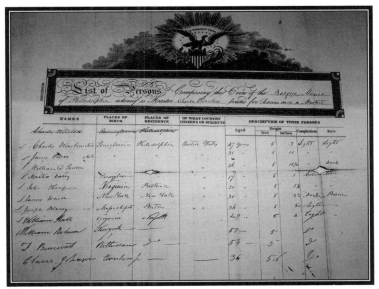

Names	Place of Birth	Residence	Citizen of	Age	Ht	Complexion	Hair
Capt. Charles Winslow	Pennsylvania	Philadelphia	United States	47	5' 3"	Light	Light
James Pieroo, Mate	"	"	"	31	5' 11"	"	"
William D. Laddn	"	"	"	26	5' 10¼"	"	Dark
Horatio Dossey	"	"	"	17	5' 1"	Colored	Man
John Thompson	Virginia	Portland	"	21	5' 5¾"	"	"
James Ward	New York	New York	"	30	5' 4½"	Dark	Brown
Joseph Blaney	Massachusetts	Boston	"	36	5' 5"	Light	"
William Hall	Virginia	Norfolk	"	27	5' 6"	Light	"
William Botisson	New York	New York	"	51	5' 6"	"	"
T. Bunwast **Replacement**	Rotterdam	Rotterdam		54	5' 6"	"	"
Clans Johnson **Replacement**	Edinburgh	Edinburgh		36	5' 6"	"	"

It is not known why the captain listed Pennsylvania as his birthplace, and not Pittston, Maine, where he was actually born. The crew appears to have been experienced, with an average age of thirty-four, compared, for example, to the *Bristol's* crew, which had an average age of twenty-four. Eight of the ten sailors who left New York aboard the *Mexico* in September 1835 were still aboard when she returned in April 1836. Two unidentified crewmen were replaced by foreign sailors. This is consistent with the average loss rate of twenty-five percent, as recorded on merchant ship crew lists that year. Losses were generally from desertion, sickness, or injury—and occasionally death.

Although the extended voyage to Sicily clearly demonstrated that Charles Winslow was a fine navigator and a competent ship's master, owner Samuel Broom could not have been happy with the results of the *Mexico's* five-thousand-mile side trip to Sicily, and her return with a bulky cargo of limited value. Spoilage in the 1,400 boxes of lemons and 318 boxes of oranges on the four-month return from Messina must have been high. Moreover, in the 1830s, Mediterranean citrus had strong competition from limes and oranges shipped to New York from the easier-to-reach Caribbean.

The fiasco of the Sicilian voyage surely was a far cry from what Samuel Broom had intended when he began his New York merchant shipping business. At the conclusion of that frustrating journey, the shipowner and the ship's master made a bold attempt to reverse their fortunes. The result would be a wrecked ship, a lost cargo, and more than one hundred passengers and crewmen frozen to death on the deck of the crippled ship.

Broom and Winslow needed a new business strategy, and they needed it fast. They decided to make quicker, more frequent trips to Europe, fill the hold with dense, higher-value cargo, and push the vessel's loads to the limit. Broom also wanted to improve business decision making aboard the ship, so he installed his teenage brother William as the ship's supercargo—the person in charge of all financial matters relating to the ship's cargo. Young William would also serve as Samuel's eyes and ears, to ensure that his older brother's wishes were being carried out.[21]

The supercargo arrangement must have been a blow to the captain. Winslow, at five feet three inches, with light hair and fair complexion, was not nearly as imposing as the giant, black-bearded masters of the packet lines or the Nantucket whalers, but he knew how to wield the power of a ship's master. Thus, he would have preferred that William Broom be taken on as the

---

[21] Various sources list young William Broom as being fourteen or fifteen. Even in 1836, this was young for the job, though not so young as it would seem today.

ship's boy, in which case the young man would be under the captain's absolute control. William's berth in an officer's cabin was a far cry from sailing "before the mast." That is where Winslow and his three brothers had begun *their* careers, living with the sailors in the forecastle.

But Winslow also knew his place. Despite having absolute command at sea, Winslow was still the owner's subordinate. Supercargo or no, his partnership with Samuel Broom would still yield a nice share in the profits of each voyage. He needed to support his wife and daughter back in Philadelphia, and he needed to catch up on lost time. Young master Broom would be tolerated.

Before shipowner Samuel Broom could put the new business plan to work, he had some public relations issues to resolve. Although his captain didn't *look* the part of a ship's master, he was well-regarded. As a result, Broom began to include Captain Winslow's name in his sailing advertisements. There was also the matter of the ship itself. The *Mexico* was small, at 279 tons; middle-aged, at twelve years; and slow—very slow. To help mitigate these deficiencies, in appearance at least, Broom rounded-up the *Mexico's* advertised tonnage to 300 tons and rounded-down her age to ten years. He certainly could not mention that the round-bottom tub leaked, which she did, but he could advertise that the barque's bottom was sheathed in the approved way, in copper, with copper fasteners, and dubbed her a "fine American Ship." After the *Mexico's* public relations make-over, this is how one of her sailing notices appeared in the *Liverpool Mercury* newspaper:

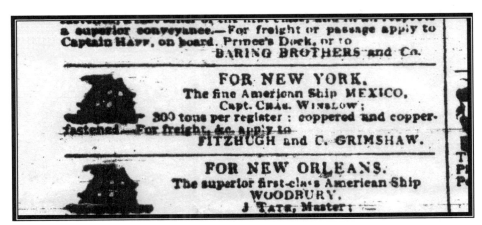

The *Mexico's* Final Sailing Notice
Liverpool Mercury, October 7, 1836.

The results were gratifying. Samuel Thompson, an important New York City and Liverpool merchant, agreed to lease virtually all the available cargo space on the *Mexico* for the transport of his own cargo from Liverpool to New York. There would also be plenty of space left for Broom's own merchant cargo. With this new business model up and running, Broom could expect the barque to make two voyages to Liverpool in the same eight months it took to make a single voyage to Sicily. Profits would more than double—for Broom and for Winslow. All they needed now was to find a cargo to ship to London, and a fresh crew to sail the ship.

To the Caribbean for a Cargo and a Crew

After the *Mexico's* Sicilian cargo was unloaded in New York and Philadelphia, the barque sailed to Portland, Maine to pick up a load of pine boards much in demand in Liverpool. A second side trip was planned before her Atlantic crossing to Liverpool—a cruise to the Caribbean. Samuel Broom was a leader in the confectionery trade in Philadelphia, so the idea of sailing to Liverpool by way of the sugarcane-growing islands of the Caribbean was particularly appealing to him.

There was another reason to sail to the Caribbean. Captain Winslow needed to fill out his crew. In July 1836, when the *Mexico* was in New York loaded with New England pine and ready to sail, not one of the crew who had made the voyage from Sicily was available. Perhaps it was the lure of higher pay offered by the New York packet lines. Maybe the crew left because they had by now been on the barque for almost a full year, and simply needed a break. Subsequent events suggest another reason for the crew's departure—the *Mexico* leaked. Not only did sailors intensely dislike manning pumps during what otherwise might be their free time, they, more than anyone, would have noticed that the leaks were progressively getting worse.

The summer of 1836 was a busy time for New York merchant shippers. Maritime traffic was at its all-time height with as many as forty ships a day leaving New York Harbor. Nine hundred and twenty large and small vessels, a record number, lined the East River and Brooklyn piers, and another three hundred twenty were tied up along the North River.[22] More

---

[22] The Dutch referred to the principal rivers of their North American territory as the North River (the Hudson) and the South River (the Delaware). The name South River was dropped completely, but the expression North River came to mean that portion of the Hudson from the Battery to about today's Tappan Zee Bridge. The name North River is still used in radio communications involving commercial shipping traffic, even in the twenty-first century.

than three-quarters of these were American ships, which in 1836 carried 75 percent of all United States imports and 90 percent of exports.[23]

Because of the huge number of ships in port, the demand for crews was high. Packet ships added to the competition for crews, as these vessels approached their peak in both size and number. Some of the packets were nearing one thousand tons, and needed more than double the crew of smaller vessels such as the *Mexico*. Other industries such as canal-boat companies, mills, and railroads were also competing for manpower. To sailors, landlubber jobs sounded attractive, especially when the alternative was eight-month-long voyages, sixteen-hour workdays, meals of salted horsemeat, and a beating from the mate simply because he was having a bad day.

The official crew list for the *Mexico's* final voyage was destroyed in the wreck, so it is impossible to know for certain which men were hired in New York. But Winslow managed to take on at least a partial crew. He then set sail for the West Indies to pick up more cargo and to round out his crew, both at bargain prices. In 1834, all slaves in the British Empire were emancipated, but they were still indentured to their former owners in an apprenticeship system. Many of these apprentices were hired out as sailors by their former masters. It is likely that Winslow hired such men in a British colony such as the Bahamas, where one of every six slaves had maritime experience. By the time the *Mexico* arrived in Liverpool, seven of her ten sailors were black men with English-sounding names.

The *Mexico's* next stop in the Caribbean was the island of St. Thomas, which was then part of the Danish Virgin Islands. In 1815, the Danes had declared St. Thomas and St. Croix to be duty-free ports in order to further stimulate the already huge worldwide demand for Caribbean cane sugar and its byproducts, rum and molasses. For twenty years there had been profits aplenty, thanks to slave labor, no taxes, and no duties. In the 1820s, European farmers discovered that sugar beets, an inexpensive alternative to Caribbean cane sugar, could be grown locally. By 1836, when the *Mexico* arrived in the Caribbean to acquire her cargo, the island sugar trade had fallen on hard times. The price of cane sugar had fallen so low, as a result of declining demand, that Danish plantation owners in St. Thomas, St. John, and St. Croix were abandoning their sugarcane fields and freeing many of their slaves because of lack of employment. The *Mexico* was able load up with

---

[23] By 1901, only 8 percent of the U.S.'s international cargo was carried on American ships, and the percentage is much smaller today.

inexpensive cane sugar, rum, and molasses—chief ingredients in the confectionery trade. Samuel Broom's plan was working.

The original crew list for the *Mexico's* final voyage listed the place of birth and residence of every crewman, but it was lost in the wreck. After the shipwreck, the New York newspapers identified all the sailors based on interviews with survivors. As a result, the *Mexico's* crew list for her final voyage can be partially reconstructed, as follows:

The Crew of the Barque *Mexico*, on Her Final Voyage

Based on survivor interviews and the captain's statements in the *New York Sun*, January 12, 1837; the *New York Commercial Advertiser*, January 5, 1837; and records in the U.S. National Archives Record Administration, New York City Office.
(William Broom, the young supercargo, would not have been considered "crew" on the official crew list, but he is included here)

Names	Place of Birth	Place of Resi- dence	Citizen of	Age	Height	Com- plexion	Hair
Capt. Charles Winslow	Pittston, Maine	Phila- delphia	United States	47	5' 3"	Light	Light
William Broom, Supercargo, Owner's brother	Penn- sylvania	Unknown	United States	14 or 15	Unknown	White	Unknown
Noah N. Jordon, First Mate	Unknown	Unknown	Unknown	Un- kn.	Unknown	White	Unknown
Edward Felix, Cook	"	"	"	"	"	Black	"
John Handsell, Carpenter	"	"	"	"	"	White	"
Stephen Simons, Steward	"	"	"	"	"	Black	"
Walter Quinn	"	"	"	"	"	Black	"
James Munro	"	"	"	"	"	Black	"
Lord Sherwood	"	"	"	"	"	Black	"
Peter Pickering	"	"	"	"	"	Black	"
Jacob Allen	"	"	"	"	"	Black	"
John Francis	France	"	France	"	"	White	"

Even though slavery was still legal in much of the Caribbean and in many parts of the United States, the black sailors aboard the *Mexico* were undoubtedly not slaves. In 1836, slavery was illegal in both England and in New York State, which meant that Captain Winslow could be prosecuted if he knowingly brought slaves into either Liverpool or New York. Indeed, Liverpool and New York were places to which free or apprenticed black sailors wanted to sail. They avoided destinations where slavery was legal because they risked being jailed, placed into forced labor, or sold into or back into slavery. According to W. Jeffrey Bolster, author of the landmark study, *Black Jacks: African American Seamen in the Age of Sail* (1997), that is exactly what happened to thousands of free black sailors in cities such as New Orleans, Charleston, and Savannah.

It is quite likely that the free or apprenticed black sailors aboard the *Mexico* expected adventure and a taste of city life in slave-free Liverpool and New York. For men with a few years of inter-island sailing experience, or even some transatlantic work by the southern trade routes, this was the opportunity of a lifetime to see places they could never otherwise see. What they got instead, was a segregated grave hacked out of frozen ground on Long Island.

Bolster writes that from the 1790s to the 1830s, one or two out of every ten sailors manning American sailing ships were men of African descent. This meant that by 1836 there were thousands of black sailors working on American ships. Often they served as cooks and stewards, but many others served as seamen, as they did on the *Mexico*. As black sailors sailed from port to port, they became important contributors in the formation of African-American and African-Caribbean society. As Bolster said in an interview in 1997:

> I will say, in terms of disseminating culture, that my vision of these black mariners [is of] men who cross-pollinated a variety of communities around the rim of the Atlantic in an age when most black people were illiterate, in an age when most black communities were not linked together by either newspapers or record albums or cassette tapes. [It was an age in] which communication between widely dispersed people of color was by oral communication, by people who physically went from one place to another.

> One of the largest groups of people who moved repeatedly during the age of slavery between these widely dispersed slave communities were mariners. Of course, there were valets who accompanied their masters on trips; there were slaves who were sold from place to place. But in terms of regular and repeated sorts of contacts, moving between the West Indian Islands, the Carolina Low Country, urban seaports like New York and

Philadelphia, metropolitan capitals like London, the group that consistently emerges doing this are black sailors.

So it's no surprise to me that the first six autobiographies published in [the] English language by black men were written by mariners. It's no surprise to me that it was mariners who were disseminating particular forms of African-inspired martial arts like stick fighting and head butting which we have ample evidence of from around the Atlantic. So I see men of color on these ships, whether sailing as cooks or cabin boys, whether as stewards or able-bodied seamen, whether as harpooners or petty officers aboard whale ships, I see these men as having a particular niche in the formation of African America.

—Author Interview conducted by seacoastNH.com (1997)
<< http://seacoastnh.com/blackhistory/jacks.html#1role>>

In 1836, at the age of eighteen, Frederick Douglass was a slave hired out by his owner to work as a caulker in a Baltimore shipyard. Douglass later wrote in his autobiography that, after working side by side with black and white sailors, he soon "knew a ship from stem to stern and from keelson to crosstrees, and could talk sailor like an 'old salt.'" This experience helped him escape slavery two years later when he borrowed papers from a free black sailor and fled first to Philadelphia and then to New York. Douglass wrote in his autobiography *Life and Times of Frederick Douglass* that he dressed up in a "red shirt and tarpaulin hat and black cravat, tied in sailor fashion, carelessly and loosely about [the] neck." So attired, he boldly boarded a train to Philadelphia. Douglass' ruse worked because he made such a convincing impression, and because it was not uncommon for free black seamen to move about in the North with relative ease.

Frederick Douglass
As a Young Man
U.S. National Archive

Despite this relative freedom to move about, free black sailors experienced prejudice aboard ship in both subtle and obvious ways. One's position aboard a sailing ship—that of captain, mate, cook, able-bodied seaman, ordinary seaman, seaman apprentice, steward, or cabin boy—determined one's status more than race did. But that by no means meant race did not matter. Although black sailors often worked alongside whites as able seamen, some jobs were generally denied to them, particularly leadership positions such as captain and mate—i.e., the ship's officers. That is how things were aboard the *Mexico*, where, following the common pattern, the officers were white.

The *Mexico's* crew does stand out for one reason. Seven blacks out of eleven total crewmen was an unusually high number. Indeed, the *Mexico* had by far the highest proportion of black sailors on any New York ship for which crew lists are available in the National Archive for the years 1835 and 1836.

When the *Mexico's* captain elected to sail across the North Atlantic with a short-staffed, largely warm-weather crew, he took two gambles: that the weather would cooperate, and if not, that the ship would remain seaworthy under his command as a master mariner. He was wrong on both counts. Moreover, a surprise awaited Winslow when the *Mexico* reached Liverpool, one which would add complications that he may not have anticipated. Owner Samuel Broom had done more than lease out most of the *Mexico's* available cargo space to Samuel Thompson. Broom had also contracted to do business with the devil—or in this case with the devils—passenger brokers William Sudlow Fitzhugh and Caleb Grimshaw.

A Deal with the Devil

The address of the firm Fitzhugh and C. Grimshaw at 10 Goree Piazzas in Liverpool brings to mind that city's long involvement in the international slave trade. Goree is a small island off the West African coast in today's Senegal. It was infamous as the centuries-long headquarters of a succession of Dutch, English, and French slave traders. Goree Piazzas in Liverpool was also a slave market. At one time, forty percent of the world's slave trading was transacted there. Although few slaves actually set foot on Goree Piazzas—most of the trades were on paper—it was a place where merchants and brokers could learn from each other how to increase profits by compressing the maximum number of human beings possible into the hold of a ship without directly killing them. The slave traders on Goree Piazzas crassly referred to the human beings they dealt in as "black ivory."

Although the slave trade was banned in England in 1807, the old compression skills of the black ivory trade became useful again in the 1830s, this time for the transport of emigrants. Only now, the brokers on Goree Piazzas called the people they transported "white cargos." They did not go so far as to force emigrants to lay side-by-side in alternating "spoon" fashion as was done with slaves, but in many ways their treatment was as bad.

According to R. G. Albion in his *Rise of the Port of New York* (1939), the New York firm of Samuel Thompson and its Liverpool affiliate, Fitzhugh and C. Grimshaw, were "outstanding" among the pioneers of Liverpool's flourishing new business of shipping white cargos. The owners of both companies were Englishmen linked by business and marriage. In the 1830s, they discovered that the Liverpool-to-New York emigrant trade was a highly profitable endeavor, but one they deemed too messy to conduct on their own ships. Perhaps the stench of the banned slave trade still lingered in their offices at Goree Piazzas. So they contracted the awful work to transient merchant vessels. Unfortunately, one of those ships was Samuel Broom's *Mexico*.

Broom was all too eager to do business with these Englishmen. When he agreed to lease the *Mexico's* cargo hold to Samuel Thompson for the transport of goods from Liverpool to New York—and still retain some space for his own merchant cargo—it must have seemed a perfect arrangement. Broom either did not know, or did not care, what Thompson's plans were for the contracted space. Thompson, in turn, sub-contracted a portion of the space to his British affiliate, Fitzhugh and C. Grimshaw. This was the 'tween deck, a temporary cargo deck just below the main deck. The plan was to house as many emigrants as could be squeezed in, over one hundred of them. The fact that the barque was a slow, leaky hulk, or that the merchant cargo might be too heavy for the small vessel was of no concern to Fitzhugh and C. Grimshaw, Samuel Thompson, or even to Samuel Broom. The cargo was insured; the ship was insured; and as for the emigrants, they were disposable.

When Captain Winslow reached Liverpool, he learned that Samuel Thompson had a large load of cargo lined up for the *Mexico*, and that Fitzhugh and C. Grimshaw had booked passage for one hundred emigrants, with more on the way. Winslow, with his thirty years of sailing experience, surely must have worried that the total load would put the *Mexico* near her absolute limit. Moreover, the cargo could not be fully loaded until the third week in October, which brought into consideration the possibility of encountering winter storms in the North Atlantic.

Although Winslow had spent the previous winter in the Mediterranean on the *Mexico's* voyage to Sicily, he undoubtedly learned on his return to New York that the winter he missed—the winter of 1835-36—had been one of the most severe in the city's history. A fire had broken out on December 16, 1835, and most of the water lines for the fire department were frozen solid, allowing a fierce wind to fan the flames, unconstrained. Seven hundred buildings, including numerous mercantile establishments, were destroyed. The temperature dropped to minus seventeen degrees, and the harbor was so frozen-over that one could walk from Brooklyn to Manhattan across the East River and then across the North River to New Jersey. The Northern Lights shone over the city for three nights, leading some superstitious New Yorkers to think the end of the world was near. A winter like that could pose terrible problems for the *Mexico* if her Atlantic crossing extended into December 1836.

Captain Winslow must have had serious concerns while he was in Liverpool, and perhaps voiced them to the *Mexico's* young supercargo, William Broom. He had a potentially excessive cargo load, growing leaks, a late sailing date, and a crew inexperienced at sailing the North Atlantic. He would soon have on board more than one hundred steerage passengers when he had never carried more that a handful of cabin passengers before. Moreover, the emigrants' passage money went directly to the passenger broker, with little accruing to the ship's master except a potential headache.

William Broom's position would have been that the passengers should be of no concern to the captain or him. They were receiving no money from the passengers, so if they went hungry, or got sick, or died, it was the passenger broker's problem, not theirs. If Winslow could help make this new business model work, there would never again be eight-month-long trips to Sicily for sulfur, rags, and boxes of rotting citrus. Broom could almost guarantee that this trip would be a big financial success—for his brother and for Winslow. Even in the unlikely event that the ship failed to make it to New York, the voyage would still be a success because the ship was insured by the Commonwealth Office of Boston, and the cargo by the State Marine of New York City and the Atlantic Office. If there were a shipwreck at sea, the ship's longboat and yawl could handle an ocean voyage. Together, the two boats could accommodate the crew and perhaps a dozen passengers. The lack of lifeboats for the remaining passengers was not the concern of the shipowner or the captain, neither of whom had any significant liability in the event a passenger was injured or died at sea.[24] This was no time for second-guesses. The *Mexico* would sail from Liverpool to New York, as contracted.

Before the *Mexico* could take Samuel Thompson's cargo aboard at the Prince's Dock in Liverpool, the crew had to unload her own cargo. The U.S. cargo, in addition to the New England pine, consisted of Samuel Broom's confectionery products and probably some raw materials such as cotton, tobacco, hides, and potash.[25] A portion of the Caribbean cargo of cane sugar, molasses, and rum was unloaded, with the remainder left on board to be carried to New York and Philadelphia for Samuel Broom's own account. The *Mexico's* sailors used the barque's yard arms as derricks to hoist the cargo up and out of the hold, and to swing it onto the dock. Then, with the help of

---

[24] The sinking of the *Titanic* seventy-five years later, in 1912, demonstrates how far nineteenth-century laws went in favoring shipowners over passengers. When that ship sank, its owners raced to the New York Federal Courthouse to file a *Limitation of Liability Proceeding* under the *U.S. Limitation Act*. That act restricted a shipowner's liability to the remaining value of a wrecked ship, *after* it sank. The only value left after the *Titanic* went down was its lifeboats, worth collectively about $3,000. Thanks to the owners' *Limitation of Liability* filing, the survivors and the heirs of the deceased passengers were permitted to divide this sum among themselves as compensation for fortunes lost in jewelry and furs, not to mention the loss of lives.

[25] Potash was used in the manufacture of glass and soap, and as a fertilizer.

Liverpudlian longshoremen, the goods were moved through customs and into merchant warehouses located within the Prince's Dock.[26] The goods would later be shipped by rail, horse-drawn wagons, barges, steamboats, and coastal sloops to cities throughout Great Britain and Ireland.

Once the unloading was done, it was time to honor Samuel Broom's contract with Samuel Thompson and his subcontract with Fitzhugh and C. Grimshaw, to load—or rather overload—the *Mexico*. As the days wore on into October, the barque sank lower and lower in the water, under the weight of the cargo. Day by day, pound by pound, inch by inch, the *Mexico* was becoming a coffin ship.

---

[26] Some of these warehouses and docks remain today, including the warehouse containing the Merseyside Maritime Museum, in Liverpool. It contains a fine research collection pertaining to nineteenth-century shipping.

Coffin Ship

During the great Irish emigration that began in the mid 1840s, the term "coffin ship" was applied to any emigrant ship where large numbers of passengers died from disease—and there were many such ships. In the 1830s, however, the word had a different meaning. A coffin ship was any merchant or naval vessel that was thought to be unsafe to sail, and which could potentially become a watery coffin to her crew. Such ships were often well insured by their cautious owners. Surprisingly, Charles Darwin's brig-sloop, the 235-ton *Beagle*, was one of the ships given this unwelcome appellation. The *New York Commercial Advertiser* of November 29, 1836 had this to say:

> His Majesty's survey ship *Beagle* has at last returned [to England] from her long employment in South America and other parts of the world. She sailed from England in 1831 from which time until 1835 she was surveying the coasts of South America, the Falklands, and the Galapagos Islands. . . Mr. Charles Darwin, a zealous, unpaid tributary to the cause of science, has laboured unremittingly. . .
>
> Not a spar has been sprung, not a sail has been split till worn too long—nor is there a sheet of copper off the vessel's bottom—yet this little ship is one of the much-abused ten-gun sloops sometimes called "coffins."

The *Beagle* was an ordinary "working" naval vessel with a design that caused her to plow through the waves with a deep side-to-side roll, keeping her deck and cabins constantly drenched. Because this type of vessel had a tendency to abruptly roll over and sink, she was declared to be one of a despised class nicknamed "coffin brigs." However, the *Beagle* was so well outfitted, so handsomely provisioned, and had such a superb crew that she performed far above expectations. Not one man was lost or injured on her four-year expedition. Other coffin ships, however, fully deserved the name. Excessive cargo loads, poor ship's maintenance, understaffing, and insufficiently trained crews were the chief ingredients in turning ships into watery coffins. The *Mexico* had all four of those problems—plus bad luck. The mixture was fatal.

Under pressure to leave Liverpool to avoid winter weather in the North Atlantic, the *Mexico's* crew worked sixteen-hour-days, seven days a week loading Samuel Thompson's British goods bound for New York. The freight advertisements published in the *Liverpool Mercury* were all too successful, because when Samuel Thompson's cargo was added to Samuel Broom's cargo, the 279-ton *Mexico* had a total load of over 500 tons—200 tons of crates and barrels, 200 tons of iron bars, and 100 tons of coal.[27]

It may seem impossible that a 279-ton wooden ship could hold 500 tons of cargo, but such loads were not only possible, they were common. In part this was because of a simplified method of calculation then in use. Historically, *tonnage* was the tax on *tuns* (casks) of wine shipped to England from Spain and Portugal. The common rule for finding the *burthen* of ships, or what was called the *builders' tonnage*, was to use a formula that took into consideration the ship's length at her keel and her breadth. This calculation gave a sharp clipper the same nominal tonnage as a bulky merchantman, even though the merchantman could carry far more than a clipper.

Mechanics Magazine, published in England in 1827, printed plans for a short, broad, sixty-four-ton merchant vessel, the *Noah*. She had a *weight* of 64 tons, registered (builders) *tonnage* of 110 tons, and a maximum *cargo capacity* of 160 tons. The simple home-experiment of placing bricks in the center of an aluminum roasting pan and floating it in a bathtub, shows how a vessel can carry far more than her weight. Make even moderate waves in the bathtub, and the pan and brick sink. The problem is that maximum cargo loads can be achieved only under favorable conditions such as coastwise trade in good weather. The *Mexico*, however, was crossing the North Atlantic in late autumn, heading into winter.

Five hundred tons of cargo in a 279-ton ship required caution in both loading the *Mexico* and sailing it. The 200-ton cargo of iron bars was the first to be loaded into her hold, using the barque's main yard as a derrick to lift, swing, and lower the bars. Loading this cargo first allowed the concentrated weight to act as ballast in stabilizing the ship in heavy weather. This would

---

[27] Source: *New York Times* (January 6, 1836). In 1836, it cost less to ship coal from Liverpool to New York City than it did to haul it overland by wagon from Pennsylvania via toll roads, toll bridges, and ferries.

have been fine if the loading had stopped with the iron bars, but Winslow still had a long way to go to fulfill Samuel Broom's merchant-shipping contract with Samuel Thompson. The *Mexico's* carpenter, John Handsell, also supervised the laying of temporary bulkheads and decking for 100 tons of coal, and to support 200 tons of Thompson's own merchandise in crates and barrels. This filled every possible space from stem to the stern, right up to the bottom of the 'tween deck where the steerage passengers would reside.

With an excessive load such as the *Mexico's*, a ship rides so low in the water that her sailing characteristics are altered. Such a vessel becomes particularly unstable in rough seas because her center of gravity is so much higher relative to the keel than on a well-ballasted, less-loaded ship. Contributing to the barque's handling problems were its rounded bottom, the massive top-heavy weight of her three masts, and the additional twenty-ton weight of over one hundred passengers, their belongings, and provisions. Altogether, this was a formula for disaster.

While William Broom, the young supercargo, was responsible for financial and contractual matters, Captain Winslow had full authority regarding all matters related to sailing the ship. This included making any determination that the barque was being overloaded. But Winslow had made an agreement with shipowner Samuel Broom, and he decided to live with it, for better or worse. If the excess load proved to be a problem at sea, at least he had the owner's younger brother along as a witness that he was simply fulfilling a legal contract. However, there were other potential witnesses that the captain should have considered. His decision to sail a heavily-loaded ship gambled with the lives of 123 people aboard the *Mexico*. Indeed, his decision to sail his vessel out into the North Atlantic sealed the fate of 115 of her passengers and crew.

In 1836, there were no regulations in the United States or Britain regarding load limits for ships. Shipowners such as Samuel Broom and merchants such as Samuel Thompson were not overly concerned that too much cargo robbed a vessel of its mobility and caused it to roll dangerously in heavy seas. Their main concern was that the ship and its cargo were sufficiently insured. The loss of a crew or passengers was incidental. Ships leaving British ports could be overloaded as much as the owners wished—so long as they could find officers and crew to sail the deathtraps. Finding a crew was not difficult because once a man signed on for voyage he no longer had a choice in the matter. If he later had concerns that the ship was being overloaded, and deserted, he could be put in prison.

The situation was not remedied until 1876, when the *British Merchant Shipping Act* was passed thanks to Samuel Plimsoll, Member of Parliament. He recognized that there was a problem with overloaded ships—and that there also was a solution. He engaged a task force of maritime engineers to determine precisely the point where any vessel reaches its maximum safe loading. The legislation he sponsored required that every merchant ship have an official mark painted on its hull—a circle with a horizontal line through it—such that the waterline could not be higher than that mark. This mark, which is still used today, got the name "Plimsoll mark." Samuel Plimsoll has been known ever since as "The Sailor's Friend."

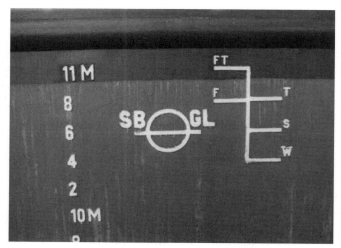

The Plimsoll Mark on a Merchant Vessel.
The Institute of Chartered Shipbrokers

When a ship rides so low in the water that the waterline reaches the Plimsoll mark on the side of the ship, that vessel is at its maximum carrying capacity. A ship's calculated load limit depends in part on external conditions: saltwater vs. freshwater (freshwater lakes generally having better sailing conditions than oceans), latitude (tropical conditions generally being less severe than non-tropical), and season (winter generally being the most difficult time to sail). The salinity-latitude-seasonal-variation marks are: FT (freshwater tropical), F (freshwater), T (tropical), S (summer), and W (winter). The letters SB-GL at the circle of the Plimsoll mark shown above indicate the classification society, Germanischer Lloyd, that surveyed this particular ship. The Plimsoll mark on this vessel indicates that when this ship is sailing in summer in salt water, it must not be loaded so much that it draws more than 10.6 meters below the waterline. In winter, the mark for this ship drops to 10.4 meters, which means it can carry considerably less cargo than in summer. In tropical conditions, it can draw as much as 10.8 meters.

There is often an even lower mark, WNA, not shown in the above example. It covers the *most dangerous sailing conditions in the world*, winter, North Atlantic—which is *when*, and *where*, the *Mexico* was sailing. The barque's five-hundred-ton cargo would surely have placed her waterline over the WNA mark. However, there were no such marks in 1836, and so the barque set sail with a crew that had little idea of the difficulties that lay ahead. Also aboard were 111 passengers who were so eager to get to America, and yet so poor, that they gave little thought to how they would get there, other than to do it cheaply. They were the *Mexico's* "white cargo."

White Cargo

Numerous contrasts can be drawn between the *Bristol* and the *Mexico* in terms of their owners, captains, number of crewmen, tonnage, age, and design, with the *Bristol* generally coming out ahead. (See Summary on page 9.) But if there is one consideration that truly separates the two, it is the manner in which the passengers were treated. The *Bristol's* passengers in first cabin, second cabin, and steerage received the relatively comfortable accommodations promised by the firm of Woodhull and Minturn. Moreover, when the *Bristol* grounded on Rockaway Shoals, Captain McKown demonstrated that his primary concern was the safety of his passengers. The central concern of the *Mexico's* owner and her captain was to make a profit, and in the case of Captain Charles Winslow it was, in the end, to save himself. The barque's passengers were viewed as a low-value cargo that did not enter into any of the owner's or the captain's calculations. Sadly, there was a set of ready, compliant victims: the poor of Ireland, England, Scotland, and Wales—specifically the 111 men, women, and children who bought inexpensive passage to the United States aboard the *Mexico*.

In the summer of 1836, when passenger broker Fitzhugh and C. Grimshaw published the *Mexico's* sailing notices in the *Liverpool Mercury*, the Great Irish Famine was still a decade away. However, circumstances were already conspiring against many of the poor, caught as they were in the whipsaw-effect of high unemployment and localized famines. William Sudlow Fitzhugh, Caleb Grimshaw, Samuel Thompson, and Samuel Broom were among the first to take full advantage of these desperate people.

The depression of the 1820s had destroyed the once-flourishing cottage industries such as weaving and lace-making throughout the United Kingdom of Great Britain and Ireland. This was followed by the negative effects of the Industrial Revolution, which eliminated most of the cottage work that was left, and employed fewer workers in factories than the ones displaced. The combined effect was devastating. Arthur Gribben gives an example to show that the severe unemployment problem in Ireland was decades in the making:

> Between 1821 and 1841 the proportion of Kilmacshalgan's parishioners working in industry and other non-farm pursuits fell from 57% to 18%.
> —*The Great Famine and the Irish Diaspora in America* (1999)

Several of the *Mexico's* passengers were from County Cavan, which is near Kilmacshalgan, and may have been just such displaced workers hoping to find opportunities in New York. Other passengers were from Dublin and Cork, where there also was high unemployment. According to Stanley Johnson in his *History of Emigration* (1913), the supply of workers so exceeded demand in Ireland and Scotland that by 1838 wages were less than half the amount paid in 1820.

Farm families were suffering too. Although most researchers date the Irish Potato Famine as beginning in September 1845, a significant potato blight struck isolated areas of England, Scotland, Ireland, and Wales ten years earlier. For example, in the summer of 1836, as the *Bristol* and the *Mexico* were on their way to Liverpool, Long Island's *Hempstead Inquirer*, citing "foreign sources," reported that 100,000 people had been displaced from their farms in the British Isles because of the blight. That same year, the *Liverpool Mercury* noted that there were 10,000 displaced farmers in western Scotland alone.

A third problem—in addition to unemployment and blight—was the explosion in population, particularly in Ireland. Again, Arthur Gribben gives an example:

> As [County] Sligo's poor became almost exclusively dependent on the land and the potato for employment and sustenance [because of industrial unemployment], the county's population increased from 146,000 in 1821 to nearly 200,000 by the Famine's eve.

These problems were small individually, at least by the awful scale of the Great Famine, but there were regions of Great Britain and Ireland where these negative effects converged with destructive force: jobs lost because of a business depression, jobs displaced by the Industrial Revolution, population growth, and increased demand for food. When localized potato blights destroyed both the food supply and the safety net of farming as a source of employment and income, there was nothing left. Stanley Johnson cites cases where desperate men went to distant towns to arrange for their emigration to America, "in order that their home liabilities might be shirked."

In 1837, an Irish school teacher named Patrick M'Kye sent a "memorial"—a written statement of facts accompanying a petition—to the Lord-Lieutenant of Ireland, an Englishman. M'Kye's bold intention was to inform the English overlords of the hardships certain parts of Ireland were enduring, and of which the English seemed unaware or uninterested. M'Kye wrote the following:

To His Excellency the Lord-Lieutenant of Ireland,
THE MEMORIAL OF PATRICK M'KYE
MOST HUMBLY SHOWETH,

That the parishioners of the parish of West Tullaghobegly, in the Barony of Kilmacrennan, in the County of Donegal, are in the most needy, hungry, and naked condition of any people that ever came within the precincts of my knowledge, although I have traveled a part of nine counties in Ireland, also a part of England and Scotland, together with a part of British America; I have likewise perambulated 2,253 miles through seven of the United States, and never witnessed the tenth part of such hunger, hardships and nakedness. . . There are about 4,000 persons in this parish, and all Catholics, and as poor as I shall describe, having among them no more than:

One cart	Eight chaff beds
No wheel car	Two stables
No coach or other vehicle	Six cow-houses
One plow	One national school
Sixteen harrows	No other school
Eight saddles	One priest
Two pillions	No other resident gentleman
Eleven bridles	No bonnet
Twenty shovels	No clock
Thirty-two rakes	Three watches
Seven table-forks	Eight brass candlesticks
Ninety-three chairs	No looking glasses above 3d.
243 stools	No boots, no spurs
Ten iron grates	No fruit trees
No swine, hogs, or pigs	No turnips
Twenty-seven geese	No parsnips
Three turkeys	No carrots
Two feather beds	No clover

Or any other garden vegetables, but potatoes and cabbage, and not more than ten square feet of glass in windows in the whole, with the exception of the chapel, the school-house, the priest's house, Mr. Dombrain's house, and the constabulary barrack.

None of their either married or unmarried women can afford more than one shift . . . and more than one half of both men and women cannot afford shoes to their feet, nor can many of them afford a second bed, but whole families of sons and daughters of mature age indiscriminately lying together. . . And worse than all that I have mentioned, there is a general prospect of starvation at the present prevailing among them, and that originating from various causes, but the principal cause is the rot or failure of seed in the last year's crop. . .

—University of Wisconsin Digital Collection
<http://uwdc.library.wisc.edu/Collections.shtml>

Although *The Memorial of Patrick M'Kye* was one of the very few written descriptions of the awful conditions of poverty in the Irish countryside, the Irish people could easily see it for themselves. Indeed, tens of thousands left their farms in 1836 and headed to the cities. M'Kye was also not alone in having discovered that things were vastly different in America. Word was spreading all across Ireland that the economic situation was altogether better in the United States, especially in New York State after the completion of the Erie Canal in 1825. Most of the Erie Canal had been dug by Irish laborers using pickaxes and shovels. These men were brought to America by canal contractors who provided free passage in exchange for a six-month work contract. The pay was one dollar a day for hard labor from dawn to dusk, a wonderful wage for these emigrants. Many were able to save enough to send for their relatives and friends.

Thanks to the canal, the value of merchandise flowing through the Port of New York increased from $84 million in 1825 to $146 million in 1836, and New York City experienced labor shortages. Demand for labor also rose in the Hudson Valley, Albany, Rochester, and Buffalo. Largely because of this demand, the number of emigrants entering through the Port of New York rose from 12,000 in 1825, to 21,000 in 1827, and to 75,000 in 1836.

The opening of the Erie Canal had profound consequences on local economies along its entire route and beyond. Before the canal was dug, wheat and corn grown on farms in the Hudson Valley and on Long Island had little competition when sold in the grain markets of New York City. That was because it cost one hundred dollars a ton to carry the same products by horse-drawn wagon from the large farms of western New York, Ohio, and western Pennsylvania. The canal brought these transportation prices down to as low as six dollars a ton. Local farmers could no longer get the prices to which they were accustomed. So they switched to the more labor-intensive, higher-value, market-gardening of perishable fruits and vegetables: spinach, strawberries, peaches, cherries, tomatoes, lettuce, and peppers. They also began to specialize in seafood—especially scallops, clams, and oysters from the bays of the North Shore and South Shore of Long Island.

Long Island's two-year-old railroad company created jobs, too. In the spring of 1836, using mostly Irish labor, the Long Island Rail Road (LIRR) began extending tracks eastward along the center of Long Island from Jamaica to Greenport. Passengers and freight were carried out to Greenport by train, and then were transferred to ferries across Long Island Sound to Stonington, Connecticut. There they were transferred to a rail line to Boston. The new rail-ferry-rail link was, for a short time, the fastest way to travel from New York City to Boston.

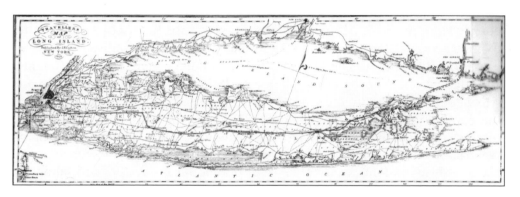

Long Island Rail Road's Combined Rail and Sea Link Connecting Brooklyn, Jamaica, Hicksville, Greenport, and Connecticut
Travelers Map of Long Island (1848)

That same year, 1836, the LIRR ordered rails of the highest quality to be shipped from Liverpool to New York City for construction of the new line. It is possible, but not proven, that some of the iron rails the *Bristol* and the *Mexico* carried from Liverpool were ordered by the LIRR. The ships may also have been carrying laborers who would lay the rails. If so, it would be ironic if both the rails and the laborers ended up at their intended destination, Long Island—though buried in its sands. Two or three months after the wrecks of the *Bristol* and the *Mexico*, the LIRR suspended all work because of financial difficulties, with tracks reaching only to Hicksville. The line to Greenport was eventually completed in 1844.

In the early 1800s, it was only natural that more Europeans emigrated to New York City than did to Boston, Philadelphia, or any other port in the United States, regardless of their final destination. They simply went with the flow, by booking passage aboard the numerous cargo ships sailing the long-established, transatlantic trade route. In the first two decades of the nineteenth century, the relatively small numbers of emigrants aboard each ship received food and accommodations at least on a par with what the crew got. These early emigrants were generally skilled workers looking for better opportunities. However, as the number of emigrants increased dramatically in the mid-1830s, and as their condition of poverty worsened, the manner in which they were treated declined until they were considered no more than human cargo. The 111 emigrants who bought passage on the barque *Mexico* were among the first to be so ill-treated.

In 1836, fifty-eight thousand British and Irish passengers—almost double the number from the year before—took passage to New York, many in response to the predatory tactics of English passenger brokers such as Fitzhugh and C. Grimshaw. The brokers used every method at their disposal to drum up business. The following is an emigrant canal engineer's contemporaneous description of how this was done in the 1830s:

> [T]here were hand bills, placarded on every corner, tree, pump and public place in the city of Dublin, and for forty or fifty miles in the surrounding country, stating, in substance, that the people were fools not to leave the country, where there was nothing but poverty staring them in the face. That laborers were so much wanted in America that even women were employed to work at men's work. . . There is one or more agent in every principal town in Ireland.
>
> —Quoted by R. G. Albion, *The Rise of New York Port.*

As emigrants streamed into Liverpool looking for passage, brokers asked shipowners to find new ways to squeeze more steerage passengers onto their merchant ships. The phrase "steerage" originally referred to a close, airless space in the stern, where squeaking and groaning levers and ropes connected the ship's helm to its rudder. This was always the least expensive passenger accommodation aboard any merchant ship, but space there was limited. By 1836, the expression "steerage class" had come to mean the lowest passenger class, whether berthed in the steerage space or, more commonly, on the 'tween deck.

Use of the 'tween deck became the method of choice for cramming emigrants in without sacrificing too much cargo space. This deck was just under the main deck, allowing about five-and-a-half feet of vertical clearance to the overhead. Anyone of above-average height had to remain bent over while standing. Prisons of the day had more overall space for their inmates.

In 1835, Britain became concerned about the mistreatment of emigrants, and updated their *American Passengers Act* with this express purpose:

> [T]o secure, as effectually as possible, the health and comfort of emigrants on board of passenger ships.

One of several provisions in the law stated, "Where there are 100 passengers, a medical practitioner is to be carried." The *Bristol*, which left Liverpool two weeks before the *Mexico* with two physicians aboard, had a statutory requirement under this law to provide one doctor for her 127 passengers, but carried two. The *Mexico*, with 111 passengers listed on her customs form—i.e., eleven over the threshold of 100—was able to meet the legal requirement by providing *no doctor at all*. Passenger brokers Fitzhugh and C. Grimshaw had become expert at working along the gray edges of the law. They used the following exception clause in the British *American Passengers Act of 1835* to avoid the medical requirement completely:

> In the enumeration of passengers, two children above seven, but under fourteen, or three under seven years of age, are to be reckoned as ONE passenger. Infants under twelve months are not to be included in the enumeration.
> —*American Passengers Act of 1835*. (British Law)

Why lawmakers in 1835 considered children to be less important than adults by counting them as one-half or one-third of a passenger in determining medical requirements, defies any modern logic. In any event, Fitzhugh and C. Grimshaw used this reckoning to their advantage. After allowing for children at their fractional value, they counted the 111 listed passengers aboard the *Mexico* as just 93 people—well below the 100-passenger threshold requirements for a paid doctor.

There is some evidence that Fitzhugh and C. Grimshaw may *still* have been in violation of the medical-doctor requirement by concealing the names of as many as twenty-eight passengers and leaving them off the *Mexico's* official Liverpool Customs House Record. These additional names were provided by the captain after the wreck, and none of them match the 111 names on the official customs list. The additional passengers, even allowing for some of them being children and infants, would have put the count well over the medical threshold figure of 100.

Twenty-eight *Additional* Passengers aboard the *Mexico*
(Names *not* on the Official Liverpool Customs House List)
Sources: *New York Sun,* January 6, 1837 and
New York American, January 12, 1837.

Name	Residence
Joseph Arford	Unknown
Terence Barry	Ireland
Joseph Brooks	Scotland
Ellen Delaney	Ireland
John Evans	New York State
John Ewing	Unknown
John Ewing's wife	Unknown
John Ewing's daughter	Unknown
Thos. Hanrihan	Longford, Ireland
Thos. Hanrihan's sister	Ireland
J. Hardy	Ireland
John Hays	Ireland
Peter Hays	Ireland
Thomas Henderson	England
Thomas Henderson's older sister	Ireland
Thomas Henderson's younger sister	Ireland
George Howland	Ireland (Cavan)
Catharine Lawrence	Ireland
Thomas McNulty	Ireland
William Roberts	New York City
Mary Simmons	Unknown
Sidney Thompson's wife	Unknown
Stanford Thompson	England (Cambridge)
John Urill	Ireland
John Urill's wife	Ireland
John Urill's older child	Ireland
John Urill's younger child	Ireland
John Walsh	Unknown

None of the contemporaneous newspaper reports investigated or even commented on the discrepancies between the Customs House Record and the captain's list. Some of the names may simply be errors in Winslow's recollection following the trauma of the wreck. But if the extra names are in fact accurate, there were not 111 passengers aboard the ship, but 139, and there were not 105 deaths, but 133. However, absent additional proof, the total stands at 111 passengers aboard the *Mexico*, and 105 deaths in the wreck.

Before the *Mexico's* human cargo could be loaded, the 'tween deck had to be prepared. The necessary construction was probably completed by carpenters provided by Fitzhugh and C. Grimshaw. Indeed, this firm was expert at creating the sparest accommodations imaginable. Using rough boards and posts, they built rows of two-level wooden berths along the ship's sides.

Here again the *American Passengers Act of 1835* provided woefully bad guidance, in this case by dictating how the bunks were to be constructed. By law, the lower of the two berths had to be at least six inches above the deck, so that spilled or vomited fluids would not immediately run onto the passengers' bedding. If one allows a few inches for a straw mattress and bedding on each of the two-up bunks—which the passengers had to provide for themselves—there was a little over two feet of vertical space in each bunk, just room enough to roll over without one's shoulder rubbing the planks of the bunk above. The minimum required width of each bunk was eighteen inches, so that any broad-shouldered person had to sleep on his side. Wider bunks were shared. The berths were more like animal pens than bunks.

Everyone slept in their clothing, often the same garments for the entire trip. If a passenger carried no bedding aboard, he or she slept on the bunk's bare boards. This all seems so strange and primitive today, but at the time it was common in the slums of Liverpool and New York City for a half-dozen people to share a single bed.

Lawmakers had not yet finished designing their improved hellhole for emigrants:

> Nor, whatever may be the tonnage, is there to be a greater number of passengers on board than after the rate of one person for every ten superficial feet [i.e., square feet of deck to be walked on] of the lower deck or platform unoccupied by goods or stores, not being the personal luggage of the passengers.
>
> —*American Passengers Act of 1835.* (British Law)

This remarkable provision allowed the *Mexico* to provide a little more than one square yard of deck area for each passenger over fourteen years old to stand on, half that area for a child seven to fourteen to run about on, a one-foot square piece of deck for a child from one year old to seven years old to play on, and no space at all for an infant under one year. Presumably infants were to be held in their parents' arms and therefore needed no deck space. The ten square feet of deck space the law allowed each passenger, plus, in many cases, just a share of a bunk, was not much more than the fifteen square

146

feet Michael Hogan, Esq. allotted his slaves when he transported them from Africa to South America thirty years before.

It stretches the imagination in wonderment at what was in the mind of the lawmakers in the mid-1830s to write such laws with their self-stated "humane intentions." Yet these were in fact *improvements* over what had been unregulated, inhumane conduct. At least now the inhumane conduct would be regulated. Changes were being made not just at sea but in the cities of New York and Liverpool as well. Laws were being passed, for example, to limit open sewage near tenements, and to reduce factory workdays from sixteen hours to twelve.

There were also restrictions on how many passengers a ship could carry, and the *Mexico's* passenger broker was aware of precisely what that legal limit was. The *U.S. Passenger Act of 1819* (which was still in effect in 1836) said that no American ship traveling between the United States and a foreign port could carry "a greater number of passengers than two for every five tons of such ship or vessel." The 111 passengers the 279-ton *Mexico* carried—that was the tonnage and the number of passengers listed on her customs form—was precisely the maximum number permitted by law (279 divided by 5, times 2 = 111.6).

The British *American Passengers Act of 1835* also had requirements regarding food provisions on board. The law stated:

Passenger ships are to be provisioned in the following proportion:

- Pure water, to the amount of five gallons to every week of the computed voyage, for each passenger, the water to be carried in tanks or sweet casks;

- Seven pounds weight of bread, biscuit, oatmeal, or bread stuffs, to every week for each passenger;

- Potatoes may be included to one-third of the extent of supply, but seven pounds' weight of potatoes is to be reckoned equal to one pound bread or bread stuffs.

- The voyage to North America to be computed at ten weeks, by which each passenger will be secured fifty gallons of water, and seventy pounds weight of bread or bread stuffs for the voyage.

   —*American Passengers Act of 1835*. (British Law)

Fitzhugh and C. Grimshaw twisted the intent of the Act's provisioning requirement. In order to free the crew from any responsibility pertaining to storage and weekly distribution of the passengers' food, the broker required that the *passengers themselves*—not the ship's crew—store and ration the food for a ten-week crossing. This had a devastating effect on the *Mexico's* passengers when the voyage neared the maximum number of days allowed for. With eleven days remaining before reaching New York, the passengers had no food left. By the time of the wreck, they were in a state of near-starvation.

Things were different for the officers and crew. The week before departure from Liverpool, Edward Felix, the ship's cook, and Stephen Simmons, the steward, were especially busy. They had to store sufficient provisions for the captain's table, where Charles Winslow would dine with first mate Noah Jordon and young Mr. Broom. They also needed to lay up enough food for nine hungry crewmen for seventy days. In all, this was about 2,500 meals. The task was made easier by the fact that the crew got little variety beyond biscuits, potatoes, and salted meat. The captain's table was another matter. Like the provisioning for first cabin on the *Bristol,* the *Mexico* had livestock pens, fresh vegetables, cheeses, tea, wine, rum, brandy, and flour for baking bread. Young William Broom probably arranged for his favorite confections as well. Of course, none of this food was to be shared with the crew, and certainly not with the passengers.

The captains of packet ships were so determined to leave port on schedule that they routinely set sail without a full load of cargo or passengers, and even paid for steam tugs to tow them from port when the tide and wind were unfavorable. However, Captain Winslow had no such luxury. With William Broom looking over his shoulder—a realistic metaphor in the case of the five-foot-three-inch captain—Winslow had to watch his ship's operating expenses. He waited for the cargo to be fully loaded, and for the wind and tide to be right, before picking up his passengers and departing the Prince's Dock. The 111 men, women, and children who had waited patiently, day after day, at the nearby passenger dock were of less concern than if they were a last-minute cargo of sheep to be herded aboard.

Not everyone approved of such tactics. One of the partners of James Beckett & Sons, a Liverpool and New York shipping company established in 1815, was outraged at the way English passenger brokers treated departing emigrants. On March 12, 1837, he wrote the following letter to *The New York Sunday Morning News*:

> The disadvantages under which emigrants labor are too numerous to require comment. Those who emigrate from Liverpool are frequently detained a considerable time before the sailing of the vessel and various pretexts and excuses are made by the Brokers and Agents for such detention; but in most cases these excuses

are frivolous and vexatious in the extreme. Most of the persons whose passages have been engaged in America, are not permitted to embark until the winter months, when the weather is most inclement, and when they are sure to experience a boisterous passage. These brokers, having sufficient business during the spring (the proper season for emigration), do not send for their paid passengers during that season, but hold off until winter, when they have no other business to attend to, and then they write for their paid passengers, and ship them off in any kind of ship, or in any sort of weather (thus exposing the poor people to every sort of vicissitude of suffering, and inflicting on them the greatest hardships that their reduced circumstances enable them to endure.) Such is the way in which some of the Brokers act who have houses in America for engaging passengers.

—*The New York Sunday Morning News*, March 12, 1837.

Unhappily, the *Mexico's* passenger broker was one of the firms the letter writer was condemning. William Sudlow Fitzhugh was already a notorious Liverpool broker when, in 1832, he joined Caleb Grimshaw to form the partnership, Fitzhugh and C. Grimshaw. The firm took advantage of the naïve and unsuspecting on both sides of the Atlantic, assisted by the firm of Samuel Thompson in New York City. It took time for their brutal methods to be exposed. In 1842, Charles Dickens sailed as a first-cabin passenger aboard a New York-to-Liverpool packet, accompanied by a shipload of steerage-class passengers. He wrote this about the brokers' tactics:

> Above all it is the duty of any Government, be it monarchy or republic, to interpose and put an end to that system by which a firm of traders in emigrants purchase of the owners the whole 'tween-decks of a ship, and send on board as many wretched people as they can lay hold of, on any terms they can get, without the smallest reference to the conveniences of the steerage, the number of berths, the slightest separation of the sexes, or anything but their own immediate profit.
>
> — Chapter 16, "The Passage Home," *American Notes* (1842).

The abusive situation Dickens describes is precisely the arrangement that existed among Samuel Broom, Samuel Thompson, William Sudlow Fitzhugh, and Charles Grimshaw. European emigrants or their relatives in New York sent bank draft prepayments to these unscrupulous brokers in response to misleading advertisements. The Liverpool brokers then searched for the cheapest shipping arrangements they could find, in this case, the *Mexico*. Once they succeeded in leasing a 'tween deck, they sent travel vouchers out to anxiously waiting emigrants in Aberdeen, Armagh, Belfast, Cavan, Chester, Cork, Dublin, Edinburgh, and other cities throughout Great Britain and Ireland. The travel vouchers included prepaid travel to Liverpool by coastal steamer, along with one-way passage to New York. Fitzhugh and C. Grimshaw maintained financial relations with bankers in New York, England, Scotland, Ireland, and Wales for just this purpose.

On arrival in Liverpool, steerage passengers often had to wait days or weeks because of overbooking, late arriving ships, or late arrival of the ship's cargo. The additional expense of this unexpected delay—the cost of housing and food—was always borne by the passengers. And so it was for the *Mexico's* passengers, when the ship's departure was delayed for a full week. Swindlers lay in wait near the Liverpool docks, ready to separate the emigrants from the life savings they carried with them. Boardinghouses charged double and triple rates for waiting passengers, and threatened to hold their trunks if they were not paid. Purveyors of food and other supplies for the voyage sold poor quality goods at unconscionable prices. Worst of all, some dishonest ticketing agents accepted passage money, and then simply disappeared.

A third of the steerage passengers on the *Mexico* were women and children unaccompanied by men. They included Mrs. Mary Metcalf and her four children, from Ireland; Mrs. Margaret Evans and her four children, from England; Bridget Devine, traveling alone from County Cavan, Ireland; and Mrs. Ballentine, traveling alone from Scotland. These women had probably traveled farther getting to Liverpool than they had ever journeyed in their lives. Once there, they became targets for "helpers," and had to fight their way through the den of thieves surrounding the docks and the passenger broker's office. Even when they were aboard the *Mexico*, they were not completely safe, because there was the very real threat of abuse from male passengers and crewmen. However, these courageous women could at least look forward to seeing their brothers, husbands, and fathers who had sailed to New York before them, who had secured jobs, and found places for them to live. Sadly, however, not one of these women would make it to New York alive.

Another third of the passengers were family groups accompanied by men. Among them were the Hopes and their four children, from Dublin, and the Peppers with their six children, from England. These families were willing to risk everything to emigrate together as a family to this great new land, America. Not one member of these families would reach their destination alive.

The final third of the passengers were men traveling without families. Many of them were leading the way for others back home. They were mostly farm workers and laborers who had waited to book passage until their harvesting and seasonal work was done. Only three of these men—a farmer, a laborer, and a weaver—would survive.

The passengers aboard the *Mexico* were so desperate to emigrate that the danger of a late fall crossing on such a small vessel was less important than saving a pound or two of their limited funds. Indeed, few of them had resources beyond a dream for the future and a vision that they could somehow establish themselves in America, and do well. That dream became a reality for thousands of emigrants who came through Liverpool in 1836, though not for those aboard the *Mexico*.

The English overlords in Ireland, Scotland, and Wales were happy to see these emigrants leave. After all, these "labouring poor," as they were called, were considered to be a virtual under-caste that could never rise out of their miserable condition. An editorial in *Dublin University Magazine* (1835), a British-leaning periodical, defined a typical Irish dwelling as "a seminary for the education of pigs." Not content with that insult, it added:

> Much of the misery in Ireland is apparent, not real; and many of the privations under which the people labour, and which, to a stranger, would seem to imply much suffering, proceed from an utter indifference about comforts and decencies, which, in England, would be deemed indispensable, and which a very ordinary effort of industry or ingenuity would be more than sufficient to supply.

It is commonly thought that Irish emigrants had better opportunities to flourish in the United States than they did anywhere in the British Empire. That assumption is rooted in the history of abusive treatment the Irish received in their homeland by their British masters. Frank Welsh in his book, *The Four Nation*s (2003), rejects that notion. His study of employment patterns in North America and Australia demonstrates that Irish emigrants to Canada and Australia achieved a greater degree of success, and did so sooner, than they did in the United States. Sadly, there was no "American welcome" awaiting these emigrants beyond the family or friends who had preceded them. Just a few months before the *Mexico* set sail, New York City's largest newspaper, *The New York Sunday Morning News*, printed a prominent editorial entitled "European Emigrants." It was bluntly critical of emigration. That editorial, which is reprinted on the following page, is a distant echo of views held by many people in the U.S. today. This 1836 editorial could be read aloud on many of today's conservative radio talk shows with just a few substitutions such as "illegal aliens" for "emigration," "Latin America" for "old world," and "Mexico" for "England and Ireland."

European Emigrants

An editorial in the *New York Sunday Morning News,*
May 22, 1836.

The tide of emigration from the demoralized communities of the old world, which has been constantly setting towards this country, is from year to year, and from day to day, becoming stronger. Can no means be taken to check it? How much longer are we to sit quietly and suffer this moral pestilence to roll unrestrained over this land? We establish quarantine regulations to guard against the introduction of the miasma of contagious diseases. We enforce them in the strictest manner, and at great expense, and yet offer no obstruction to the free admission of social and political infection. What inconsistency! Disease at the worst will lay waste to but a small portion of the country – destroy a few hundred or a few thousand of our inhabitants, while the unrestricted admission of the ignorant, lazy and vicious emigrants from England and Ireland, will in time entirely blight the fair fruits of our free institutions, and debase to the low standard of European pauperism the present high moral and intellectual character of our people.

Within a month past, several thousand of degraded beings, who would be a disgrace to the social and political state of the most barbarous nation on the globe, have arrived at this port [the Port of New York]. Every vessel that arrives comes crowded with them, and many thousands more are collected at Liverpool and other English ports, waiting for passage. We might, were it not for them, dispense entirely with our prisons, our penitentiaries, and our alms-house establishments. At least three-fourths of the inmates of the alms-house at Bellevue are foreign paupers, who have been sent over for us to support, by the poor-masters of England and Ireland.

When and where is this state of things to end? Are we to go on forever importing European vagrants in increasing ratio – a ratio out of all proportion to the increase in our native population? Will no one of our legislators take the subject in hand, and endeavor to restrain an evil, compared with which the plagues that affected the hard-hearted monarch of Egypt, were but trifles! If not, the people must do it for themselves – and they must do it soon, too.

In the 1830s, Americans were not only increasingly anti-emigrant, they were becoming anti-Catholic. Popular fiction of the day described priests seducing women in the confessional booth, booklets told of nuns cutting infants from the womb and then tossing them to dogs, and "Break the Pope's Neck" was a favorite children's game. In 1834, a convent was burned in Charlestown, Massachusetts after a vicious anti-Catholic sermon. In 1836, Samuel F. B. Morse—at a time when he was still developing the telegraph—ran for Mayor of New York City on an anti-emigrant and anti-Catholic platform. His unsuccessful run came on the heels of a series of articles and a book he published claiming the United States would soon fall under the yoke of Catholic despotism.

Samuel Thompson, the New York partner of Fitzhugh and C. Grimshaw, had no love for emigrants beyond the money he could squeeze from them. In 1832, his uncle Francis, the head of the firm, had died of cholera. The disease, as everyone in New York believed, and in this case it was true, came from Europe aboard the emigrant ships. For the captain and crew of the *Mexico*, transporting passengers to New York was unpleasant at best. The fear of contagion was one more reason to keep as much distance as possible from the filthy "white cargo" on the 'tween deck. Besides, the officers and crew had more than enough to worry about without concerning themselves with "ignorant, lazy and vicious emigrants" aboard their ship. They had an ocean to cross, and winter was fast approaching.

The Captain and Crew of the *Mexico*

As the *Mexico* prepared to sail from Liverpool, the only crewmember from the Sicilian voyage still aboard the barque was her fair-haired, fair-complexioned captain, Charles Winslow. The senior crewmen from his home state of Pennsylvania, along with the other sailors, had departed before the barque set sail from New York. But the character of the ship was set by the captain, not by the crew. Winslow was not like the captains of the packet lines. They were well-known men who mingled with the wealthy merchant families of Liverpool, London, and New York. They were men known for their social skills and their intelligence, men who could discuss fine wines and good music along with tide tables, winds, and currents. Winslow was one of the many captains of the early 1800s who "came up from before the mast," meaning he rose from the ranks of able-bodied seamen who slept in hammocks in the forecastle. Such captains were not much more civilized than the rough crews they commanded.

James Fenimore Cooper wrote about one of these harsh captains and two merciless mates in his biography of a sailor, *Ned Myers; or, A Life Before the Mast* (1843):

> [I]n the forecastle . . . was a man who had shipped as an ordinary seaman. He had been a soldier, I believe; at all events, he had a medal, received in consequence of having been in one of the late affairs between his country [Holland] and Belgium. It is probable this man may not have been very expert in a seaman's duty, and it is possible he may have been drinking, though to me he appeared sober at the time the thing occurred which I am about to relate.
>
> One day the captain fell foul of him, and beat him with a rope severely. . . . [T]he captain letting him go, told him to go forward.

As the man complied, he fell in with the chief mate, who attacked him afresh, and beat him very severely. The man now went below, and was about to turn in, as the captain had ordered—which renders it probable he had been drinking—when the second mate, possibly ignorant of what had occurred, missing him from his duty, went below, and beat him up on deck again. These different assaults seem to have made the poor fellow desperate. He ran and jumped into the sea, just forward of the starboard lower-studdingsail-boom. The ship was then in the north-east trades, and had eight or nine knots way on her; notwithstanding, she was rounded to, and a boat was lowered—but the man was never found.

What captains such as these lacked in polish they made up for in navigation skill, with its invariable, mathematically-derived rules. They also had willingness, even eagerness, to use their absolute power of command to the full. Owner Samuel Broom had just the man he needed in the unyielding Charles Winslow. It was a dirty business hauling cargos of iron, coal, crates, and lice-infested emigrants across the North Atlantic, especially with a crew of warm-water sailors from the Caribbean. Unlike Captain Alexander McKown of the *Bristol*, who led by example, Captain Charles Winslow would demonstrate on this voyage that his word was law, and that was all anyone aboard his ship—passenger or crew—needed to know.

A ship's crew could expect at least a partial day off on "The Lord's Day" whether out at sea or tied up at a dock. But by setting sail on Sunday captains ensured that their crews would be denied their customary time off. When a ship sailed from port, all hands were required to work the entire day. A sailor would not dare to complain to a mate about losing his day off, for fear of being knocked off his feet. It is no surprise that the *Mexico* left Liverpool on a Sunday.

The work of sailing a ship was physically challenging. The rising and plunging of a tall ship through heavy seas makes tasks such as stowing and replacing a split sail extremely dangerous, and can require the participation of all hands, including those not on watch. To change a sail, several men had to climb out along the yardarm sixty feet and more above the deck, clinging to hand lines and foot ropes, reaching and fisting bulky sailcloth until they got it under control. They always had to be aware that a sudden gust of wind could whip a sail out of control and in an instant pitch a man head over heels to the deck below.

When not on watch or otherwise working, the *Mexico's* sailors resided in the forecastle, the forward-most portion of the ship, at the impact point where the bow meets the oncoming seas. In a violent storm the forecastle drops twenty feet or more from wave crest to trough in just three seconds. This makes the entire ship shudder and appear to lose all her forward motion. Normal conversation is impossible because of the booming noise, and the continual blast of seawater against even heavily-caulked planks gradually leads to enough seepage to soak the sides, the bulkheads, and the deck.

The crews on merchant ships generally had heavier workloads and worse food than sailors aboard naval vessels, primarily because of parsimonious shipowners—and the *Mexico* was certainly no exception. The crew's cold breakfast and cold evening meal consisted of hard biscuits and salt beef or salted horsemeat. The only pleasure to be taken from these meals was a twice-daily allowance of hot tea sweetened with molasses and a daily allotment of grog. For midday dinner, the crew sometimes received what Richard Dana in *Two Years Before the Mast* (1840) called "a rare treat." This was "scouse," a hot mixture of dry biscuits pounded up fine, salt beef cut into small pieces, a few peeled potatoes, and a chopped onion, all boiled together and seasoned with salt and pepper. At mealtime, a younger crewman went up to the cookhouse to get the watch's total allotment of scouse. He carried it to the forecastle in a "kid," a wooden serving vessel with high sides. All the watch-mates, black and white, senior and junior, gathered around the kid with spoons in hand, and ate. The cook had another way to relieve the men's dietary boredom, besides preparing scouse. He would sometimes substitute salt pork for the usual salt beef or salted horsemeat.

Sailors aboard merchant vessels often described their service as slavery, which of course it was not, because any sailor, white or black, could wave goodbye to his captain at the conclusion of a voyage, whereas a slave was bound for life. But a sailor was a slave in the narrow sense that he could not leave his ship once he had contracted to sail on a specific voyage, usually a round trip. Leaving the ship at mid-voyage was deemed desertion and was punishable by whipping, or imprisonment, or both.

In the 1830s, American ships with racially mixed crews such as the *Mexico's*, were workplaces where blacks and whites worked, ate, and slept together in a way that was impossible anywhere else in the United States, in any of the states, free or slave. In a supreme irony, the crewmen who shared a life aboard the *Mexico*, who slept in adjoining hammocks, and who ate from the same kid, were separated in death. They were buried in separate graves— one for blacks, the other for whites—all within a common enclosure called "The Mariners Burying Ground," in the village of Lynbrook.

American shipowners took great pride in sailing their ships with about half the crew that French, Spanish, or Italian ships used. The usual number of men needed to sail a medium-sized American merchant ship with three square-rigged masts—the *Bristol* was one such ship—was probably a captain and sixteen men. Often, ships were re-rigged as barques with a fore-and-aft sail on the mizzen to require less handling. This meant that one or two men could be trimmed from the crew, bringing the minimum down to fourteen. Winslow set sail from Liverpool on the barque *Mexico* with only ten men under his command, the same number he had sailed with on his eight-month voyage to Sicily. But this voyage was different, and the lack of reserve manpower would prove fatal. On the previous voyage he spent the winter months sailing in the Mediterranean, not the North Atlantic, and he had an experienced crew, unlike the current crew he had assembled at the last minute. He had carried a light cargo of powdered Sicilian sulfur, rags, nuts, and fruit, as compared to his current cargo of five hundred tons of iron bars and coal. Moreover, on the voyage home from Sicily he had just two passengers, both men of means, who had dined with him at his table. Now he had 111 emigrants berthed on the 'tween deck.

Although the vessel was proudly advertised in the Liverpool newspapers as "The fine American Ship *Mexico* – coppered and copper-fastened," this had little to do with the unseaworthiness of the overloaded, undermanned barque. Sheathing the bottoms of ships was done as far back as Roman times when lead sheets and copper fasteners were used on vessels belonging to Emperor Trajan. Sheathing prevented incrustation from barnacles and seaweed, which often grew to a thickness of half a foot around the entire wooden hull. It also prevented invasion by shipworms—known as *teredos*—a burrowing marine mollusk that drills into a ship's wooden planks. But lead was not durable, and the practice was abandoned. In 1761, the British Admiralty experimented with copper sheathing but found problems with both its durability and its electro-chemical reaction with seawater, all of which seriously degraded the copper in just three years. By the 1830s, however, reasonably good results were being obtained using copper fasteners and attaching bars of zinc to the hull.

The eleven-year-old *Mexico's* warm-water trips to the Mediterranean and the Caribbean may have had unseen costs from within the ship—dry rot, a fungus that seeks out warm, moist, dark spaces. Creeping, white, fungal fingers of dry rot penetrate a ship's hull from the inside, weakening the interior of the wood while leaving the outer surface intact to all appearances. Despite the *Mexico's* copper sheathing, copper fasteners, and anti-electro-chemical zinc bars, the barque's minor leaks would become so grave a problem at sea that even the passengers began to realize the seriousness.

Winslow should have seen it all coming. As the *Mexico* sat at the Prince's Dock in Liverpool, the experienced, forty-seven-year-old captain should have made allowances for the difficulties that lay ahead for his ship, perhaps by refusing to load some of the cargo, or turning away some passengers. But owner Samuel Broom had already trumped Winslow's objections. If Broom was confident enough to place his younger brother William aboard the ship, how could Winslow now falter? The *Mexico* would sail; the contracts with Samuel Thompson and with Fitzhugh and C. Grimshaw would be honored.

The *Mexico* Sails

On Sunday, October 23, 1836, exactly two weeks after the *Bristol* left port, the *Mexico* was ready to depart. Her cargo was loaded, and in a few hours the tide would be right for sailing down the Mersey. At dawn, the barque was rope-hauled to a nearby passenger dock for taking on passengers. For a week now, the emigrants had gathered at the dock, waiting for word from Fitzhugh and C. Grimshaw that the *Mexico* would sail. At each postponement of the sailing date, they had returned to their miserable, overpriced lodgings. By now, some of them had probably been so "gulled" by the sharpies of Liverpool that they had little or no money left. Others, forewarned, still had gold sovereigns in their money belts or sewn into the linings of their coats. Finally, the time had come, and they stood at dockside with their possessions. Their trunks, boxes, and bundles were filled with clothing, bedding, and cooking utensils. The passenger broker's food supply stood by, waiting to be loaded, enough for an unlikely seventy-day voyage. At least it was *assumed* the supply would last that long.

Boarding the passengers was a simple matter for the officers and crew of the *Mexico*. The passenger broker led the group up the gangway and down the ladder to the 'tween deck. All the adult passengers had paid the same rate of three pounds ten shillings, about $400 today. For this they would be transported from Liverpool to New York in the same manner as if they were barrels of merchandise. Indeed, the barrels deep in the *Mexico's* hold received more attention than the passengers did because the barrels had to be physically loaded and unloaded by the crew, and they were insured against loss.

As the hour of departure approached, there was the tumult of late arrivals from the boarding houses. Hectic scenes were common at the

Prince's Dock because passenger brokers were more eager to take their fees than to ensure that their ticket purchasers had time to reach the ship. Even after the gangway was removed, a large family might present itself at dockside, flushed and panting, with a cart carrying all their worldly goods. If the gangway was already pulled up, the family's belongings were pitched across the gap onto the ship, and then pitched again from the main deck down the ladder to the steerage deck. Family members scrambled aboard by grabbing for the ship's rail and rigging, eagerly accepting the assistance offered by fellow passengers. Bundles, chests, and boxes, and even people fell overboard with enough frequency that the dockmaster at the Prince's Dock assigned a small boat to stand by and retrieve fallen possessions and individuals.

Unlike the *Bristol*, which was a relatively new ship designed for both passengers and cargo, the *Mexico* had no passenger-friendly features. There were no bull's-eyes to add natural light below decks, no round-house on the deck, and no tables and benches on the 'tween deck. Passengers on this ship had to sit on their bunks or on their trunks. There were no partitions to separate families or women and children traveling alone. Aboard the *Mexico*, everyone was packed onto the single deck with no privacy at all. Any improvements in this open arrangement had to be accomplished by the passengers themselves, by using blankets or lengths of old sailcloth—if they could get it—hung between bunks as dividers or in front as curtains.

Ocean voyages under such circumstances were particularly hazardous for young women traveling alone. The *Mexico* had eleven women unaccompanied by men, ranging in age from fifteen to thirty. Crewmen and male passengers took such delight in preying on unattached women in steerage, that the women had no choice but to band together for self-defense. By the 1850s, things were so bad that a law was passed by the United States Congress levying a fine against shipowners for each woman raped and made pregnant aboard an emigrant ship.

The passengers stacked their worldly goods in the center of the 'tween deck, and tied them down, with none of the skill needed for severe storm conditions. Charles Dickens, writing in *An Emigrant's Letter* about his own voyage six years later, described "passengers tumbling about one over another; our boxes dashing first to one side and then to the other and many broken to pieces." Storms like the one Dickens described would batter the *Mexico* for two months, almost without ceasing.

The sail down the Mersey was short and pleasant, aided by the outgoing tide. There was no need for the customary *Roll-call of the Passengers* and the *Search for Stowaways* because the captain and crew had no interest in how many people were below decks. The *Mexico* lay at anchor for several hours at the shoal-guarded mouth of Liverpool Bay until the high tide returned. Packet ships, operating on tight schedules, were willing to pay for pilots to guide them through the sandbars, but with a twenty- to thirty-foot tide change providing a comfortable margin for safety, Captain Winslow could save money by crossing with the high tide.

As was the tradition on all tall wooden ships, the initial sea-watch belonged to the first mate, Noah Jordan. The ocean voyage started out badly, with a difficult passage south, even under the lee of the Irish coast. Once the *Mexico* rounded Cape Clear, at the southern end of Ireland, the spray began to fly off the tops of the waves into the helmsman's face. From then until the barque reached New York there was barely a day with favorable winds. For the most part, the only sails that could be carried were the fore-and-aft sails—the jib, fore staysail, and fore-and-aft spencers—because the square sails that normally provided the barque's primary wind-driven power were useless in such head-on weather.

The three male passengers who survived the wreck had little to say about how badly the *Mexico* fared on her Atlantic crossing. They simply blamed the miserable voyage on the extremely bad weather. Although this is certainly true, these were the observations of non-sailors. There is much more to the story of the barque's difficulties at sea.

**Joseph Clement Delano
Captain of the *Roscoe***

<webpages.charter.net/mcarolan/
ThomasCarolan.html>

The *Morning Courier and New York Express* of November 24, 1836, reported on its "Marine List" that the packet *Roscoe,* two days after leaving Liverpool, sailed "in co[mpany] with [the] barque *Mexico*," and that she hailed the barque as she passed by. The fact that the *Mexico* had a two-day lead out of Liverpool, and was passed in just two days, means that the *Mexico* was traveling at about half the speed of the *Roscoe*.

The *Roscoe*, at 620 tons, was built in 1832 by Smith & Dimon of New York. She was 134 feet long with a beam of 32 feet, compared to the *Mexico's* 279 tons and approximate dimensions of about 100 by 26 feet. Though relatively new, the *Roscoe* was not one of the truly modern, sharp-designed clippers such as the *Rainbow* and the *Sea Witch*, but she was a well-designed and well-crewed ship with a famous captain at the helm, Joseph C. Delano.[28] The *Roscoe* was able to maintain her rate of speed of more than twice the *Mexico's* for the entire Atlantic crossing. As a result, the *Roscoe* arrived off Sandy Hook in just thirty days compared to the *Mexico's* crossing of sixty-nine days.

There is additional evidence of the *Mexico's* incredibly labored voyage. The *New York Herald's* "Marine Intelligence Report of Jan 4, 1837 – Recent Ship Arrivals off the Hook," reported that two days after the *Mexico* arrived off Sandy Hook, an unnamed vessel arrived after a thirty-eight-day crossing from Liverpool. This vessel had given the *Mexico* a month-long lead, had encountered many of the same storms as the *Mexico*, and arrived in New York at about the same time. The Atlantic crossings of the *Roscoe* in thirty days and the other vessel in thirty-eight days were typical winter westbound crossing times. They prove beyond any doubt that the overloaded *Mexico* was unseaworthy in winter storm conditions in the North Atlantic.

Full-rigged barques such as the *Mexico*, constructed in the 1820s, were broad in the bow (referred to as "apple-cheeks bows") broad amidships, and broad in the stern. They were built for cargo capacity, not performance. These vessels could not knife through heavy seas as the clippers could. Nor could they handle moderate waves as efficiently as the newer, sharper-designed ships such as the *Bristol*. Instead, the *Mexico* had to bull her way through even moderate seas, creating large bow and stern wakes.

As the *Mexico* headed out past Ireland into the North Atlantic, thirty knot headwinds pushed twenty-foot seas in her face. The overloaded wooden vessel creaked and groaned in protest as she labored into, up, and over each oncoming swell. On reaching each crest, the bow plunged downward into the next wave, almost bringing the ship to a stop. Seawater surged over the deck and the cycle began again as the next wave approached. The effort to keep the barque closely pointed into the wind was exceedingly difficult for the crew, especially at night, when the mountainous waves were unseen until the white froth at their peaks met the bow and rushed along her sides like a rolling avalanche of foam.

As each new day brought a new round of storms and ever colder weather, it become obvious to Captain Winslow that the vessel had serious problems. With a more nimble ship, he could change his course southward to avoid the brunt of the storms. Many ships sailing out of Liverpool did just

---

[28] The *Roscoe's* captain, Joseph Clement Delano, was a distant relative of President Franklin Delano Roosevelt. The captain's father's brother was FDR's great grandfather. FDR said in 1944, "What vitality I have is not inherited from the Roosevelts. . . [M]ine, such as it is, comes from the Delanos." Coincidentally, Robert Minturn, one of the owners of the *Bristol*, also owned the *Roscoe* under The Line of Packets.

that, often sailing hundreds of miles south across the Gulf Stream, before resuming a course west. Such a maneuver could cost days but gain weeks. But the *Mexico* could not alter her westward course because she could not handle the heavy beam seas she would then encounter. The sad fact is that the 279-ton vessel with her 500-ton load was not seaworthy under those conditions. Her high center of gravity (relative to the keel) made the barque laterally unstable. If she pointed away from the wind, powerful windward seas could roll the *Mexico* to the point of putting half her lee deck underwater, tearing away her lifeboats, cookhouse, and rigging, and even snapping off her lower spars. Such rolling could also cause the cargo to shift, with potentially disastrous results. Winslow, forced as he was by the weather and by the limitations of his ship, had no option but to continue sailing, close-hauled and westerly, into the teeth of the wind.

The Barque *Mexico*
The *New York Sun*,
January 12, 1837.

Winslow's crew of mostly warm-water sailors was sufficient in number to handle a fair-weather crossing; but the cold, stormy North Atlantic combined with the barque's sailing limitations revealed the crew's inadequacies in both number and skill. There was little Winslow could do about his manpower problem except threaten or administer whippings, and shuffle assignments. A few weeks out of Liverpool, the captain designated a new arrival, John Francis, as second mate. Francis, a French citizen, had signed on in Liverpool. However, the demands of heavy-weather sailing quickly exposed the man's incompetence and forced Winslow to dismiss him and take the larboard watch himself. Francis was summarily evicted from the officer's quarters and returned to the forecastle.

A serious problem emerged as the vessel experienced progressively worse leaks. There was a variety of causes, all related to the hull: severe stresses from the extraordinarily heavy cargo, a lack of freeboard on the low-lying barque, the constant pounding of the waves, and possible damage from dry rot. The already overworked crew had to man the pumps in addition to their regular duties. Stephen Simmons, the ship's steward, served the needs of the ship's officers and also provided a bare-bones, but profitable level of service to the passengers by selling rum and whiskey to them. Now he too had to man the pumps.

Captain Winslow dealt with his problems with the dogged determination of a master mariner with thirty years' experience at sea. Like all ships' captains, he could tell his vessel's position either by dead reckoning—using just a compass, a timepiece, and a log line—or by shooting the sun or stars with a sextant. He could identify the Gulf Stream simply by smell, even when it was far beyond the horizon. In a dense fog he could scrape up a bit of sand from the ocean bottom and know if he had reached Georges Bank. Winslow had survived storms so severe that his experiences cannot be understood by a non-mariner. He was convinced that he and his ship would survive this voyage.

The passengers, on the other hand, had no control of their destinies, and had to remain in total submission to the captain's and the mate's orders, and to the forces of nature. After the wreck, the three surviving passengers provided little information about how the *Mexico's* problems at sea affected the lot of their fellow emigrants or themselves. All they said was that it was a "boisterous crossing" on "a terrible ship." However, the awful conditions the passengers endured can be surmised from other details.

The *Mexico* had a bare main deck except for her small cookhouse and her two boats, and was open to the elements. The passengers had no choice but to remain below in bad weather, which was just about every one of the sixty-nine days it took for the *Mexico* to reach New York. Had the weather been better, the deck hatches could have been left open to admit fresh air to the 'tween deck, and the passengers might have been permitted to come up on the main deck to cook food on the open stoves, wash clothes, or simply walk about. But with "boisterous" conditions, and seawater surging across the deck of the overloaded barque, the hatches remained battened down. The only people permitted on deck were the crew, while the passengers were confined like prisoners.

Like many American ships of the day, the *Mexico* had a cookhouse that was presided over by a black man, in this case Edward Felix. Cooks on American merchant ships were generally called "Doctor" by the crew. This appellation had nothing to do with the dispensing of medicines—the first mate kept the medical chest. Instead, it was a gesture of the crew's familiarity with and feigned respect for the man who fed them. Felix's galley was only about six feet by five feet, containing a stove, a coal bin, and storage shelves. Pots and pans were hung on hooks. No passengers were ever permitted to enter the cookhouse because this was where the captain's and the crew's meals were prepared. On the rare occasions when the weather calmed down enough for the passengers to come up on deck, their heads undoubtedly would turn toward the smell of the captain's roasted pork or chicken dinner coming from the cookhouse stovepipe. The cook and the steward had to keep a sharp eye on the animal pens that were secured inside the ship's small boats. They could see the passengers' longing glances cast in the direction of the livestock.

No fires were permitted below decks, so passengers had to cook their meals on the ship's stoves on deck. These open stoves were attached to flat stone bases and lashed down to a hatch cover. Not only did the rolling and pitching of the ship make cooking difficult, the stoves had no protection from wind, sea-spray, and rain. Because so many people had to use the same stoves, the best one could hope for was to quickly boil up some water before moving out of the way for the next person on line. For weeks at a time, conditions were so bad that the passengers could not cook at all, and were forced to eat cold meals of biscuits, salted meat, and water. Hot tea was a rare luxury.

As the voyage wore on into mid November, the stench of unwashed bodies, rotting food, seasickness, and spilled-over human waste must have become a torture to the passengers. The flow of unhealthy fluids across the *Mexico's* 'tween deck tested to the full the *American Passengers Act's* requirement that the lower bunk be at least six inches above the deck to keep effluence out of the bunks. It is difficult to judge from afar whether the smell of the male passengers' cheap pipe tobacco—which was mixed with tea leaves—added to or subtracted from the overall foulness of the air. Perhaps worst of all were the lice that swarmed over the passengers' bodies. Although the *Mexico's* survivors spoke only in general terms about the terrible conditions aboard the barque, other sea travelers of that era have been more specific. Ralph Waldo Emerson crossed the North Atlantic on a packet ship that was infinitely more luxurious than the *Mexico*. He wrote:

> [T]he confinement, cold, motion, noise and odor . . . the floor of
> your room sloped at 20-30 degrees. . . upset, shoved against the
> side, rolled over. . . suffocated with bilge and mephitis [stench].
> —"English Traits - II. Voyage to England" <<Bartleby.com>>

Except for the steward, members of the *Mexico's* crew were forbidden to enter the 'tween deck. The passengers were responsible for such tasks as emptying waste buckets and mopping the deck with pails of seawater. But even the mopping was impossible for days at a time because the hatches were kept closed and therefore seawater could not be obtained.

The lack of personal bathing was less of a problem because no one aboard really expected to take a bath until they reached New York.

Herman Melville wrote about the awful situation below decks in *Redburn: His First Voyage*, a semi-autobiographical novel. Melville, who traveled across the Atlantic as a crewman, described the hatchway leading to the 'tween deck:

> We had not been at sea one week, when to hold your head down the fore hatchway was like holding it down a suddenly opened cesspool.

It was like that on the *Mexico*. Within a few weeks out of Liverpool, much of the 'tween deck—including clothing, bedding, and trunks—was soiled by sea spray, rain, sea sickness, human waste, and spilled food. There may not have been one day of the sixty-nine-day crossing when it was calm enough for the passengers to bring their clothes and bedding up on deck, to wash them in seawater, and hang them up to dry in the sun. For the last weeks of the voyage it didn't matter, because the wash would have frozen stiff in minutes.

Such conditions take a severe physical and mental toll. As maritime historian W. S. Lindsay writes about life on the 'tween deck:

> It was scarcely possible to induce the passengers to sweep the decks after their meals or to be decent with respect to the common wants of nature; in many cases in bad weather, when they could not go out on deck, their health suffered so much that their strength was gone, and they had not the power to help themselves. Hence, 'between decks' was a loathsome dungeon.
> — W. S. Lindsay, *History of Merchant Shipping* (1876)

There is no record of how many passengers died aboard the *Mexico* before she reached Sandy Hook. Under similar circumstances as many as one quarter of steerage passengers died from disease—cholera, typhus, plague, tuberculosis, dehydration, and influenza. Burials at sea, especially of children, were not only common, they were expected. In the 1830s, one shipping line even bragged in their advertisements that they had more births than deaths aboard their ships—a dubious advantage. The United States government's underwhelming response to these tragedies was to fine sea captains ten dollars for every shipboard death. The effect of this punishment was to turn most of the dead person's passage money over to the government.

In mid-December, after seven weeks of this living hell, conditions aboard the *Mexico* worsened. Fierce North Atlantic headwinds still buffeted the vessel, but now the sea spray was cold enough to leave a thin coat of ice on the decks, spars, sails, and ropes. Ashes from Edward Felix's cook stove were scattered on the deck to prevent dangerous falls. Every sail change and every course change was a painstaking and impossibly dangerous task, further taxing the crew. Below decks, the leaks became more severe, and the hand-pumps had to be manned twenty-four hours a day. Winslow could no longer force his crew to operate the pumps because they were having too much difficulty dealing with the adverse conditions on deck. As a result, Winslow asked for passenger-volunteers to do the pumping, which they did, perhaps earning a few hot meals in the bargain.

Captain Winslow had to reduce sail even further. If a sail split in the wind now, it would be a virtual death sentence for any crewman ordered to climb up the icy mast, cling to ice-encrusted safety lines, haul down a torn and frozen sail, and bend a new one to the yard.

The Caribbean sailors aboard the *Mexico* were at a particular disadvantage. Sailors out of New York always brought heavy winter clothing with them, including woolen pea jackets, flannel underclothes, woolen mittens, southwester caps, and insulated boots. The Caribbean sailors may well have had to draw on the ship's "slop chest" of used clothing and other provisions sold aboard ship. Improperly dressed, unaccustomed to dealing with extreme cold, and mistreated for complaining about it, these sailors paid a huge price. Of this there is no doubt. They were the first of the crew to experience the early stages of frostbite.

Although the *Mexico's* black sailors were weathering the same gales and manning the same infernal pumps as the white crewmen, they now received the brunt of the captain's frustration. There was a long tradition for this. Jeffrey Bolster's *Black Jacks* quotes an early nineteenth-century black seaman, a veteran sea-cook: "[The white mates] used to flog, beat, and kick me about the same as if I had been a dog." Bolster provides other examples of such race-based mistreatment, telling of a cook and steward tied back to back, of a cook struck with a board, and of disproportionate floggings given to black seamen.

A surviving passenger reported, without elaboration, that some of the black crewmen became "troublesome." How could things be otherwise? These men had not bargained for a berth on a leaky, wallowing, frozen, coffin ship. Their goal in shipping aboard the *Mexico* was to work hard, earn a little money, and see places their friends and family could only dream of. They had never contemplated frostbite or being beaten with a knotted rope if they balked at climbing an icy mast with half-frozen hands and feet.

The passengers, too, had not planned on such a long, cold voyage. When icy December weather set in, the passengers began eating more than their usual daily allotment of food, simply to keep warm. Although the steward had plenty of provisions in his larder for the captain and crew, the passengers were less fortunate. By December 20, two months into the voyage, all their food had either been consumed or had spoiled, and the captain was estimating a week to ten days before reaching port. The emigrants were now starving.

In desperation, forty-one men and women made an appeal to the captain in the form of a letter, which they all signed, many with "X's." Miraculously, the letter survived the wreck, and was printed in the *New York Sun* of January 12, 1837. The passengers' petition, which is reprinted below, was hand delivered to the captain by William Robertson, a passenger who did not survive the wreck.

TO CAPTAIN WINSLOW:

20th December, 1836

SIR—We, the undersigned passengers in the barque Mexico under your command, being reduced to a very deplorable state, for want of provisions, and unable any longer to bear the privation, take this means of proposing the only plan that can be adopted to preserve the lives of ourselves, our wives and children. We are fully aware of some provisions being on board, such as Biscuits and Herrings.

We propose to purchase a sufficient quantity of the same, and to give you a deposit equal to their current price at New York, and this will secure you in the value of such part of your cargo as we may consume.

We respectfully submit this for your consideration and request a reply in the course of the day.

—*New York Sun*, January 12, 1837.

If a crewman aboard the *Mexico* had approached the captain with such a letter, Winslow would have had him whipped. Richard Dana describes a similar situation in his book, *Two Years Before the Mast,* where a crewmate made a modest request of the captain and was severely beaten. Now one of those foul-smelling, strongly-accented pieces of "white cargo," someone calling himself a representative of the passengers—people Captain Winslow was supposed to have no responsibility for—dared to address him! The passengers, however, had carefully selected their messenger. William Robertson was a powerfully built blacksmith. As he approached, he loomed over the much shorter captain, giving the appearance of being able to throw Winslow over the side of the ship in an instant. Robertson stood and waited for the captain's response. But Winslow would have none of this; certainly not from such riffraff. A surviving passenger said that Winslow gave Robertson the following challenge in response:

Do you want to take command of the ship!!!
—*The New York Sun*, January 12, 1837.

Surprisingly, Captain Winslow relented. He had already seen signs of trouble among his crew; and Robertson's physical size was a reminder that he did not also need problems with rebellious passengers. Perhaps it was young William Broom who reminded the captain that his older brother Samuel was earning a good sum by leasing both the cargo hold and the 'tween deck to Samuel Thompson, and that some allowance should be made. In any event, the very next day the captain ordered that supplies be drawn from the ship's stores for the benefit of the passengers. He issued a daily food allocation in rotation as follows: day one, a biscuit for each passenger; day two, a biscuit and a herring; day three, a handful of flour. Although this was literally a starvation ration, the captain ordered that no other ship's stores were to be consumed by the passengers. The ship's crew remained on their normal rations. The price paid by the passengers would be terrible. Eleven days later, when one last opportunity to live or die would come, only the strong would survive. The rest would perish.

On December 25, 1836, Christmas Day, when the rotation of the passengers' daily food ration should have been a "Day Two" biscuit and a herring, Captain Winslow ordered Edward Felix to prepare something special for the passengers. Surviving passenger John Wood spoke about this after the wreck, calling this Christmas dinner a "great treat." In fact, it was an abbreviated version of a crewman's daily allocation: a biscuit, six small potatoes, and a quarter of a pound of salt pork. Passenger Wood remarked:

We thought a great deal of this meal, and were very glad and thankful for it.
—*New York Herald*, January 6, 1837.

As the *Mexico* labored on toward New York, day after painful day, the passengers were so weak from hunger, seasickness, and cold that they could barely function. The insides of the barque were now coated in ice from the passengers' moist breath. They were literally starving and freezing to death in the hold of the *Mexico*. In all likelihood some died before the wreck, but there is no record of that. After another week of this, they received the awful news that the temperature had moved down into single digits. This, however, was tempered by other, *electrifying news*: the Navesink Twin Lights of New Jersey had been sighted.

The *Mexico* Reaches New York

The *Mexico's* approach along the South Shore of Long Island was agonizing. Headwinds forced the barque to beat back and forth in the New York Bight for days, until she finally neared the New Jersey coast. At 11 PM on Saturday, December 31, 1836—New Year's Eve—the lookout spotted the Navesink Twin Lights gleaming atop the Atlantic Highlands, the highest headland along the Atlantic coast south of Maine. Captain Winslow told a crewman to open the 'tween deck's hatch cover and yell down to the passengers that the Twin Lights were in view, and that within a few hours the barque would be lying off Sandy Hook awaiting the arrival of a pilot.

New Year's Eve aboard the *Mexico* was bittersweet, despite the good news. The temperature recorded in Manhattan that night was five degrees above zero, so no one wanted to step outside onto the icy deck. Passengers contented themselves by climbing up the ladder one by one and poking their heads out the hatch. They strained for just a moment to see the Navesink Lights and any other lights on the shores of New Jersey, Staten Island, Brooklyn, or Long Island, before quickly retreating to their cold beds. The only other observers of the scene were the sailors on watch, wrapped in all the layers of pants, shirts, and jackets they could muster, and with a blanket over that. Because of the intense cold, crew members continually interrupted their watch by ducking into Edward Felix's cookhouse for a few moments, to soak up the warmth from the glowing coals, and to drink a cup of hot water.

At six o'clock in the still-dark morning of New Year's Day, the lookout sighted the Sandy Hook Light. Soon they were off the bar. All around them in the dim light of early dawn was an incredibly beautiful scene. Almost forty other tall wooden ships were lying at anchor off the Hook, each one displaying brightly-lit lanterns from its yards. The lights swung back and forth as the seas rocked the ships. The slapping sound of the rigging created percussive music. However, Captain Winslow was not fooled by the placid scene. The only thought in his mind was: Why are so many ships standing by? Where are the pilots?

On Sunday morning, the passengers were up at first light "in great spirits," as a survivor said, taking quick turns on deck, and looking at the ships and the shore. First Mate Noah Jordan advised the passengers that as soon as a pilot was taken aboard, the *Mexico* would sail past the Sandy Hook Shoals, round the elbow of the Lower Bay, then cruise along the shore of Staten Island, through the Narrows, past Governors Island, and up to dockside in Manhattan. With luck they might arrive that very evening. Six weeks earlier, the passengers aboard the *Bristol* had been given the same hopeful prediction.

The mate informed the passengers that once the barque reached the dock, anyone who did not have a place to stay in the city could remain aboard for one night only, to allow time to find other arrangements. If they chose to stay aboard they would be required to sleep on bare boards, because once the ship passed Staten Island there would be no bedding left on the ship. This, the mate advised them, was necessary to avoid being held in quarantine.

Ever since the cholera epidemic of 1832, any ship from a foreign port carrying forty or more passengers was subject to inspection by a medical officer, and could, if necessary, be put into thirty-day quarantine at Staten Island. Filthy, vermin-infested ships with cargo to deliver—that is, ships such as the *Mexico*—tried to avoid quarantine. Their captains ordered the passengers to toss all their bedding overboard in advance of any inspection, scrub the 'tween deck with sand and holystones, and mop every surface including the bunks. The mate would then order all the passengers out onto the main deck with their trunks and bundles. Finally, the crew would carry covered pans filled with smoky, burning coals down onto the 'tween deck so that the entire space could be fumigated under closed hatches. The reason for these procedures was to conceal from the medical-inspection officers the degrading conditions of filth the passengers had lived in for the previous two months.

The announcements about discarding the bedding and cleaning the 'tween deck did not upset the passengers. Instead, songs and shouts of joy rang throughout the ship, prayers of thanks were offered, friends and family members hugged each other, and tears were shed. This was a true New Year's Day celebration for the exhausted emigrants, a day to be spoken of again and again to their children and grandchildren. This was not simply a day to bring in another new year, 1837; this very day would bring a new life, in a new country, America. Their sixty-nine days of hell aboard the *Mexico* were over.

It was a happy day for the sailors, too, especially for those who had received the brunt of the captain's frustration on this voyage. They had spent days and nights manning the pumps, climbing out onto ice-encrusted yardarms, beating frozen sails with their fists, and when they balked, being beaten themselves. The captain may even have increased the crew's grog ration that day.

The passengers and crew of the *Mexico* had completed an excruciatingly difficult voyage to reach the entrance of New York Harbor. But as hard-earned as their arrival celebrations were, they were premature. Dante wrote in his *Inferno*: *Se tu segui tua stella, non puoi fallire a glorioso porto.* (Translation: If you follow your star, you will surely find your glorious harbor.) Close as they were, they had not yet reached their harbor, their *glorioso porto*. Still ahead of the *Mexico's* passengers were three days in hell, the last one of which would be straight out of the frozen Ninth Ring of Dante's *Inferno*.

For the moment, however, there was great anticipation among the passengers as they excitedly readied their baggage for disembarkation, many of them retracing the steps of the victims aboard the *Bristol*. They took out the "Sunday-best" clothing they and their children expected to wear later that evening when they walked down the gangway in New York, waving to their friends and relations. The parallels to the *Bristol* were almost complete— except for the *Mexico's* longer voyage, the terrible sailing conditions, the hunger, and the bitter cold. In a surreal repetition of the *Bristol's* disaster, the harbor pilots were again not at their posts.

Captain Winslow could see massive ice floes drifting past the Hook and out to sea, rhythmically rising and falling in the ocean swells, occasionally bumping into the ship's sides as they passed. He stood on the open deck in worried contemplation. The previous winter, pilots had guided vessels into the Lower Bay, right through the ice floes, despite the fact that the North River and the East River had frozen over. The thought may now have crossed Winslow's mind that perhaps the freeze-over was worse this year; perhaps the pilot boats were locked in ice at their Staten Island and East River piers. Perhaps they could not come out.

This was quickly proven not to be the case. Two small ships appeared off Staten Island, slowly picking their way through the ice in the direction of the *Mexico*. Great excitement arose when the vessels were seen to be schooners coming out through the channel and sailing among the waiting ships. Surely, these were pilot boats off-loading their pilots. One of the schooners approached the *Mexico*, and the schooner captain hailed the barque with his megaphone. The long days and nights of suffering appeared to be over; but they were not. The following words, as reported in the *Morning*

Courier and New York Express of January 4, 1837, were exchanged between the two captains. The sound of them was devastating to everyone aboard the *Mexico*, both passengers and crew:

> **From the schooner**: "Ship ahoy! What ship is that pray?"
>
> **Answer from Captain Winslow**: "The Barque *Mexico*, 70 days from Liverpool, with 165 passengers, short of provisions and water; we have lost sails and are in a leaky condition. We must have a pilot immediately."[29]
>
> **From the schooner**: "We have no pilot aboard."

The schooner captain explained that the two schooners were news boats, collecting ship-arrival information for the New York newspapers. He wrote down the barque's information and left.

Although the harbor pilots were unwilling to venture out into the ice-choked channel that New Year's Day, the news boats had done so. The intrepid news boat reporters had begun their difficult work in the late 1820s, when two New York papers, the *Courier* and the *Journal of Commerce*, decided to get a jump on their competitors. They contracted with a rowboat crew to gather information from incoming ships in the Lower Bay, particularly those that were stalled below the Narrows waiting for a fresh breeze or for the tide to change. The rowboat maneuvered from ship to ship, recording vessel names, captains, cargos, and ports of origin. Their chief objective, however, was to collect the foreign and domestic newspapers that these vessels carried from port cities around the world. They then delivered the consolidated European news, national news, and ship arrivals to their editors for publication. This news boat cooperative anticipated Reuters and the Associated Press by more than two decades.

So eager were merchants, insurers, bankers, and the general public to get this out-of-town and overseas news, that by the time the *Mexico* stood off the Hook in January 1837, eight New York papers had organized themselves into three news-gathering associations, each one with a fast-sailing, ocean-going schooner. A dozen years later, in a short-lived experiment, some tall ships arrived with carrier pigeons pre-trained to fly to their home coops in New York City. Capsules attached to their legs contained brief news summaries. This gained a few hours on the news boats.

---

[29] It appears that Winslow exaggerated the officially listed total of 111 passengers, or possibly the news reporter aboard the news boat misheard the number. The same reporter also wrote Winslow's name down incorrectly. Even after including potentially unlisted passenger names, the total would be only 139. Shipowner Samuel Broom also later denied the *Mexico* was ever short of water.

The news boat for the *Morning Courier and New York Express,* the *New York Herald,* and the *New York Times* recorded that the *Mexico* and thirty-eight other vessels were off the Hook:

Marine Intelligence Reports of January 3-4, 1837

—New York Herald, New York Times, and *Morning Courier*

Type of Ship	Ship Name	Captain	Sailed From
Packet	*Montreal*	Champlin	London
"	*George Washington*	Holdredge	Liverpool
"	*Sully*	Not reported	Havre
Ship	*Unicorn*	Redman	Liverpool
"	Wallace	Not reported	Spain
"	*Tamarac*	Kane	British
Barque	*Mexico*	Not reported	Liverpool
"	*Cruickston Castle*	(Br) Ferguson	Greenock
"	*Brazil*	Parker	London
Brigs	*Victory*	Bourne	Darien
"	*Harbinger*	Savage	Fayal
"	*Commerce*	Dashield	Belize
"	*Victory*	Lard	Darien
"	*Macon*	Bibbins	Darien
"	*Orontes*	Cole	Philadelphia
Brig	*Julia & Helen*	Thorndyke	New Orleans
"	*Victress*	Dickenson	Mobile
"	*Frances*	Hart	Savannah
"	*June*	Babidge	Charleston
"	*Veto*	McNear	Hamburg
Galliot	*Flora*	Weyneman	Bremen
Schooner	*Gov. Brooks*	Lincoln	Eastport
"	*Venus*	Coggins	Bath
"	*Claudia & Maria*	Rubin	Washington
"	*Perseverance*	Johnson	New Bern
"	*Bounty*	Conklin	New Bern
"	*Ann Eliza*	Not reported	Norfolk
"	*Sybill*	Musgrove	Sydney
"	*Orient*	Phillips	Cape Haytien
"	*Adeline*	Morrill	Boston
"	*Ambassador*	Tinker	Porto Rico
"	*Select*	Conklin	New Bern
"	*New York*	Hoxie	New Bern
"	*Exchange*	Frehorn	New Bern

(Continued on the next page)

Marine Intelligence Reports (Continued)

Type of Ship	Ship Name	Captain	From
Schooner	*Marja*	Woglan	Baltimore
"	*Gil Blas*	Seely	Virginia
"	*Nonpareil*	Sturdevant	North Carolina
"	*Expeditious*	Jones	Virginia
"	*Franklin*	Brown	Virginia

The next morning, on the assumption that all thirty-nine ships had by then been piloted across the bar at Sandy Hook and had entered port, the papers reported them as "arrivals" in their "Marine Intelligence" columns. The reports were premature. Three of the listed ships never made it to port. The brig *Veto*, out of Hamburg, was blown ashore at Sandy Hook with no loss of life. The British ship *Tamarac* was blown ashore at Fire Island with the loss of one life. The *Mexico* was blown ashore at Long Beach with the loss of 115 lives.

After the disappointing departure of the news boat, Winslow initiated some action himself. He approached another tall ship, the 627-ton packet *George Washington*, owned by Grinnell & Minturn (Minturn was an owner of the *Bristol*), and hailed her captain, John Holdredge. The speedy packet had left Liverpool one month after the *Mexico*, yet reached New York the same day the *Mexico* did. Winslow pleaded with Holdredge to lead the *Mexico* across the shoals, "if he had any knowledge at all of the way through." Holdredge refused. He told Winslow he was not a licensed pilot, and could be fined and censured for piloting another ship through the channel. Furthermore, he said the *George Washington* was "too heavy" and "too valuable" to run the risk, but advised the *Mexico*, which drew less water, to attempt it on her own. Declining Holdredge's suggestion, Winslow hailed two other vessels and asked each of them to escort the *Mexico* through the channel. They, too, refused.

Unknown to Winslow, a potential rescuer—Captain Brown of the lighter *North America*—was passing nearby. Brown's vessel was a small, flat-bottomed, cargo boat, and so he was not limited by a ship that was too heavy or too valuable to risk crossing through the shoals. However, Brown later testified that he felt constrained from guiding the *Mexico* in because of the fear created by the harbor pilots that anyone acting in their place would be fined. A New York State law passed at the request of the Board of Pilots assessed large fines to any captain who attempted to guide a vessel into New York Harbor without a pilot's license. The pilots claimed that lives and property would be lost if non-licensed pilots did their work. The effect was to create a legal monopoly, since the only way to get a license was through the Board of Pilots.

The *New York Gazette* (January 5, 1837) reported that Captain Brown observed the *Mexico's* numerous distress signals and signals for a pilot. He said he knew the channel quite well and would have piloted the barque to safe anchorage inside the Hook, except for the potential fine. In a sad footnote to this lost opportunity to save the *Mexico,* Brown stated that when he passed the barque on his way into the channel, he was returning from a salvage operation at the wreck of the brig *General Trotter*, which had gone ashore a week earlier, "in consequence of not being able to procure a pilot."

The New York Morning Courier (January 7, 1837) reported a surviving passenger's recollection of what Winslow said when all his signals and pleas for help went unanswered. He said the captain spoke of "a degree of anxiety that was not to be expressed." Contributing to Winslow's anxiety was all the bad luck that had befallen him on this voyage: unfavorable winds, temperatures near zero, and a crossing of sixty-nine days—longer than any crossing he had experienced. He also had to consider the shipowner's younger brother, William, who was aboard as his brother's eyes and ears, and ready to second-guess the captain's every move.

Charles Winslow's statements, his actions, and his inactions at this critical stage of the voyage suggest that he was descending into a state of depression and despair. The *New York Times* (January 5, 1837), offered the excuse that he was "not sufficiently acquainted with the coast to enter on his own judgment." But with so many lives at stake, this was not a valid explanation for Winslow's failure to act. He should have taken Captain Holdredge's advice and crossed the shoals. Winslow had a calculation different from that of the other captains off the Hook. He had 111 starving passengers aboard his overloaded, unseaworthy vessel—and he had a troublesome, frostbitten crew. Captain Holdredge of the *George Washington* could afford to wait things out in his superbly-outfitted, well-crewed packet. Winslow had to get his ship in, and do it *now*. Time had run out.

Captain Winslow was an experienced navigator out of the Port of Philadelphia, and did not need a pilot to guide him up the Delaware River to his home pier. But here at Sandy Hook, the risk of grounding his ship on the shoals must have seemed too great, despite the starvation and frostbite aboard his ship. The idea of deliberately sailing his ship across an unfamiliar shoal was simply unacceptable to Winslow. Someone as rigid in his thinking as he would prefer to plot a course to the end of the earth and back—sailing single-handedly if necessary. Come hell or high water, Charles Winslow would not risk grounding his vessel on the shoals, in the plain view of dozens of other captains. He would wait for a pilot.

Captain Winslow's Last Chance

Late on New Year's Day, Captain Winslow's final opportunity to save his ship arrived in the form of a paddlewheel tugboat, one of the many steam-powered workboats that were expanding business from the Hudson River and New York Harbor out to the open sea.[30] He hailed the tug as it cruised past, towing a tall ship out from the harbor; but there was no response. The tug released the vessel it was towing, turned, and headed back into the Lower Bay. Because of its shallow draft, the tug sailed over the shoals without much regard to the channel. It was as if its captain had not seen or heard the *Mexico's* signals. John Wood, a surviving passenger, said with great understatement that everyone aboard the *Mexico* viewed the tug's departure "with sorrow and disappointment" (*New York Herald*, January 6, 1837).

Clearly, someone aboard the tug had a pilot's knowledge, even if he was not a registered pilot. After all, the tug had just towed a deep-draft vessel out through the channel. Winslow had missed his last chance. He should have done what he failed to do when hailing the news boat earlier, that is, launch the ship's yawl and intercept the vessel—with a bag of shipowner Broom's silver and gold coins in hand to pay any fee requested, along with a promise to reimburse any fine that the tug's captain might incur for violating the pilots' self-serving rules. There certainly was sufficient money aboard the *Mexico* to bribe either the tug captain or the news boat captain. William Broom had a strongbox in his cabin containing the proceeds from the sale of

---

[30] For a discussion on the steamboat business in and around New York Harbor, see the Appendix.

the *Mexico's* American and Caribbean cargos in Liverpool.[31] The payment might have been more than the *Mexico's* owner might like, but there was too much at stake. Starvation and frostbite were justification enough.

In 1836, desperate captains occasionally bribed unlicensed pilots to take them over the bar. Two months earlier, for example, Captain Bigsbee of the ship *Steiglitz* flew signals for a pilot for fourteen hours, and finally paid a news boat $15—half the pilot's rate—to take him in. When the pilot association saw Bigsbee's admission in the newspapers, their response wasn't to sheepishly apologize for failing to be on station; it was to demand that Bigsbee pay them the other half of the $30 pilotage fee, for doing nothing.

The news boat that Winslow spoke with earlier that day provided convincing evidence that he had let an opportunity slip away. The *New York Commercial Advertiser* of January 4, 1837 reported in its daily "Marine List" that its news boat, after speaking with the *Mexico* on January 1, led the packet ship *Unicorn* across the bar to an anchorage just inside the Hook. The news boat also placed food supplies aboard that vessel and placed men on board to assist in handling the ship. This was exactly the help the *Mexico* needed.

Surely there was no ship standing off the Sandy Hook bar that was in greater distress than the *Mexico*, as the news boat captain learned from his megaphone-conversation with Winslow. Why then help the *Unicorn*, and not the *Mexico*? A clue comes from the rest of the *New York Commercial Advertiser's* report about the *Unicorn*. It says that Captain Redman and ten of the *Unicorn's* men rowed to the news boat, and that Redman himself boarded the boat. The rest of the story must be surmised: that Redman enhanced his request for assistance by also opening his purse. A pistol tucked into the captain's belt may have provided further inducement. That is what Winslow should have done; but it required a sense of confidence with equals, and a feeling of obligation to his passengers, both of which he lacked. Winslow was from a different school from Redman. His maritime upbringing was "before the mast," in a world where a man was taught that you could beat a subordinate to a pulp and treat emigrants like cargo, but treat officers with respect.

Winslow stood on his icy deck, anxiously watching the tug pick its way through the ice floes and cross the bar. As the sun set over the New Jersey Highlands, the tug's paddlewheel churned a white froth and its chimney belched smoke and sparks into the cold evening air. Along with the tug went the final chance at life for 115 passengers and crew of the *Mexico*.

---

[31] The money chest survived the wreck of the *Mexico*, but its whereabouts today are not known.

The captain once again fired his ship's gun, flew his distress signals, relit his lamps, and waited—for a pilot who would never come.

At ten o'clock in the evening of New Year's Day, Winslow's run of impossibly bad luck took another sharp turn for the worse. The wind began to increase, becoming a violent gale from the northeast, and bringing with it a blizzard. He desperately wanted to keep his ship on station off the Hook, but his "troublesome" crew was so debilitated by overwork and the awful cold that they would not—they could not—perform the necessary sail changes and maneuvers. The only alternative was to allow the ship to be blown out into the New York Bight and somehow find a way back to the Hook the next morning.

Six sailors—John Francis, Lord Sherwood, Peter Pickering, Jacob Allen, Walter Quinn, and James Munro—on seeing that the captain had no intention of crossing the bar and that he was preparing to set out to sea, took a stand. They remained in their berths in the forecastle, wrapped in their blankets, exhausted, sick, half-frozen. In reality, it was no longer a question of willingness on their part, but as a surviving passenger stated, "they were unable to do duty" (*New York Commercial Advertiser*, January 5, 1837).

For the five Caribbean sailors, the voyage was not at all what they had bargained for when they signed articles for a summer-and-early-autumn crossing to Liverpool and on to New York. They now understood why they were chosen to fill out the *Mexico's* crew. Their labor was cheap, and their half-frozen limbs and indeed their very lives were expendable. The malingering French sailor, John Francis, who was pointedly described by surviving passenger Thomas Mollahan as "not good for anything," had a different motive for remaining in the forecastle. He was doing what he had done for most of the trip: avoiding work as much as possible and staying as warm as he could.

Passenger Mollahan presented another view of the six sailors, calling them: "mutinous" and "insufficient." The second of these descriptions, "insufficient," gets to the root of the problem. The short-handed crew had spent too many hours on watch, too many hours manning the pumps, and too many times being awakened for emergencies such as torn sails and cracked spars. There was never time to warm themselves or dry out their wet and frozen clothes or spend half of a Sunday at leisure. Not only were they spent, the sailors had the first stages of frostbite—all but Seaman Francis, that is.

With most of his crew now mutinous, there was little the captain could do to direct the ship in any purposeful way. After all, he had to sail in a blizzard, in zero visibility, in single-digit temperatures. The *Mexico* was carrying a mixed set of storm sails: a close-reefed main topsail, a reefed foresail, two reefed trysails, and a fore-staysail. These sails were frozen stiff, and the sheets that controlled them were inflexible rods of ice. Moreover, he had only four crewmen left to manage the ship: the mate, Noah Jordan; the ship's carpenter, John Handsell; the cook, Edward Felix; and the steward, Stephen Simmons.

Desperate for hands, Winslow sent Noah Jordan to ask if any passengers had sailing experience. The captain was finally acknowledging that the emigrants were more than just "cargo," but only if they could help sail his ship. However, none had any experience. Jordan advised the passengers that the barque would be pushed far out to sea unless he could find at least a few men willing to perform seamen's duties on deck. The work would be cold and dangerous, but the lives of all aboard were at stake.

Three men—Richard Owens, a twenty-six-year-old farmer; Thomas Mollahan, a twenty-six-year-old laborer; and John Wood, a twenty-three year-old weaver—volunteered to come up on deck. None of these men had family members aboard the ship, and all three were willing to risk their lives in the performance of dangerous tasks totally unfamiliar to them. The prospect of three hot meals a day and a berth in the forecastle, or perhaps even in an officer's cabin, were inducement enough to pack their gear and get off the foul-smelling 'tween deck. The captain would eventually reward them in a way they could never have anticipated, when he included them among the very few that he allowed to live.

With Herculean efforts and remarkable leadership, the makeshift crew sailed the barque out into the Bight that night, and then took her back to the Hook, arriving at seven o'clock Monday morning, January 2, a half hour before sunrise. Winslow instructed the mate to fire a signal gun and rocket five times, at fifteen minute intervals. He also ordered pennants to be hung upside-down from the mast, the internationally recognizable distress signal. Again there was no response from a pilot boat. The weather was so bad that not even the news boats came out that day. Winslow made repeated attempts to stand off the Hook, but the wind, the cold, and the frustration of finding no pilots made each effort more difficult than the one before.

Crossing the shoals now would be suicidal. The driving snow obscured the view of the coast, the cross-currents were vicious, and the rise and fall of the mountainous seas could cause the *Mexico* to bottom-out. Moreover, if the barque grounded, no other ship would dare send its small boats to provide assistance in this weather. In desperation, the captain fired his rockets and guns again, with no response. Reluctantly, as evening fell, he turned the barque out to sea.

Winslow could not have known at the time that help was on the way, albeit unreachable. The news boat that had assisted Captain Redman and the *Unicorn* the previous day had by this time returned to its pier at New York.

The *Mexico's* owner, Samuel Broom, received word that his barque was off Sandy Hook with distress signals flying. Worried for William, his younger brother, Broom immediately chartered a steamboat and put a pilot aboard with specific instructions to "find and bring up the *Mexico*, at any rate, without regard to cost" (*New York American*, January 6, 1837). Three hours later, the chartered steamboat and pilot returned to the pier and reported that there was so much snow, wind, and surf that no vessel could cross the bar. For the two days December 31 and January 1, there had been no pilot boats, and the way was clear for passage. On January 2, with Samuel Broom's paid pilot at the ready, he could not cross. There was nothing more to be done. The *Mexico's* fate was sealed.

When Charles Winslow set out across the Atlantic from Liverpool with his overloaded ship, he had gambled that he would make the late-season crossing safely despite the odds. The stakes were an insured ship, an insured cargo, and the lives of 123 people. Now, with all options gone, he had to keep sailing or lose his most important stake, his own life.

The Wreck of the *Mexico*

The Wreck of the *Mexico*
New York Sun, January 12, 1837.

Winslow had seven men—the mate, the cook, the steward, the carpenter, and three passengers—to sail the huge ship again out into the Bight, this time in a blizzard. The frostbitten sailors in the forecastle came up to help from time to time, but as one of the passenger-sailors, Richard Owens, later said in an interview, "the sailors were bad, and I helped the vessel very much myself" (*New York Herald*, January 6, 1837). Because the cook and steward had to keep the cookhouse in operation around the clock, they could spell the other men only intermittently. Some barques of the period had small stoves in the captain's cabin, but there is no direct evidence that the *Mexico* did. However, Captain Winslow and Mr. Broom managed to remain physically fit during the entire ordeal, while the three passenger-sailors wound up in the hospital with frostbite. This suggests that Winslow and Broom were not only keeping themselves well-fed, but warm as well.

Each of the two watches had three or four men on duty, excluding the captain and William Broom, and half of them had no sailing experience. With so few hands working in such awful conditions, the square-rigged sails were unmanageable, so the captain ordered them cut down. The barque then sailed under jibs and staysails in weather so cripplingly cold that each man could stay at the wheel or stand lookout for only one half hour at a time before requiring a few minutes' shelter in the cookhouse.

Winslow was forced to adjust his sailing tactics. Every change in the ship's heading required men who were off-watch to come out on deck to help with the painful task of repositioning the ice-clad sails. In order to conserve the crew's energy it was necessary to extend his tacks and take the risk of maneuvering closer to the shore. To reduce the danger of ending up stranded on a sandbar off Long Island or New Jersey, he ordered that depth-soundings be taken regularly with a lead-line.

At 4 AM on the morning of January 3, 1837, First Mate Noah Jordan came on deck to stand watch. The temperature was three degrees. He cast the lead-line and reported to the captain, who was retiring to his cabin, that the depth was fifteen fathoms. Winslow calculated that based on the compass heading and the gradually sloping seabed off Long Island as shown on his charts, the ship could remain on this tack for at least two hours longer. The captain gave an order to that effect and went to bed, telling Jordan to wake him in two hours for the next course change.

Winslow's calculation seemed reasonable, but the information he had received was incorrect. The ice-encrusted lead-line had made it appear that the depth was fifteen fathoms (ninety feet) when in fact it was probably no more than three fathoms (fifteen feet). A quarter of an hour later, the *Mexico* struck bottom with great force. The ship continued to thump heavily on the bar, pointing head-on across it. Whenever there was a lull in the storm, an unmistakable sound could be heard out of the blackness: waves pounding an unseen shore.

Winslow came on deck immediately. The passengers below felt the shaking and thumping, but Winslow kept the hatches battened down. He did not do this for their safety, which was of no concern to him, but so that he and his men could work on deck unencumbered. Huge waves blasted against the stern and side of the ship and sent icy seawater and foam down her length. For two hours, Winslow and his crew desperately tried to work the ship off the bar in an attempt to escape laterally to deeper water by way of a trough. At 6 AM, this effort came to an abrupt halt when, in the winter morning darkness, a wave knocked the rudder off, thus ending all chance of maneuvering the ship to safety. At this point Winslow ordered that the ship's wreck gun be fired to attract potential rescuers.

The captain directed the crew to play out the jib and boom, in the hope that the billowing sail would pull the ship closer to shore. If he succeeded, the crew would have an easier time getting to the beach in the ship's boats, and his chances of salvaging the cargo would improve as well. After the *Mexico* dragged and bounced on the bottom for several more minutes, she settled. Like the *Bristol* before her, she was fixed in place by the dead-weight of hundreds of tons of cargo deep in her hold.

Winslow knew the leaky barque could not endure the pounding of the waves for long, so he sent word to the passengers that the *Mexico* must be abandoned, that she might break up. But he ordered them to stay below until the boats were ready to be launched. First, there was work to be done on deck. The ship was listing badly with her masts angled out over the sea. Their massive weight could lever the ship over onto her side and destroy any chance of lowering the ship's small boats, so he ordered the mainmast cut away with axes. The cutting and clearing was done in stages, with the jury-rigged crew working outside for a few minutes at a time, and then ducking into the cook house for warmth. By this means, the mast was cut away and the ship was stabilized.

The captain had little idea what shore this was. Some crewmen thought Long Island; others, New Jersey. Not until morning light could it be seen that the barque was grounded off a low, barren barrier beach on Long Island's South Shore. The *Mexico* was a cable-length (200 yards) off the beach, so close that it seemed one could hurl a marlinspike to dry land, yet so terribly far because of the awful surf. [32]

---

[32] The location of the *Mexico* wreck: The *Morning Courier & New York Express* of January 5, 1837 called the wreck site, "Hempstead Beach." This very general location could place the wreck anywhere from today's Atlantic Beach to Lido Beach. A report from the *New York Sun Supplement* of January 12, 1837 placed the wreck at "twenty-six miles from Sandy Hook." This puts the wreck at today's Jones Beach State Park. Other reports stated that when rescuers arrived they crossed the frozen bay for ten miles from what is today Freeport. This places the wreck as far as Jones Beach to the east or Long Beach to the west. Charles Ellms, *The Tragedy of the Seas* (1841), records that the dead were carried "four or five miles" to Lott's barn. The barn was in today's Baldwin. This last reference is quite specific, and strongly suggests that the wreck was at the barrier island of Long Beach. Finally, Daniel Treadwell wrote in 1842 in his *Personal Reminiscences of Men and Things on Long Island* that the *Mexico* came ashore at Long Beach.

The Historian of the City of Long Beach, Roberta Fiore, is aware of a long-standing oral tradition on the island that the wreck occurred just offshore of where today's Lincoln Boulevard meets the beach. She is supported by Long Beach bayman and diver, William

Long Islanders—including the local wreck-master, James Smith, of Raynorstown (Freeport today)—heard the ship's wreck gun from afar, and walked across the frozen bay to Hempstead Beach (today's Long Beach). The weather was so severe that all they could do was build a shelter out of canvas and driftwood, light a large fire behind it, and watch and wait. But Winslow had finally had enough of waiting. He would not make the mistake he had made when he stood off Sandy Hook scanning the horizon for a harbor pilot who would never come. This time there was no anxiety or hesitation. He would effect his own rescue.

Running aground before the eyes of thirty fellow sea captains would have been a humiliation, but wrecking a ship in a vicious storm off a barren beach was no disgrace for a ship's master. Many captains had done so and continued their careers, proudly telling their wreck and rescue stories over cigars and glasses of sherry. Charles Winslow was energized. He was now a man of action with a clear plan. Having done all that he could to stabilize the vessel, he set about conducting a rescue using the ship's boats. Undoubtedly he was pleased to see people on the beach. Once he made it ashore, he would need immediate warmth and shelter from the extreme cold. Assistance would also be required to maneuver the *Mexico's* boats back and forth from ship to shore, to continue the rescue operation for the passengers and the crew.

Mountainous waves, sea spray, snow, gale winds, and the build-up of layers of ice on every surface of the *Mexico* made launching the ship's boats a huge challenge. The slippery, angled deck could barely be stood on. Even the ashes strewn about for traction were repeatedly washed away or covered with more ice. Small ropes grew to the size of a hawser from the accumulation of ice. Winslow ordered the tarps removed from the ship's boats, and had them cleared of the barrels and empty animal pens stored inside. The chickens, lambs, and pigs had long since been eaten by the captain, the mate, and young master Broom.

The captain's plan was straightforward. The longboat, with a capacity of a dozen or more, was the larger of the ship's two boats. It was to be launched first, and rowed to shore with a hawser attached to her stern. The hawser would be played out from the deck of the *Mexico* as the longboat was rowed to the beach and unloaded. A second rope would be attached from

---

Burchianti, who says that a fellow bayman and diver, John Daly (now deceased), often maintained that he dived the *Mexico* wreck in the 1950s and 1960s. He did this when the ocean sand bars off Long Beach shifted enough to expose the *Mexico's* huge timbers. According to Daly, the wreck site is about fifty yards southwest of the ocean-end of the Lincoln Boulevard jetty. Burchianti notes that sand has once again built up off Long Beach, and today covers the timbers Daly spoke of.

shore. Men aboard the *Mexico* would then haul the boat back out to the barque by means of the hawser, and repeat the ferrying process until all were rescued.

Winslow's plan was identical to the one the captain of the British ship *Tamarac* successfully employed that very day, some thirty miles to the east, when his 600-ton vessel was wrecked in the same storm. But conditions were different on the *Mexico*. The barque had a severely debilitated crew, and she had a captain who understood perfectly well the *power* of command, but had no concept at all of the *responsibility* of command.

Longboat – Capacity about Twelve.
Vergulde Draeck <www.voc.iinet.net.au>

The crew successfully launched the longboat and pulled it along the leeward side of the barque toward the bow, using a light line. The *Mexico's* bow was the highest point of the ship as she lay on the sandbar, and it provided the best—albeit scant—protection from the wind and waves. This was the best place to load the boat. It was also where the plan collapsed. The cold and exhausted crew was not thinking clearly. They had neglected to immediately tie on the hawser. As the empty longboat was hauled under the bowsprit for loading, it was caught by a breaking wave and violently driven away. The sailors holding the single line could not hang on. One report said that the boat was simply mishandled and slipped away; another, that the ice-encrusted line snapped like a thread. Whatever the cause of the mishap, the crew and the passengers peering out from the hatches watched in agony as this hope for rescue floated away to shore, empty.

Before the second boat could be launched, the captain ordered the crew to cut down the foremast, because the ship was once again listing dangerously. Winslow called on the three passenger-crewmen—Thomas Mollahan, John Wood and Richard Owens, all of whom knew how to wield an axe—to cut away the foremast, which they did.

Having lost the longboat, the crew next launched the smaller yawl and pulled it toward the bow, this time using a line attached to the boat's bow and another to her stern. The passengers could no longer be kept below deck. They anxiously edged closer to the yawl. Captain Winslow ordered them to stand back, which they did—except for one female passenger, the reports do not give her name. Distraught at having seen the empty longboat drift to the beach, she inched closer. As the yawl was brought up alongside the *Mexico's* bow, she darted across the icy deck and leaped into the boat.

Yawl – Maximum Capacity about Eight
Longhope Lifeboat Home Page - <http://www.longhopelifeboat.org.uk/>

One of the survivors of the wreck told the *New York Sun* that the woman's daring act "enraged the Captain." Winslow stopped everything. He would allow no one to get into the yawl until she got out. But the woman went into a fetal position in the bottom of the boat, wedged herself under a seat, and refused to move. Winslow, pulling himself up to his full five-feet-three-inches, stood firm. This woman had violated his direct order, and a captain's order must be obeyed.

However, this was no time for a principled standoff. The enemy was not the terrified woman lying in the bottom of the yawl; it was the raging surf, the near zero-degree cold, the ice, and the gale winds. Already the longboat had been lost, and time was of the essence. But Winslow could not let such an act of defiance pass. Instead of ignoring her and moving on with his rescue plan, he ordered the first mate and a sailor to board the yawl and drag the woman out by force.

While the two men were pulling the resisting woman out of the yawl, attention was not paid to a huge wave that surged up around the ship. The wave lifted the boat and its occupants up onto the *Mexico's* deck. As the water receded, it began to pull the yawl back off the deck, but the boat caught on a piece of deck equipment and overturned, dumping the three occupants— the woman, the mate, and the sailor—out onto the deck. [33]

The wave pulled the half-submerged yawl away with such force that the sailors were unable to hold onto the painter or the safety line. And so the empty yawl drifted shoreward, as the longboat had before, taking with it any chance the captain had to rescue himself, his crew, and his passengers. When the submerged boat reached the beach, a final punctuation mark was added to the fiasco. The yawl was dashed to pieces by the surf.

Winslow's feelings of anxiety quite likely returned, for he was once again in the unhappy, passive situation he had been in at Sandy Hook. There was nothing to be done now but wait, hope, and pray for a rescue from shore. If and when those rescuers appeared, however, he would make certain that no crazed female passenger, or anyone else, would interfere.

Richard Owens, one of the three passenger-sailors who were ultimately saved, said that the captain continued to have some hope that something could be done from shore:

---

[33] It is interesting to speculate as to who the daring, unidentified woman was who leaped into the yawl in defiance of the captain's order. It is perhaps less likely that she was a mother with a child aboard, or a woman with a sister, a brother, or a husband aboard. If that assumption is correct, many names can be eliminated. There were twelve women on the *Mexico* not accompanied by family. It may have been one of these who jumped into the boat:

Isabella Ballentine	28	Rose Hughes	15
Bridget Brennan	17	Mary MacCafferty	30
Catharine Collins	16	Sally Maguire	18
Bridget Farrell	18	Martha Mooney	22
Catharine Galligan	25	Catharine Ross	20
Mary Higgins	50	Eleanor Tierney	18

Generalizations about highly-stressful situations are problematic. Perhaps the names of all the women, including those accompanied by family, should be considered. After all, when the *Bristol* was wrecked five weeks earlier, the person who climbed out on a fallen mast in order to be the first to be rescued was a servant girl who left an adult male relative behind on the ship.

> The tide being now making [rising] and the wind setting in-shore, the Captain said there was no chance of saving the vessel, but he still thought every hope of saving all hands.
>
> —*New York Times,* January 5, 1837.

The statement may be less optimistic than it seems. The captain expressed hope of saving "*all hands*," not "*all those aboard*." This appears to exclude the passengers. Winslow's full intention cannot be gleaned from a single paraphrased statement, but his subsequent actions demonstrated that his primary aim was indeed to save the men who had helped him sail the ship for the past two days in a blizzard, and to save the money chest, William Broome, and himself.

Raynor Smith's Heroic Rescue

On the morning of January 3, the pounding waves gradually began to separate the twelve-year-old barque's planks at the waterline. The sound of seawater pouring into the cargo hold below was an alarming development, and the squeal of rats scurrying beneath the 'tween deck was a terrifying confirmation of what was to come. The passengers' refuge would soon be lost. When the captain was informed of the worsening situation, he instructed the crew and male passengers to begin preparing rough shelters on deck and in the mizzenmast's rigging. The mizzen was the only mast still standing. Sailcloth and ropes were made available, but few passengers were in any condition to accomplish the difficult work. The roughly-constructed shelters were poor at best. Women and children were told to put on as much clothing as they could, and to wait below, near the ladder, as long as possible.

Three hours later, at 11 AM, icy seawater began to bubble up through the boards of the 'tween deck. Rats, seeking to escape the rising flood, crawled out through small openings, and up onto the passengers' bunks. As the water rose about them, the terrified emigrants reluctantly climbed the ladder and stepped out onto the barque's open deck. In the process, they entered what would become the closest thing to Dante's Ninth Ring of Hell that anyone can find on earth. When most people think of "Burning Hell," they are not taking into consideration that the Ninth and last Ring of Dante's *Inferno* is a place of icy wind and frozen tears. Indeed, in the fourth and final circle of the Ninth Ring, near where Satan himself is trapped in ice, sinners are completely encapsulated in ice and distorted in all conceivable positions.

The agony of the starving and seasick men, women, and children can only be imagined, as they were suddenly exposed to wind, sea spray, and near-zero-degree cold. They gathered around their captain, "imploring his assistance and asking if hope was still left to them" (*New York American,*

190

January 5, 1837). There was nothing the captain could do but to tell them to shelter themselves, and wait.

The captain, his working crew, and William Broom retained for themselves the privilege of the cookhouse, the only permanent shelter on deck. From the beginning of the voyage the passengers had not had access to the cookhouse, and they would not get in now. The bow lay a bit higher than the rest of the ship, so some of the crew—the malingerers and mutineers, to Winslow's mind—remained inside the forecastle in hammocks they had repositioned and suspended above the rising water.

Small as the cookhouse was, with nine men packed inside, the captain found room for two important items: the supercargo's strongbox and his own saber with its belt and scabbard. The sword may be the one that had been in the Winslow family since 1778, when, during the American Revolution, a British raiding party entered his grandfather James Winslow's house and demanded food:

> His wife [Anna] was obliged to make a hasty pudding, but before the unwelcome guests had completed their meal they were constrained to leave in a hurry. One left behind him a silver spoon and another an iron-handled sword, which have been preserved as heirlooms in the family. [34]
>
> —William Richard Cutter. *Genealogical and Personal Memories Relating to the Families of the State of Massachusetts* (1910)

As the oldest of the nine Winslow boys, Charles probably inherited the sword. Now, at this perilous moment, he might have simply wanted to preserve the heirloom. However, when the captain, at five-foot-three, strapped on his thirty-nine-inch-long weapon, at such a desperate time as this, it must have been puzzling. But Winslow had reasons he would reveal later.

Like the wreck of the *Bristol* at Rockaway Beach, the wreck of the *Mexico* was off a barren, wind-swept, barrier beach, in this case Hempstead Beach. Behind the beach were a few hundred yards of low-lying sand dunes, beach grass, shrubs, and stunted trees. A wide, frozen bay separated the island from the mainland. Unlike the Rockaway Peninsula, which was connected by a road to the mainland and was populated with fishermen's

---

[34] Hasty pudding is a corn, wheat, or oat mush, which, unlike its name, should be slow-cooked. If, as is likely, Anna's cooking was rushed, the British soldiers departed not only without their sword and spoon, but with upset stomachs. As a practicing doctor, and the only one in Pittston, Maine in whom the settlers had any confidence, "Granny" Winslow would have known the effects of a hastily-prepared pudding.

cottages and a luxury hotel, the island where the *Mexico* lay was a desolate place, especially in winter, when one had to cross miles of bay ice to get there.

Raynor Rock Smith

Seven Men from Raynorstown who Conducted the Rescue of the *Mexico*.

Captain Raynor Rock Smith (51)
Zopher R. Smith (Raynor Smith's son, 30)
James R. Smith   (Raynor Smith's son, 28)
Oliver R. Smith   (Raynor Smith's son, 24)
Oliver C. Smith
Samuel Raynor
Willet Smith

If not for Raynor Rock Smith (1785-1869), a fifty-one-year-old Long Island boat captain, fisherman, and father of eighteen children, the *Mexico* would have had no survivors. Smith and his six-man boat crew, including three of his sons, dragged a surfboat for several miles—one report says ten miles—from Raynorstown, across the frozen bay to where the crippled ship lay. It is likely that he used a horse to pull the boat. Other boatmen from nearer points on the mainland were already out on the beach with their boats, but no one was making a move to initiate a rescue.

The situation was discouraging, beginning with the sight of the *Mexico's* yawl lying in pieces on the beach. The problems facing the rescuers were daunting. It was so cold on the beach, open as it was to the cutting wind, that even with a good fire going, and with a shelter, they were fearful of frostbite. The cold was so intense that the seawater along the beach had frozen into slurry, referred to as slush ice—difficult for any boat to penetrate. The most fearsome obstacle was the waves, which one observer described as "high as a house." This was the kind of surf to keep boats on the beach in any weather.

For over thirty years Raynor Smith had earned a living sailing and fishing off the South Shore of Long Island. In that time, he had assisted in several sea rescues. He and his boat crew had, as he said, "never shrunk from the surf." But this was different. The awful conditions provided reason enough for any man to stay on shore. However, over the noise of the wind and waves, Smith could hear the pitiful cries of the men, women, and children on the *Mexico* only two hundred yards away. He could see them desperately sheltering themselves in the mizzenmast rigging. This went on for an hour, until Smith could stand it no more. At two o'clock in the afternoon, he asked his boat crew whether they were willing to risk an icy death. If so, he would lead them out to the stricken ship. They agreed to join him.

Smith used his own surfboat because it was large, had a high prow and stern, and had buoyancy chambers to help it float in the event it was swamped. A rope was attached to the stern so that the boat and men could be quickly pulled back to shore if it overturned. For the time, this was a superb combination of men and rescue equipment in extremely dangerous surf. With the assistance of other fishermen, Smith and his six comrades launched their boat and fought their way out to sea through the waves and slush ice. The ice resisted the pull of the oars and limited the boat's forward progress. Layers of ice built up on the oars, making them feel like logs. Wind and waves tried to force the boat back to shore, and the riptide threatened to push the boat west, past the ship. With great strength and skill, Smith and his crew rowed the two hundred yards out to the *Mexico*.

It was now near three in the afternoon. The passengers had been out in the open for four hours. The people up on the mast were the first to see the rescue boat approach. The captain and his deck-hands were still huddled in the cook house, and the other sailors were in the forecastle. On hearing the shouts, they all came out to see. Winslow knew that there was a serious risk to the rescue boat, not just from the raging sea, but from a potentially chaotic surge of passengers if they moved toward the place where they thought the surfboat might pull in. Discipline had to be maintained or the rescue boat could be swamped by panicked men, women, and children. The captain attempted to create some order on deck, but this was impossible as half-frozen, terrified people surged around him, clutching infants and children, pleading with him to save them.

Their pleas meant little. Any right the passengers had to enter the rescue boat was forfeited hours ago when the female passenger disobeyed his direct order and caused the loss of the yawl. He would see to it that neither she nor anyone else would interfere this time. At his signal, he and the men in the cookhouse moved quickly across the foredeck and out onto the bowsprit. As Raynor Smith drew near the *Mexico* in his surfboat, he could see from the saber Winslow was waving that this was the captain telling him where to approach, under the barque's bows. The surfboat had some leeward protection there, and access to it could be controlled. Smith skillfully maneuvered his boat under the tip of the bowsprit, where a sailor was dangling a long chain for him to grab. Smith stood up and seized the chain on the second try. Holding tightly to the chain, he could keep the surfboat on station while keeping its prow pointing in the direction of the oncoming waves.

To the surprise of Captain Winslow, the sailor out on the end of the bowsprit, the man passing the chain down to Raynor Smith, was not his first mate, Noah Jordan, the man he had ordered to be there. Instead, he was the malingering sailor, John Francis. Francis had anticipated where the rescue would be made, and had scrambled out from the forecastle and onto the bowsprit ahead of the captain and his men. The canny sailor knew where he stood with the captain, and willingly risked both Winslow's condemnation and his likely loss of pay—if he could just get into the rescue boat.

The Wreck of the *Mexico* [35]
Unknown artist in Thomas Bingley's *Tales of Shipwrecks and other Disasters at Sea* (1842).

Although John Francis was able to anticipate the captain's move, none of the passengers did. Before they could react to this changed situation, ten men—Francis, the first mate, the ship's carpenter, the three passenger-sailors, William Broom, the captain, the steward, and the cook—were all out on the bowsprit. This was no easy task, because everything was covered with a layer of ice. Wet sea spray made the ice even slicker, but the rigging provided handholds.

Francis did not wait for instructions from the captain. He could guess what the order would be: "Come back to the ship immediately!" This would be followed by a blow to his head. Instead, as soon as Raynor Smith had hold

---

[35] The print shows two masts—the foremast and the mizzenmast—still standing when the rescue was in progress. However, by then, both the foremast and mainmast were down, leaving only the mizzenmast standing.

of the chain, Francis slid down into the surfboat, landing with a crash. Winslow did not order that Francis be removed from the surfboat; apparently he had learned something from his misguided attempt to remove the frightened woman from the yawl.

The first mate was next. Jordan either mistimed the rise and fall of the surfboat or slid down the chain too fast. As a result he bounced off the surfboat's gunwale, fell into the sea, and sank out of sight. The third man out, one of the passenger-sailors, dropped too quickly into the heaving surfboat, fell against the gunwale, and then veered into Raynor Smith. This made Smith lose his grip on the bow chain, and in seconds, the rescue boat was carried off by the surf and had to be rowed back. One by one, three more men—the two other passenger-sailors and the carpenter—dropped into Smith's boat. Captain Winslow was acutely aware of the two most important things on board the *Mexico*, besides himself. He lowered young Master Broom into the surfboat, followed by the ship's cash box. He then slid down the chain himself.

Edward Felix, the cook, was out on the icy bowsprit behind the captain, with Stephen Simmons, the steward, right behind him, expecting to be next into the rescue boat. The passengers were pressing hard behind them, shouting to be saved. Before Felix or Simmons could get into the boat, however, it began to move away toward shore. It may have been that Raynor Smith did not want to overload the surfboat in such vicious seas, and had to pull away. Perhaps it was by coincidence that Winslow had arranged for his white crewmen to go off first. Perhaps it was racism. Whatever the reason, through an incredible act of desperation and boldness, Edward Felix managed to save himself. The *New York Gazette* reported in summary fashion what happened next:

> The cook, as we are informed, jumped overboard from
> the bowsprit, swam to the shore boat, and was picked up.
> —*New York Gazette and General Advertiser,* January 5, 1837.

Like most black men of the 1830s, Edward Felix had probably spent a good part of his life being alternately ignored by or humiliated by whites. On this voyage, however, the "Doctor" had been an essential part of the crew, especially in the final critical weeks when hot food and a warm fire kept the men going. Now, when his desperate pleas were ignored, and his true status aboard the *Mexico* was exposed, Felix's leap off the bowsprit was an all-or-nothing, high-stakes gamble for his life, a gamble of the type few people will ever be offered, no less take. That he was a strong swimmer is evident from the fact that he swam fully clothed through enormous, roiling seas, and somehow made it to the surfboat. So much could have gone wrong: a breaking wave could have submerged him, a blast of wind or a wave could have pushed the rescue boat out of his reach, or he could have simply been left behind.

Once in the water, Felix lost the option of returning to the ship. Even if he did make it back aboard, that would have been the end of him. His soaking-wet clothing would have frozen hard, and hypothermia would have set in. Raynor Smith's crew stopped rowing for a few moments, long enough for Felix to reach the stern. They hauled him in. Edward Felix was the last person to leave the *Mexico* alive.[36]

The Wreck of the *Mexico* and the Rescue of Captain Winslow.
Unknown artist, in Charles Ellms' *Tragedies of the Seas,* (1841).

---

[36] Unfortunately, nothing more was written about the cook, Edward Felix, and his fate is not known. Even though he reached the shelter and fire on shore, there was still a risk of hypothermia and frostbite, because of his wet clothing. The three passenger/sailors, none of whom got wet, ended up in the hospital.

Death by Freezing Aboard the *Mexico*

Thus perished, one by one, that pilgrim crowd.
The silver haired, the beautiful, the young:
Some were found wrapp'd, as a crystal shroud
Of waves congeal'd, that tomb'd them where they clung.

Some on the sand, the sounding breakers fling,
Link'd in affection's agonized embrace;
And to the gazer's eye the warm tears spring,
As he beholds two babes—a group of grace,
Lock'd in each other's arms, and pillowed face to face.

—Written about the victims of wreck of the *Mexico* by an
unknown poet. In Benjamin Thompson's *History of Long
Island* (1839).

The rescue boat nearly capsized as Raynor Smith and his crew fought their way to shore with eight survivors. The waves, wind, and slush ice were more hazardous than even the experienced Smith had expected. Once he was back on shore, near the fire, he was finished. Raynor Smith would not put his sons and his friends through such danger a second time. But there was still a last hope for the men, women, and children aboard the *Mexico*. When the surfboat came ashore, it trailed a line all the way back to the stricken vessel, where Smith had attached it to the bow chain. In theory, this line could be used to save the others. The men still aboard the *Mexico* had to pull Smith's empty surfboat back out to the ship, trailing another rope from shore. By this means the surfboat could be ferried back and forth from ship to shore using the pull-ropes.

All the elements were there for the rescue to proceed, except for one overwhelming omission. Winslow, in taking into the rescue boat the few men who were anywhere near fit to work, left only one able man behind, the steward, and it is uncertain that he was fit. By now the capstan was an immovable block of ice, and could not be used to crank the surfboat out to the *Mexico*. No, the task would require several fit men to pull hand-over-hand against the powerful forces of wind, waves, slush ice, and riptide. However, four hours of outdoor exposure to near-zero-degree cold, wind, and icy sea spray—combined with the lack of food, water, and protective clothing—eliminated any chance that there were people still aboard the *Mexico* in a condition to haul the ice-clad line. Thus, the surfboat lay immobile at the sea's edge, as a slack line stretched dishearteningly out from its bow to the wreck.

The *Mexico* Rescue

By Weldon Bedell
(Acrylic, undated
– mid-20th Century)

The Phillips House
Museum
Rockville Centre, NY

The three surviving passenger-sailors were far from happy with the rescue. They thought more should have been done to save the others. The *New York Sun* later reported their unanimous condemnation of Captain Winslow's inaction as he sat on shore warming himself at the fire, guarding the strongbox, and not casting even a glance in the direction of his ship. They said that the captain alone among those who had sailed the ship was not frostbitten, yet he did nothing to encourage a further rescue. Their criticism was withering:

> The [three surviving passengers] all condemn the conduct of Captain Winslow. When Captain W. did reach the shore, he manifested very little anxiety for the lives of those on board. It is said that had he but offered even a dollar a head for all who could be brought on shore alive, there were several hardy boatmen on the spot who would doubtless have ventured to the task.
> —*New York Sun,* January 12, 1837.

Cries were still heard from the *Mexico* through pauses in the howling wind. The passengers had seen one rescue boat come out. Perhaps there would be another. However, night was falling and it was getting colder. The *Morning Courier* described the tragic end aboard the barque:

> And now, the horrors of the scene were indescribable. Already, had the sufferings of the unhappy beings been such as to surpass belief. From the moment of the disaster, they had hung around the Captain, covered with their blankets thick set with ice, imploring his assistance and asking if hope was still left to them.
>
> When they perceived that no further help came from the land, their piercing shrieks were distinctly heard at a considerable distance, and continued through the night until they one by one perished. The next morning the bodies of the many unhappy creatures were seen lashed to different parts of the wreck, embedded in ice.
> —*Morning Courier & New York Express*, January 5, 1837.

It must have been dreadful for the parents and children aboard the *Mexico* that night. The youngsters had placed their trust in their mothers' and fathers' decision to make this life-changing voyage to America. Now, in a final caring act, their parents could do no more than hold them close, listen to their sobs, pray over them, and promise that all would be well—as they felt the warmth of their children's lives escape with each breath and with each new blast of freezing, coating, sea spray. As night came, the realization must have come to those still alive on the *Mexico* that there would be no nighttime rescue, and that by morning they would all be dead. There was nothing they could do but literally hold on to one another as their lives flickered out.

News reports identified all 108 passengers who huddled that night on the icy deck or up in the rigging of the *Mexico*. A complete list of the victims of the wreck of the Mexico appears at the end of this chapter. Many of them were complete families, such as William and Judy Pepper from England with their six children ranging in age from 4 to 14, and Bridget and John Write with their 2-year-old son and their infant. Saddest of all, if only because of their family name, were the Hopes—John, a carpenter from Dublin, his wife Mary, and their four young boys.

There were also women and children whose passage had been paid for by their husbands and fathers already settled in New York. They included Elizabeth Wilson and her two children; Margaret Evans of England with her infant son and three older children aged 6, 9, and 10; and Mary Metcalf, also of England, with three little girls and a boy.

Groups of brothers and sisters, traveling together without their parents, clung to each other in the rigging. They included the Lawrence siblings: Elizabeth, 19, James, 11, and Catharine, 9, all from Scotland. There were the three Carpenter girls: Mary, 30, Margaret, 25, and Miles, 24, along with their cousin Mary, 25, all of them from Ireland.

Mountain climbers have occasionally come close to the point of freezing to death, and lived to tell the tale. This is how one climber described it:

> I was growing colder and colder. I'd lost my right glove. My face was freezing. My hands were freezing. I felt myself growing really numb and then it got really hard to stay focused, and finally I just sort of slid off into oblivion.
>
> —*Into Thin Air*, by Jon Krakauer.

This terrifying observation was made by Beck Weathers, a climber of Mount Everest. He had his right arm amputated halfway below the elbow, lost the fingers and thumb of his left hand, and had his nose amputated, all from frostbite. Weathers' experience of sliding "off into oblivion" likely describes the final hours of the passengers and crew aboard the barque *Mexico*.

The National Oceanographic and Atmospheric Administration has identified the clinical effects of hypothermia, the situation where the body loses heat at a faster rate than it can burn calories to compensate:

> Initially, as the body temperature starts to drop, shivering begins. At the same time, the brain begins to reduce the amount of blood that is circulated to the extremities of the body in order to conserve heat for the vital organs near the body's central core. If

the central core of the body continues to cool, uncontrollable shaking, memory loss, disorientation, incoherence, slurred speech, drowsiness and apparent exhaustion may develop. These are all signs of a very serious situation. If the body core temperature drops below 95 degrees Fahrenheit, just 4 degrees below normal, immediate care is needed, as the person will likely become irrational. Once the body core temperature drops below 90 degrees, the person loses muscle control, and outside help is the person's only hope for survival. If that help is not available, heart and/or respiratory failure and death will eventually follow as the core temperature continues to drop.

—<http://www.noaanews.noaa.gov/stories2004/s2154.htm >

Perhaps the poet Emily Dickinson understood best how it might feel to be at the point of death by freezing, even though it was far beyond her experience to know. She described it in her great poetic meditation on pain and loss, written in 1862:

After great pain

This is the hour of Lead
Remembered, if outlived,
As Freezing persons, recollect the Snow —
First, Chill, then Stupor, then the letting go.

The next day, January 4, waves washed across the *Mexico's* decks and through the now almost horizontal rigging, casting ice-encrusted bodies into the sea and nudging them shoreward. The corpses bobbed in the ocean until they were at last thrown up onto the beach, singly and in clusters. Brothers, sisters, mothers, fathers, children, and close friends were frozen fast to their loved ones, in icy death-grips. Even after one or more of a family's members were dead, the others had refused to let go, as the ice welded them together in misshapen, crystalline forms.

A reporter from the *Morning Courier & New York Express* walked the beach and witnessed frozen corpses being pulled from the surf and laid on the sand. He reported that the hands of some of the dead seemed to still grip some long-gone rope or spar. No coroner was needed to advise him on the cause of death. He stated the obvious conclusion in his news report the following day: "None, it is believed, drowned, but all frozen to death."

William and Judy Pepper, the parents of six children who died aboard the ship that terrible night, were apparently unable to hold onto their children; and so, near the end, the couple simply clung to each other. When the couple's bodies washed up on shore, they were so locked together by ice, by the intertwining of their arms, and by *rigor mortis*, that they could not at first be separated. This was done later, with great difficulty, for the purpose of identifying them. When they were found to be man and wife, their still-frozen bodies were rejoined, locked again in their final embrace. They were buried that way, together, in an oversized coffin, in the Old Sand Hole Cemetery.

The weather finally cleared, allowing surfboats to go out to the almost completely destroyed wreck. Under the supervision of the coroner, frozen bodies were pried from icy perches on the mizzenmast, which now lay partly in the sea. Several passengers' bodies were recovered with gold coins sewn into the linings of their coats. Crates and barrels of valuable cargo also washed ashore. In order to prevent the kind of pilferage experienced at the wreck of the *Bristol*, wreck-master James Smith guarded the beach with sixteen hand-picked men. He also had the assistance of the coroner and an agent from the *Mexico's* insurance company. This time, there would be no thefts of cargo or personal property.

The coroner placed the recovered bodies crosswise on horse-drawn sleds, and carried them over the ice and snow four or five miles inland to Hick's Neck (Baldwin today). The frozen corpses were then arranged on the floor of a barn located in an orchard behind Major John I. Lott's tavern. People came from miles around to see the macabre sight of dozens of frozen bodies lying in rows. One of the witnesses to this awful scene wrote a letter to a friend in Boston, describing what he saw. His moving account was published in the *New York Commercial Advertiser* on February 10, 1837:

> On reaching Hempstead, I concluded to go somewhat off the road, to look at the place where the ship *Mexico* was cast away. In half an hour, we came to Lott's tavern, some four or five miles this side of the beach, where the ship lay; and there, in his barn, had been deposited the bodies of the ill-fated passengers, which had been thrown upon the shore. I went out to the barn. The doors were open, and such a scene as presented itself to my view, I certainly never could have contemplated. It was a dreadful, a frightful scene of horror.
>
> Forty or fifty bodies, of all ages and sexes, were lying promiscuously before me over the floor, all frozen and as solid as marble—and all, except a few, in the very dresses in which they perished. Some with their hands clenched, as if for warmth, and almost every one with an arm crooked and bent, as it would be in clinging to the rigging.
>
> There were scattered about among the number, four or five beautiful little girls, from six to sixteen years of age, their

cheeks and lips as red as roses, with their calm blue eyes open, looking you in the face, as if they would speak. I could hardly realize that they were dead. I touched their checks, and they were frozen as hard and as solid as a rock, and not the least indentation could be made by any pressure of the hand. I could perceive a resemblance to each other, and supposed them to be the daughters of a passenger named Pepper, who perished, together with his wife and all the family.

On the arms of some, were seen the impressions of the rope which they had clung to, the mark of the twist deeply sunk into the flesh. I saw one poor Negro sailor, a tall man, with his head thrown back, his lips parted, and his now sightless eye-balls turned upwards, and his arms crossed over his breast, as if imploring heaven for aid. This poor fellow evidently had frozen while in the act of fervent prayer.

One female had a rope tied to her leg, which had bound her to the rigging; and another little fellow had been crying, and was thus frozen, with the muscles of the face just as we see children when crying. There were a brother and a sister dashed upon the beach, locked in each other's arms; but they had been separated in the barn. All the men had their lips firmly compressed together, and with the most agonizing expression on their countenances I ever beheld.

One little girl had raised herself on tiptoe, and thus was frozen, just in that position. It was an awful sight; and such a picture of horror was before me, that I became unconsciously fixed to the spot, and found myself trying to suppress my ordinary breathing, lest I should disturb the repose of those around me. I was aroused from the reverie by the entrance of a man—a coroner.

As I was about to leave, my attention became directed to a girl, who, I afterward learned, had come that morning from the city to search for her sister. She had sent for her to come over from England, and had received intelligence that she was in this ship.

She came into the barn, and the second body she cast her eyes upon, was hers. She gave way to such a burst of impassioned grief and anguish, that I could not behold her without sharing in her feelings. She threw herself upon the cold and icy face and neck of the lifeless body, and thus, with her arms around her, remained wailing, mourning, and sobbing, till I came away; and when some distance off, I could hear her calling her by name in the most frantic manner.

So little time, it appears, had they to prepare for their fate, that I perceived a bunch of keys, and a half eaten cake, fall from the bosom of a girl whom the coroner was removing. The cake appeared as if part of it had just been bitten, and hastily thrust into her bosom, and round her neck was a ribbon, with a pair of scissors.

And to observe the stout, rugged sailors, too, whose iron frames could endure so much hardship—here they lay, masses of ice. Such scenes show us, indeed, how powerless and feeble are all human efforts, when contending against the storms and tempests, which sweep with resistless violence over the face of the deep. And yet the vessel was so near the shore, that the shrieks and moans of the poor creatures were heard through that bitter, dreadful night, till towards morning, when the last groan died away, and all was hushed in death, and the murmur of the raging billows was all the sound that then met the ear.

—*New York Commercial Advertiser*, February 10, 1837.
The author is unknown.

Some New Yorkers began to realize that the wreck of the *Mexico* should not end the way maritime disasters had in the past—with no meaning beyond the recognition that one's fate at sea is subject to forces greater than mankind can ever hope to comprehend, no less resist. The sight of dozens of frozen corpses laid out in Lott's barn was powerful to those who had either seen it or read about it. Lists of the dead, 115 in all, appeared in the newspapers. The lists took up column after column. All this occurred while the memory of the wreck of the ship *Bristol*, just weeks before, was still fresh. Each of the two wrecks, taken separately, was the worst, accidental mass-death in the history of the United States up to that time. Taken together, they were incredible twin tragedies. Perhaps, this time, there would be repercussions. Indeed, questions were being asked: Who was to blame? Was it the captain's fault? Was it the pilots? Could the system be changed? How should the dead be remembered?

A Summary of Life and Death aboard the Mexico

Wrecked on Hempstead Beach on January 3, 1837

	Total Aboard the *Mexico*	Rescued	Died
Captain, Crew, and Supercargo	12	5	7
Passengers, Per Customs List	111	3	108
Total	**123**	**8**	**115**

The Eight Survivors from the *Mexico*

Name	Other Information
Charles Winslow	Captain – Philadelphia – 47 years old.
William Broom	Ship's supercargo – 14 or 15 years old – brother of shipowner Samuel Broom of New York City.
John Francis	Seaman – a French citizen.
John Handsell	Ship's carpenter.
Richard Owens	Passenger – a farmer – 26 years old.
Thomas Mollahan	Passenger – Irish - a laborer – 26 years old.
John Wood	Passenger – a weaver – 23 years old.
Edward Felix	Ship's cook.

Source: *New York Sun*, January 12, 1837.

The Crew of the Barque *Mexico*

Based on survivor interviews and the captain's statements in the *New York Sun*, January 12, 1837. Also the *New York Commercial Advertiser*, January 5, 1837; and the U.S. National Archives Record Administration, New York City Office.

Names	Place of Birth	Place of Residence	Citizen of	Age	Ht	Complexion	Status
Capt. Charles Winslow.	Pennsylvania	Philadelphia	United States	47	5' 3"	Light	Rescued
William Broom, Supercargo	Pennsylvania	New York	United States	14 or 15	n/a	White	Rescued
Noah N. Jordan, First Mate	n/a	n/a	n/a	n/a	n/a	White	Fell to his death and drowned
Edward Felix, Cook	n/a	n/a	n/a	n/a	n/a	Black	Swam to Rescue Boat
John Handsell, Carpenter	n/a	n/a	n/a	n/a	n/a	White	Rescued
Stephen Simmons, Ship's Steward	n/a	n/a	n/a	n/a	n/a	Black	Frozen
SEAMEN:							
John Francis	France	n/a	France	n/a	n/a	White	Rescued
Walter Quinn	n/a	n/a	n/a	n/a	n/a	Black	Frozen
James Munro	n/a	n/a	n/a	n/a	n/a	Black	Frozen
Lord Sherwood	n/a	n/a	n/a	n/a	n/a	Black	Frozen
Peter Pickering	n/a	n/a	n/a	n/a	n/a	Black	Frozen
Jacob Allen	n/a	n/a	n/a	n/a	n/a	Black	Frozen

The 111 Passengers Aboard the *Mexico*
Customs House, Liverpool.
All froze to death, except three men, as shown.
Printed in the *New York Sun*, January 12, 1837.
Supplemental data from *New York American* January 5, 1837.

Names	Age	Occupation	Country
Thomas Anderton	36	Farmer	Unknown
Ellen Anderton	30	None	Unknown
William Babbington	30	Clerk	Ireland
Isabella Ballentine	28	None	Scotland
Margaret Barrett	25	None	Ireland (Cavan)
Joseph Barrett	Infant	None	Ireland
Samuel Blackburn	23	Laborer	Ireland (formerly of NY)
Samuel Blackburn, Jr.	19	Laborer	Ireland
John Blanchard	20	Farmer	Unknown
Andrew Boyd	17	Laborer	Unknown
Bridget Brennan	17	None	Ireland
Joseph Brooks	28	Paper Maker	England (Derbyshire)
Terrance Burns	28	Laborer	Ireland
Miles Carpenter	24	None	Ireland
Margaret Carpenter	28	None	Ireland
Mary Carpenter	30	None	Unknown
Mary Carpenter	25	None	Unknown
Catharine Collins	16	None	Ireland
Mary Delaney	22	None	Ireland
Bernard Devine	20	Laborer	Ireland (Cavan)
Patrick Devine	20	Laborer	Ireland (Cavan)
Bridget Devine	20	None	Ireland (Cavan)
Margaret Dolan	18	None	Ireland
Christopher Dolan	40	Laborer	Ireland
Owen Durneen	30	Farmer	Ireland
Thomas Dwyer	27	Laborer	Ireland
Thomas Ellis	20	Laborer	Ireland
James Ellsworth	52	Tailor	Poughkeepsie
Martha Ellsworth	13	None	Poughkeepsie
Margaret Evans	32	None	England
George Evans	10	None	England
William Evans	9	None	England
Margaret Evans	6	None	England
John Evans	Infant	None	England
Bridget Farrell	18	None	Ireland

Names	Age	Occupation	Country
Catharine Galligan	25	None	Ireland (Cavan)
James Handlin	18	Laborer	Ireland
John Harden	22	Laborer	Ireland
Joseph Harford	30	Laborer	Unknown
John Hayes	30	Laborer	Ireland (Cork)
Joanna Hayes	30	None	Ireland (Cork)
Mary Hayes	4	None	Ireland (Cork)
John Hayes	Infant	None	Ireland (Cork)
Mary Higgins	50	None	Ireland
John Hope	36	Carpenter	Ireland (Dublin)
Mary Hope	32	None	Ireland (Dublin)
Wm. Hope	14	None	Ireland (Dublin)
Frederick Hope	11	None	Ireland (Dublin)
Thomas Hope	9	None	Ireland (Dublin)
Henry Hope	7	None	Ireland (Dublin)
Rose (or Rosa) Hughes	15	None	Ireland
John Jones	30	Laborer	Unknown
Wm. Jones	23	Laborer	Unknown
Charles Jones	26	Laborer	Unknown
Lewis Jones	25	Laborer	Unknown
Hannah Jones	18	None	Unknown
Bridget Kerr	22	None	Unknown
Maria Kerr	20	None	Unknown
Elizabeth Lawrence	19	None	Scotland
James Lawrence	11	None	Scotland
Catharine Lawrence	9	None	Scotland
John Leonard	25	Farmer	Ireland
Mary MacCafferty	30	None	Ireland
Sally Maguire	18	None	Unknown
Thomas Maloney	23	Laborer	Ireland
Matthew Martin	30	Steward	Ireland
Bartholw. McGlinn	40	Laborer	Ireland
Mary Metcalf	42	None	England
Barbara Metcalf	13	None	England
Harriet Metcalf	9	None	England
Elizabeth Metcalf	7	None	England
Emanuel Metcalf	3	None	England
Thomas Mollahan	26	Laborer	Ireland (Rescued)
Martha Mooney	22	None	Ireland (Dublin)
Michael (or Patrick) Murray	28	Laborer	Ireland (Cavan)

Names	Age	Occupation	Country
Ellery Nolan	32	None	Unknown
Richard Owens	26	Farmer	Unknown (Rescued)
William Pepper	33	Farmer	England
Judy Pepper	33	None	England
Joseph Pepper	14	None	England
William Pepper	12	None	England
Rebecca Pepper	10	None	England
David Pepper	8	None	England
Mary Ann Pepper	6	None	England
Joseph Pepper	4	None	England
John Reilly	27	Laborer	Ireland (Cavan)
Peter Rice	22	Laborer	Ireland
Wm. Robertson	35	Smith	Unknown
Catharine Ross	20	None	Ireland
Edward Smith	25	Laborer	Ireland (Cavan)
Mary Smith	25	None	Ireland (Cavan)
Elizabeth Smith	30	None	Ireland (Cork)
Robert Smith	16	None	Ireland (Cork)
William Smith	12	None	Ireland (Cork)
John Sullivan	20	Clerk	Ireland
Bridget Sullivan	18	None	Ireland
James Thompson	27	Laborer	Unknown
Sydney Thompson	27	Laborer	Unknown
David Thompson	25	Tailor	Unknown
Eleanor Tierney	18	None	Ireland (Cavan)
Elizabeth Wilson	30	None	Unknown
Thomas Wilson	7	None	Unknown
Margaret Wilson	3	None	Unknown
James Wilson	25	Laborer	Unknown
Mary Wilson	24	None	Unknown
James Wilson, infant	½	None	Unknown
John Wood	23	Weaver	Unknown (Rescued)
John Write	28	Laborer	Unknown
Bridget Write	28	None	Unknown
Nicholas Write	2	None	Unknown
Catharine Write, infant	½	None	Unknown
111 total passengers per Liverpool Customs House Record.	21	= Average Age	

Part III

After the Wrecks

The Condemnation of the New York Pilots

The wreck of the *Mexico* had many underlying causes, including the captain's poor decisions, the barque's insufficient crew, her excessive cargo, and her leaky condition. Yet the *Mexico* could have escaped her fate if the harbor pilots had come out past Sandy Hook to bring in the distressed vessel. The *Bristol*, too, would have made it safely to port but for the absence of the pilots. In the winter of 1836-37, other reports kept coming in about ships that were forced out into storms, causing tremendous harm, because there were no pilots to lead them through the shoals:

> The brig *General Trotter* . . . gone ashore in consequence of not being able to procure a pilot.
> —*New York Gazette*, January 5, 1837.

> The Swedish brig *Snappopp*, from Stockholm, was off the Hook and blown off on 26 December. . . Captain Hansten, tried again on December 29. [No] pilots, sailed down to Norfolk, Virginia.
> —*Williamsburgh Gazette*, January 16, 1837.

> Disasters off the coast — The barque *C. P. Williams*, from Apalachicola, was off the Hook 1st January, and was blown to a great distance, and one of the crew was frozen.
> —*Williamsburgh Gazette*, January 16, 1837.

James Gordon Bennett of the *New York Herald* stood out as the first public figure to take a principled stand against the pilots. His own investigation of the wreck of the *Bristol* convinced him that the pilots were to blame. He quickly pointed to the source of the problem—a self-interested monopoly. Bennett pulled no punches in his editorial:

213

We cannot be silent upon the shameful remissness of the pilots, whose duty it was to have boarded the vessel. To them must be attributed the loss of the ship—to them the loss of lives—and they ought to be, as they elsewhere would be, accountable. This is owing to monopoly. Had there been a fair competition allowed, the pilots would have been on the alert, and, in all human probability, the lives of the lost and the tears and sorrow of the afflicted bereaved would have been spared.

—*New York Herald,* November 29, 1836.

When the *Mexico* met the same fate six weeks later, Bennett resumed his attack:

We have to record today another melancholy disaster, more distressing, more calamitous than even the loss of the ship *Bristol*. Again, our atrocious pilot system, or rather our want of all system, sent over a hundred human beings to a watery grave. Their blood is not obliterated from the pilots' hands.

—*New York Herald,* January 5, 1837.

The New York pilots had a long history before 1836. In 1694, eighty-five years after Henry Hudson spent two frustrating days trying to get a small boat through the Sandy Hook shoals and into the Lower Bay, the Dutch rulers of Nieuw Amsterdam got around to passing an "Act for Settlyng Pilotage for All Vessels That Shall Come Within Sandy Hook." By the time the *Bristol* and the *Mexico* arrived off the Hook, the rules had changed little, except to make things worse. In 1817, a pilot law was passed that limited the number of pilots to sixty—half for the East River passage to Long Island Sound (the "Hell's Gate" entry), and half for the passage at Sandy Hook. Between 1817 and 1836, the volume of shipping traffic in New York Harbor more than doubled, but the number of pilots remained the same, at sixty. This guaranteed that anyone lucky enough to become a pilot could retire rich. During their lucrative careers they could afford to make generous donations to friendly political parties. Once New York's politicians realized that pilots were a big source of campaign and party funds, they eagerly seized for themselves the joint responsibility—along with the Board of Pilots—of appointing all new pilots. The result was cronyism and incompetence among a group that became known pejoratively as "The Sixty."

Pilot training was good—in principle. Young pilots, typically sons, nephews, and grandsons of pilots—as they often are today—began their apprenticeship at about age sixteen and remained indentured for five years, to learn "The Art, Trade and Mystery" of pilotage. Pay was seven dollars a month, which was five dollars less than a sailor's monthly pay. The apprentice pilot agreed "not to commit matrimony" or gamble or drink. His master's responsibility was to teach him to pilot vessels to and from New York by way of Sandy Hook or, for smaller vessels, by way of the East River. On becoming a master pilot, his fee was $20 to $30 for each ship he piloted, which meant he then made as much in one day as a sailor made after two months at sea.

From the days of tall wooden ships, to the twenty-first century, much has changed in the way a pilot guides a vessel, but much remains the same. Today, when a cruise ship or container ship radios its approach near Sandy Hook, a pilot boat arrives and offloads a pilot. The pilot takes temporary command of the ship and guides it past the Hook and through the shoals toward Staten Island. Making a dog-leg to the right, he pilots through The Narrows, then across the Inner Harbor, and up to the ship's pier. Pilots know the channel so well that even without reference to channel buoys, sonar, and global positioning satellites (GPS), they can guide a ship in. As one pilot said to this author, "I look at the GPS and the other electronic data on board the ship I am piloting, and then I glance over my left shoulder to see if the Sandy Hook Light is 'in the right place.' Only then do I feel good about the course."

Today there is a system to ensure that *all* vessels from foreign ports take on a pilot, and that there are *always* enough licensed pilots on station. In 1836, however, the system for pilotage was "every man for himself." Whatever a captain chose to do—whether he used a pilot or not—the pilots always got their cut. Some bold and experienced ship captains refused to take a pilot aboard, almost as a matter of pride, and sailed their ships right up to the dock. Even so, they still had to pay a half-pilotage fee. When someone other than a pilot or a captain guided a ship into port, a fine was assessed on top of the half-pilotage fee. It was a "win-win" situation for the pilots.

According to R. G. Albion, there was a grossly insufficient number of pilots in 1836, with only thirty pilots for Sandy Hook. Even in good weather, these few pilots were unable to handle the fifty or more vessels that could arrive and depart the port on a single busy day. In bad weather, the situation was worse, because pilots had no incentive to risk going out past the Hook when they could simply wait out a storm at their piers in Staten Island or Manhattan. Then, when the storm subsided, they could go out and collect their fees, and collect half-pilotage from any captain who had risked entry on his own.

Because ships could take a full day to be piloted from Sandy Hook to Manhattan, merchants craved advance notice to prepare for their vessels' arrivals at the pier. As a result, the "telegraph" was introduced in the United States. This was a visual and mechanical device—not the electronic one patented by Samuel Morse in 1840. The device used was the Chappe telegraph developed in 1791 by two Frenchmen, the Chappe brothers. It was a tall, wooden structure with two, semaphore-like arms that could send visual messages from a distance of many miles. The use of telescopes expanded its range.

In 1829, a Chappe-style telegraph was set up next to the Navesink Twin Lighthouses, along with a second telegraph at Sandy Hook. Charles Havens, the Navesink operator, read semaphore signals from incoming ships and from the Sandy Hook station. He then relayed that information—ship arrivals, important passengers, cargos, and overseas news—to a station on Staten Island. Havens used pulleys to move the arms of the telegraph, mimicking semaphore flags. Another operator on Staten Island relayed the information to the Battery at the tip of Manhattan. The message was transcribed at the Battery and sent by foot messenger to merchants who had paid for the service. Until 1844, when Samuel Morse first sent the famous message "What hath God wrought!" over telegraph lines, the semaphore towers developed by the Chappe brothers were the only telegraphs in use.

Telegraph Tower at Navesink, Above Sandy Hook
Built in 1829 to transmit shipping news to Manhattan.
Twin Lights Historical Park.

The telegraph had a secondary purpose, one which the New York pilots despised. Several times a day the Sandy Hook station transmitted the names of all the pilot boats that had passed through the nearby channel to or from their stations off the Hook. This report was used by a group of New York City merchants to support their contention that the pilots were derelict in their duty. After the tremendous loss of life caused by the wrecks of the *Bristol* and the *Mexico*, the *New York Gazette* inquired as to how many pilot boats had been reported on station at the time the two ships stood off the Hook. The *Gazette*'s investigation revealed that the pilot reports had abruptly ceased at around the time the *Bristol* and the *Mexico* departed for Liverpool, and that there were no subsequent reports. Further investigation revealed that the Sandy Hook telegraph building, along with its signals and its equipment, had been vandalized. The editor of the *Gazette* published enough information for his readers to connect the dots themselves, without actually accusing the pilots of having done the damage:

> A former practice of the telegraph keeper at Sandy Hook has been discontinued. We refer to his custom of reporting when the pilot boats were not on their stations. On making inquiry on this subject, we have ascertained that on a certain night during last summer, the telegraph building was broken open by some unprincipled villains, who destroyed the signals, broke the telescope, and did other damage to the premises. This will readily account for the absence of any more reports about the absence of the pilots.
>
> ——*New York Gazette*, as reported in the
> *New York Commercial Advertiser*, January 11, 1837.

Even without making a clear accusation against the pilots, the *Gazette*'s story added to the storm of public anger and stirred calls for reform, including demands that the telegraph observation post be repaired and that its function of monitoring the pilots be resumed. Outrage against the pilots extended up the Hudson River as far as Albany, the final destination of many Irish emigrants in the 1830s, and also the source of most of the pilot-friendly legislation:

> The *Mexico*, like the *Bristol*, was lost for the want of a pilot. She was hailed by a news boat two days before she was wrecked. The pilots are protected in their monopoly. The pilots are Politicians. They spend their time in Porter-Houses and Club-rooms. They are protected. Young, fully trained [apprentice] pilots are refused licenses after giving seven years of their lives pursuing the business.
>
> ——*Albany Evening Journal*, as reported in
> *New York Gazette*, January 14, 1837.

217

The legally-mandated Board of Pilots was a self-regulatory organization loaded with pilots, former pilots, relatives, and political cronies. The president of the group valiantly defended the pilots in the press, citing the New York City Fire Department in an analogy:

> In speaking of the disasters of those ill-fated ships [the wrecks of the *Bristol* and the *Mexico*], were they occasioned by the elements, the want of attention of the captains, or the negligence of the pilots? If the latter, why were not the Firemen and the Fire Department brought before the public and censured, as the pilots have been, for not controlling the elements and saving that vast amount of property that was destroyed on the sixteenth of December [of 1835].
>
> —*New York Commercial Advertiser*, January 12, 1837.

The analogy would have been valid if the firemen he was comparing the pilots to had stayed home in bed on the night of December 16, 1835, when fire destroyed seven hundred buildings in New York City. But contrary to his analogy, the firemen had bravely fought the terrible fire, despite the near-zero-degree weather. Many of their water lines were frozen, thus preventing them from putting out the blaze. The fire department lost the battle, though not through lack of effort.

View of the Great Conflagration of Dec. 16th and 17th, 1835 From Coenties Slip
Published by J. J. Disturnell and J.H Bufford; from a sketch by J.H. Bufford.

The pilots' president then went so far as to invent his own version of the facts, claiming that at eleven o'clock on New Year's Eve there were two pilot boats on station off the Hook, with several pilots on each, boarding ships. This version of the events conflicts starkly with the reports of the three surviving passengers of the *Mexico,* Captain Winslow, and the captains of two other vessels, all of whom said they saw more than thirty ships standing off the Hook between the hours of eleven o'clock and midnight that night, with lanterns lit, waiting for pilots—and not one pilot boat present.

The Pilot Board's president next claimed that on Sunday, January 1, the pilots could not get out to the *Mexico* because of a heavy snowfall and lack of wind. Again, the evidence contradicts the pilots' version of events. News reports revealed that the steamboat *Hercules,* which was headed out to tow the packet *Montreal* into the harbor, towed a pilot boat out through the snow and pack ice, to a protected spot just inside the Hook. When there was not sufficient wind for the pilot boat to sail from there out to the waiting ships on its own, the *Hercules'* captain offered to take aboard his steamboat any pilots wanting to go out and be put aboard the waiting ships. The total number of pilots who came aboard the steamship was exactly two.

Damning evidence was revealed about the majority of the pilots' whereabouts on the days in question. The *New York Herald* printed the account of eyewitnesses who saw close to thirty—that is, close to *all*—Sandy Hook pilots and several customs house officials "enjoying themselves" at Riley's Inn on West Broadway. They were seen there on New Year's Eve and again on New Year's Day. Another of the *Herald's* eyewitnesses claimed the pilots were drunk both days, and that a large group of them was observed late Sunday morning, buying coffee and sandwiches and generally hanging around near the seaport, sobering up.

As evidence of the pilots' dereliction of duty piled up, the Pilot Board's president desperately sought a way out. He cited ice in the bay. The Narrows, he said, were "choked with ice," making any passage extremely dangerous. This seemed to be a good argument because New York Harbor was under a siege of ice, as everyone could see. Pack ice was floating down the North River and the East River, and was wreaking havoc. The *New York Commercial Advertiser* reported that on January 3, at one o'clock in the afternoon, a small boat with six persons aboard—two army sergeants, a soldier, a storekeeper, and two boatmen—carrying provisions for the garrison at Governors Island, was overturned by an ice floe, with the result that five men drowned. When the steamboat *New York* happened by, one man was rescued. So much ice came down the East River that it tore the brig *America* from her repair dock and drove her ashore full of water. A large field of ice drove the British barque *Cruickston Castle* from her berth alongside the brig *Commerce,* tearing off her bowsprit and flying jib-boom.

The argument, however, was bogus. At least two news boats were out off Sandy Hook on New Year's Day, with ice floes all around them, recording ship arrivals and picking up newspapers. Their presence off the Hook took the wind out of the sails of the pilots' claim that ice prevented them from going out.

Changing course toward another shoal in his discourse, the Board president cited Captain Winslow's words to explain why the pilots could not have guided ships in, in such extremely cold weather:

> The captain of the barque *Mexico* reports that the weather on the coasts has been very severe, so much so, that it was impossible for one to stay on the ship's deck for more than one half hour at a time. Query. In that case, who is to spell the pilot?
> —*New York Commercial Advertiser*, January 12, 1837.

The sharp rejoinder from the *Advertiser* was, "Who spelled the reporters on the news boats?" The Board president lamely closed his arguments with a *non sequitur*, citing the high premiums pilots must pay to insure their vessels.

The pilots, having lost in the court of public opinion, now faced a grand jury investigation. But they were not charged with any crime because they had violated no law. They *were* the law. As the public outcry continued, and as reporters persisted in asking probing questions, the pilots desperately resorted to violence, as they had after the wreck of the *Bristol*, when a pilot assaulted the *Herald's* James Gordon Bennett. This time, another pilot, Thomas Vail, assaulted a news reporter from the *Courier & Enquirer*.

None of the press's and public's outrage seemed to matter, nor did the pilots' pitiful defense. The harbor pilotage system was so corrupt and so interlocked with the New York City and New York State political systems that nothing at all was done. Suddenly, a month later, there was an abrupt political change. What finally resonated with the politicians was not the cries of freezing, emigrant children on the *Mexico* or the screams of drowning families aboard the *Bristol*. No, it was the howls of complaining merchants as insurance rates on their ships and cargos began to climb following the wrecks. In early February 1837, the legislators of the State of New Jersey—not New York, where corruption so completely dominated marine affairs—dramatically changed the regulations for the *New Jersey pilots*, and thus for *all* the pilots. Previously, the Jersey pilots, fifteen in number, were permitted to escort only those vessels that were destined for New Jersey landings, such as Raritan Bay. Now, under the new law, they could escort ships past Sandy Hook, through the Narrows, and right up to the New York City piers.

The New York pilots and the Pilot Board were outraged at the possibility of competition for their pilot fares. They immediately dispatched lobbyists and city and state officials to Washington, D.C. to plead "states' rights," so that they could retain the lucrative monopoly they were guaranteed under New York State law. What they got instead was a slap in the face far more painful than the punches the pilots had thrown at various publishers and reporters. In hearings before Congress, the pilots' negligence in contributing to the wrecks of the *Bristol* and the *Mexico* was repeatedly thrown at them. Several captains presented damning and insulting testimony, such as the following:

> It is a matter of notoriety, wherever I have been acquainted with ship-masters and commercial men that travel by sea in Europe, Africa, North and South America, the negligence and inattention of New York pilots. It is a bye-word, "As lazy as a New York pilot." You cannot say any thing more grating to a seaman. . . he will consider himself highly insulted, and I certainly think so too.

(Signed,) GIDEON PARKER
18th day of January, 1837.

> ——Pennington, et. al., *Statement of the Facts : Pilot Laws (*1840).

The New York pilots disregarded the insults. They placed all their hopes in one piece of paper—a federal law passed in 1789 and signed by George Washington, which said in part:

> *Chap. IX.—An Act for the establishment and support of Lighthouses, Beacons, Buoys, and Public Piers.*

> Sec. 4. And be it further enacted, That all pilots in the bays, inlets, rivers, harbors and ports of the United States, shall continue to be regulated in conformity with the existing laws of the States respectively wherein such pilots may be, or with such laws as the States may respectively hereafter enact for the purpose. . .

The forty-eight-year-old federal law appeared to guarantee that the monopoly could continue to thrive under the protection of New York State law. But the pilots' "states' rights" argument was undone by the concluding phrase of the act: "until further legislative provision shall be made by Congress." With the disasters of the *Bristol* and the *Mexico* fresh in their minds, Congress did act, and they did so immediately. On March 2, 1837, they passed a law stating the following:

That it shall and may be lawful for the master or commander of any vessel coming into or going out of any port situate upon waters which are the boundary between the States, to employ any pilot duly licensed or authorized by the laws of *either of the States* bounded on said waters, to pilot the said vessel to or from said port, any law, usage, or custom to the contrary notwithstanding.

—Pennington, et. al., *Statement of the Facts : Pilot Laws (*1840).

(Italics added.)

The result was dramatic, and it happened literally overnight. The very next day, the New Jersey pilots sailed out past the Hook, looking for any customers they could find, whether bound for New Jersey, Staten Island, Manhattan, or Brooklyn. The pilot system of New York Harbor would never be the same. A New Jersey official made the following observation three years later regarding the beneficial effect of opening competition between the New Jersey and New York pilots:

And I do further declare that . . . the pilots up to March 1837, were not in the habit of going to sea; and, since then, I have seen the New York and Jersey pilots seventy miles from Sandy Hook. I have no reason to know that any unusual complaint has been made by ship-masters or merchants, as to the pilots, for the last three years.

— Pennington, et. al., *Statement of the Facts : Pilot Laws (*1840),
"Statement of James Bergen, Notary Public, of New Jersey."

As Robert Greenhalgh Albion wrote in *The Rise of New York Port*, "Up to 1837, the pilots played it so safe that scarcely a single accident [to pilot boats] was recorded." When the New York pilots were forced to change their tactics, they more than met the challenge. Pilot boats had to widen their cruise radiuses in order to beat other boats to incoming vessels, and be first to a fare. These more aggressive tactics took their toll. Two years later, in 1839, the pilot boats *John McKeon* and *Gratitude* were wrecked in storms with the loss of all hands. R. G. Albion calculates that fifteen pilot boats were lost in the twenty-three years following the wrecks of the *Bristol* and the *Mexico*. Forty more pilots were lost in the fifteen years after that, according to the *New York Times* of January 23, 1870. The pilots were earning their pay, and more.

Once the monopoly was broken the pilots sailed so fast, so far, and with such maneuverability in search of vessels that their reputation soared. In 1851, a Sandy Hook pilot, Richard "Old Dick" Brown, was selected to sail the yacht *America* in a race around the Isle of Wight, against fourteen British yachts. Brown brought home the first ever America's Cup.

The Yacht *America*
Winner of the first America's Cup, in 1851; captained by a New York Pilot.
Print by Currier & Ives.

The Censure of Captain Charles Winslow

{{chain decoration}}

At the same time that New York City's newspapermen were chasing down leads to prove that the Sandy Hook pilots were derelict in their duty, they kept another target in their sights: Captain Charles Winslow of the *Mexico*. These were heady days for the new field of investigative news reporting. Both readers and reporters were discovering that it was far more interesting to learn that shipwrecks might not simply be called acts of God, but could be caused by *people*. The newspapers found plenty of grist for their mill in Charles Winslow.

A simple comparison highlights Winslow's failures. The British ship *Tamarac*, captained by Francis Kane, left her home port of Liverpool a month after the *Mexico*. Following a "pleasant voyage," the ship arrived at Sandy Hook in company with the *Mexico*. When no pilots came out, both vessels were forced out into the New York Bight, and the ships ran aground on the same day. The *Tamarac* struck bottom at Fire Island, a remote barrier island thirty miles east of the *Mexico*. A newspaper reported the situation:

> More shipwrecks for want of a pilot: The British ship *Tamarac*,
> Capt. Kane, left Liverpool on 20th November, and after a pleasant
> voyage made Sandy Hook on Saturday last. Made various signals
> and fired rockets for a pilot. She lay off under storm sails. . .
> struck bottom three miles east of Fire Island Light. . .
> —*New York American*, January 6, 1837.

Despite the similarities of the two wrecks, the outcomes were starkly different. Kane's twenty-six-man crew of fit and able seamen saved themselves and all their passengers but one, an infant who died. The *Tamarac's* crew rowed a ship's boat to shore, dragging a stern-line, and then ferried boats back and forth through the wind, waves, and slush ice. The *New York American* gave the details:

> Got out her boats and sent one with a line ashore. . . All safe except one infant who perished. . . 4 cabin, 113 steerage and crew of 26 lost everything except the clothes they wore. . . The sea was all the while making a complete breech over the vessel, and she was one complete body of ice.
>
> —*New York American*, January 6, 1837.

Captain Kane and the crew of the *Tamarac* faced the same weather at their wreck site as Captain Winslow and his crew, and were able to mount an effective rescue of passengers and crew. Winslow and his men were able to accomplish nothing—except save a few of themselves. Their failures cost the lives of 48 male passengers, 33 female passengers, 27 children, and 7 crewmen, 115 people in all. The newspapers' criticism of Winslow and the abandonment of his passengers came quickly, with the strongest coming from the *New York American*:

> Respecting the conduct of Captain *Winslow*, in being among the first to quit the wreck, and abandoning those who had no earthly reliance but on him, there should be, there can be, but one universal feeling of execration.
>
> —*New York American*, January 5, 1837.

Samuel Broom (the owner of the *Mexico*) and his brother William were among the few people who appreciated what Winslow had done. After all, he saved young William's life in preference to 115 other men, women, and children aboard the barque. The brothers immediately rose to the defense of the captain. William personally delivered a note to the *New York American's* office, demanding that any newspaper that had published the censure of Captain Winslow should now print the Brooms' statement. The newspapers gave scant attention to the Brooms' imaginative defense:

> The captain having been censured for leaving the ship, we are requested to say that he was urged to do so by the passengers, in the hope that he would effect from shore something for their rescue.
>
> —*New York Gazette and General Advertiser,* January 7, 1837.

A few days later, the three passenger-sailors from the *Mexico*, Thomas Mollahan, John Wood and Richard Owens, were interviewed in the hospital by James Gordon Bennett, publisher of the *New York Herald*. The men completely refuted the Brooms' claim that the captain had shown any interest in effecting a rescue from shore. As a result of this, the Brooms needed some fresh damage control. When a "committee of gentlemen from the City of New York" was formed to go out to Hempstead to award Captain Raynor Smith a silver tankard "in commemoration of his services to humanity," the Brooms sent an emissary along with them. This representative presented $50 to Raynor Smith and to each of his surfboat crew, as a token of thanks for their brave deed. The gifts were made in the name of Captain Winslow. The generous, total amount of $350 effectively turned over to the rescuers most of the money the emigrants had paid the Liverpool passenger broker to transport them to New York City—and not, of course, to Lott's barn where they at that very moment lay as frozen corpses.

Despite the Brooms' efforts, the *New York American* did not waver in its criticism of Captain Winslow:

> The commander that abandons his ship in peril, leaving those who confided in him to destruction, like the commander of a besieged garrison who should pusillanimously desert his post, can find no sympathy in any manly breast.
>
> —*New York American*, January 12, 1837.

Tempting as it is to declare Winslow a scoundrel, one must still examine his actions at Hempstead Beach in light of the thinking of the day. The captain cannot be held to have violated the rule of "women and children first," or "the captain is the last to leave the ship," because there was no such "rule" in the 1830s. Part I of this book provides several examples to show that was the case (see pages 93-96). However, even at a time of "every man for himself," the censure stands. When Charles Winslow took with him the only able-bodied men who could effectively continue the rescue, he condemned the others to die.

The extreme anxiety that Winslow admitted he felt at Sandy Hook surely returned as he waited for a rescue boat to come out from shore at Hempstead Beach. That nervous apprehension may explain why the captain continued to carry his saber throughout the rescue. After he had used the weapon to show Raynor Smith where to approach with his surfboat, there was no further use for it. At thirty-nine inches in length, the saber was awkward for a man only five feet three inches tall to wear, even on level ground. Indeed, it could have been a fatal hindrance to him while maneuvering out along the icy bowsprit. The captain had seen his first mate slip and fall into the sea; he had seen a passenger-sailor mistime his leap, fall hard onto the boat's gunwale, and almost tumble into the sea. Any reasonable person would have discarded the weapon long before reaching the end of the bowsprit, yet Winslow was still wearing his saber. True, the weapon may have been a family heirloom; but, whatever value it held, monetary or otherwise, it was surely worth less than his life. With his saber in hand, however, no one could stop his escape plan.

Captain Winslow's Saber and Scabbard
The author is pictured at the Lynbrook Public Library, displaying Captain Winslow's
thirty-nine-inch saber and scabbard to a group of Cub Scouts, circa 1985.
Photo by Louise Janet Campbell.

The primary responsibility for the disaster lay squarely on Charles Winslow's shoulders. The captain would probably deny it, preferring to blame the pilots and others for what had happened, but as master of the *Mexico*, he had ultimate responsibility for *everything* aboard the ship—overloading the leaking barque, packing her with emigrants, and staffing her with an insufficient crew. When presented with the opportunity to make the most important decisions of his life, he had failed miserably. He chose to sail the barque out into a blizzard rather than cross the shoals into New York Harbor on his own. He ruined his own rescue effort when he tried to remove a terrified woman from the yawl. And at the end, he sat idly on the beach, sitting atop the ship's money chest, with his saber at his side, warming himself at a fire, while his passengers and crew froze to death two hundred yards away.

Little is known about Charles Winslow after the wreck. He was forced to testify before a grand jury, but was never charged. Indeed, nothing could be legally be done beyond the censure he received in the newspapers. As a result, he continued as a ship's master. Five years after the wreck, Winslow was still commanding transient merchant ships. On September 19, 1842, the following, brief obituary appeared in the *Yarmouth* [Massachusetts] *Register*:

> 8th ult. [August 8, 1842], off Gibraltar, Capt. Charles WINSLOW of Philadelphia, late master of ship *Minerva* of New York, 52.

Later it was reported that his body was buried in the "neutral ground" that separated the British-controlled Rock of Gibraltar from Spain by the combined distance of two cannon shots. The circumstances of Winslow's death off Gibraltar are not known, nor is it known whether his saber found its way from Gibraltar to Long Island after his death, or remained on Long Island after the wreck. The truth of how Winslow's saber and scabbard ended up in storage at the Garvies Point Museum at Glen Cove may never be known, since the donor of the saber will not reveal how he or his family acquired it. Some Long Islanders believe it was forcibly taken from the captain.

The curse of Captain Charles Winslow lives on—in the form of his saber. In recent decades, the weapon was from time to time put on display in the Village of Lynbrook, where sixty-two of the victims of the *Mexico* are buried. Around the year 2000, however, the saber and scabbard, along with many other valuable items from the Nassau County Museum's collection, were found to be missing. The thief was a museum curator. He was convicted on a felony count, but the whereabouts of the saber remains unknown.

Porcelain Pitcher
Recovered from the *Mexico*
Owned by Virginia B. Stanton.

Only one artifact remains from the *Mexico*. It is a porcelain pitcher recovered from the wreck and presented to Aleta Smith of Raynorstown, in gratitude for the help she and her mother gave to the badly frozen survivors of the wreck. The pitcher has been handed down for several generations, by way of the eldest daughter.

A Mass Grave in Lynbrook

Word of the wreck of the *Mexico* spread quickly through the Town of Hempstead on Long Island.[37] The stories were appalling—victims' screams fading away in the night, bodies washing onshore encapsulated in ice, and rows of frozen corpses laid out in Lott's barn. Charles Ellms, in his book *Tragedies of the Seas* (1841), relates what the nearby residents did within days of the disaster:

> By this terrible calamity a greater number of lives were lost than by any previous shipwreck on the coast of the United States. . .
>
> The humane inhabitants of Hempstead and its vicinity, being actuated by the purest sentiments of philanthropy, held a public meeting on Friday, the 6th of January, at which the following preamble and resolutions were adopted:
>
>> The inhabitants of the town of Hempstead, feeling themselves called upon by the recent awful and distressing shipwreck, and unprecedented loss of life on the melancholy occasion, held a large and respectable meeting on Friday evening, when it was unanimously,
>>
>> *Resolved*, That since it has pleased the Great Disposer of events to cast upon our shore the bodies of many friendless fellow-creatures, suddenly deprived of life by a most

---

[37] Historical and contemporary place names in the southern part of Nassau County can be confusing, to say the least. For example, there are the Town of Hempstead and the Village of Hempstead; and there are Far Rockaway, Near Rockaway, Rockaway Beach, Rockville Centre, and East Rockaway. *The History of Nassau County Community Place-Names* (1999) by Richard A. Winsche is a fine resource into the origins of these names. Also see the Appendix (page 259) for a brief discussion on local place names.

disastrous shipwreck, we deem it a solemn duty, devolving upon us, to cause them to be decently and properly interred;

— that a committee of twelve be appointed to collect contributions for the purpose of purchasing a piece of ground, to be forever reserved solely for the interment of bodies which shall hereafter be cast upon our beach; and, also, for the further purpose of erecting a suitable monument over the bodies now to be interred.

Whereupon the following gentlemen were named as the committee:

John Bedell, Richard Carman, Nathaniel Seaman, Jacob Coles, Stephen C. Shedeker, Platt Willets, Peter T. Hewlett, Oliver Denton , John W. De Mott, Daniel Mot, John I. Lott , and Raynor R. Smith [the hero of the rescue].

The committee, having succeeded in obtaining ample funds, have purchased a lot of ground adjacent to the burial-ground of the Methodist church, [at] Near Rockaway, and to be attached to the same, under the restrictions of the resolutions; and every arrangement has been made for the interment of the bodies in a respectable manner, and with appropriate ceremonies.

The cemetery at the Old Sand Hole Methodist Church in Near Rockaway was chosen as the final resting place for the victims because of its closeness to where the bodies lay in Lott's barn. The money recovered from the victims—about $300—was held in escrow by the wreck-master, pending claims from heirs. Local contributions were used to acquire enough land to expand the Old Sand Hole Cemetery and create a Mariners Burying Ground. Peter T. Hewlett donated some of the land and Oliver Denton donated the lumber for the coffins.

The committee began arrangements for the burial of the forty-three bodies initially recovered. Women from the village of Hempstead went quickly to work, purchasing funeral garments with their own funds, and bringing them to Lott's barn. There they prepared the still-frozen bodies of the women and children, and "with their own hands enshrouded [them] in the habiliments of the grave." The male bodies were prepared by local men. As the week wore on, ten more bodies were recovered for a total of fifty-three.

Three bodies were omitted from the committee's tally of fifty "men, women, boys and girls." They were black sailors from the ship. They counted differently, as "colored." Slavery was slow to disappear in New York State, and technically still existed in the 1830s. A 1799 statute freed all slaves born after July 4 of that year. But it was freedom much delayed, because those young slaves had to wait twenty-five or twenty-eight more years (until 1824 for enslaved women and 1827 for enslaved men) to receive their promised freedom. An 1817 statute gave freedom to all slaves born *before* July 4, 1799—but those slaves had to wait ten years, until July 4, 1827, at which time all New York slaves were made free. Well . . . not quite. Even then, slavery was not entirely repealed, for there was an exception: nonresidents could enter New York and remain there with their slaves for up to nine months at a time. New York's "nine-months law" stayed on the books until 1841.

In 1837, racism was deeply embedded on Long Island. Although the white residents of Hempstead, Hempstead South, and Near Rockaway were generous in preparing the white victims for burial, they were unwilling to prepare the bodies of the black sailors. Charles Ellms tells us how their bodies were cared for:

> The colored bodies were committed to the care of the colored
> people of the neighborhood, and interred at the same time, and
> within the same enclosure.
>
> —*Tragedies of the Seas* (1841).

Although the black sailors were to be buried within the Mariners Burying Ground, they were not permitted to be buried in the same long grave where the whites were to be laid shoulder-to-shoulder in their coffins. The black men would get their own, separate grave. Further reinforcing the inferior status accorded to anyone of African descent, the committee posted an official, segregated, order-of-procession for the carriages that transported the bodies three miles from Lott's barn to the cemetery:

> The Clergy.
> Committee of Arrangements.
> The Corpses.
> {Women,
> Men,
> Children,
> Colored.}
> Pall-Bearers.
> Friends and Relatives.
> Citizens.

The wagon procession on Wednesday, January 11, 1837, was the longest Long Island had ever seen—three hundred horse-drawn carriages and wagons. Fifty-two farm wagons carried the coffins, one body to a coffin except for Mr. and Mrs. Pepper, who were together. (The funeral ceremony is recounted on pages 13-14.)

Over the next few weeks, more of the *Mexico's* victims washed up along the South Shore of Long Island, making a total of eighty-three recovered bodies. Relatives and friends claimed some of the bodies, including those of Patrick Murray, Rosa Hughes, Samuel Blackburn, Catharine Galligan, James Lawrence, and William Evans. They were buried elsewhere. In all, sixty-two bodies were interred in the Mariners Burying Ground. Of those buried there, the names of only a few are known for certain. They are William Pepper, his wife Judy, and two of their daughters, Rebecca and Mary Ann; Martha Mooney; Stephen Simmons (the ship's steward); and Noah Jordan (the mate).

Six weeks before the January 11 burial ceremony, the unclaimed bodies of the victims of the wreck of the *Bristol* had been hastily buried at Rockaway Beach, at a discreet distance from the Marine Pavilion. The possibility of eventually moving those additional seventy-seven victims to the Near Rockaway burial site probably influenced the committee's decision to acquire such a large plot as they did. But it was not until 1839 that victims of the wreck of the *Bristol* were removed from their temporary graves at Rockaway Beach and re-interred with ceremony at the Mariners Burying Ground.

In 1840, using local contributions and $300 of still-unclaimed funds taken from the bodies of the victims—which funds the legislature of the State of New York had finally released—a monument committee authorized the purchase of a memorial to be placed at the Mariners Burying Ground. Peter T. Hewlett of East Rockaway wrote in his diary that he headed the group that went to the village of Sing Sing (today's Ossining), New York to commission the carving of a white marble obelisk. The monument was carried to East Rockaway by coastal sloop, and then taken by horse-drawn wagon up Ocean Avenue to the cemetery. It was erected on November 28, 1840, where it stands today, marking the mass grave of 139 victims.

The Mariners Burying Ground at the Rockville Cemetery
Formerly the Old Sand Hole Cemetery.
Lynbrook, New York.

A piper plays *Amazing Grace* at a memorial ceremony in 1999.
The eighteen-foot-tall white-marble monument marks the mass grave
of 139 victims of the wrecks of the *Bristol* and the *Mexico*.

Photo by Arthur S. Mattson.

Text Engraved on the *Bristol* and *Mexico* Monument:

(On the South side)

To the memory of 77 Persons chiefly Emigrants from England & Ireland,
being the only remains of 100 souls composing the Passengers and crew of
the American ship *Bristol*, Capt. McKown, wrecked on Far-Rockaway beach.
Nov. 21, 1836

(On the West side)

All the bodies of the *Bristol* and *Mexico* recovered from the Ocean
and decently interred near this spot, were followed to the grave by a large concourse
of Citizens and Strangers and an address delivered suited to the occasion from these
words, "Lord save us, we perish," Matth. 8. 25. v.

(On the North side)

To the memory of sixty-two persons chiefly Emigrants from England and Ireland;
being the only remains of 115 souls, forming the passengers
and crew of the American *Barque Mexico,* Capt. Winslow, wrecked
on Hempstead beach. Jan. 2. 1837 [38]

(On the East side)

To commemorate the melancholy fate of the unfortunate sufferers belonging to the
Bristol and *Mexico*, this monument was erected; partly by the
money found upon their persons, and partly by the contributions of the
benevolent and humane, in the County of Queen's.

---

[38] The obelisk gives the date of the wreck of the *Mexico* as January 2, 1837. This is correct so long as the night of January 2 is taken to include the still-dark, early-morning hours of January 3, when the vessel actually struck the bar off Hempstead Beach. This was common usage in the early nineteenth century, and is accepted by this author. Contemporaneous newspaper accounts report that the *Mexico* was in fact wrecked on Tuesday, January 3, 1837 at about 4AM or 5AM. The *New York Sunday Morning News* (January 8, 1837), *New York Herald* (January 5, 1837), the *Supplement to the New York Sun* (January 12, 1837), and the *New York Morning Courier* (January 5, 1837), all give January 3. Two contemporaneous historians also give the morning of January 3, 1837 as the date and time of the wreck. See Benjamin Thompson's *History of Long Island,* Vol. II (1843) and Charles Ellms' *Tragedy of the Sea* (1841).

Also on the base, on the North side, the following lines are inscribed:

> In this grave, from the wide Ocean doth sleep,
> The bodies of those that had crossed the deep,
> And instead of being landed, safe on the shore,
> In a cold frosty night, they all were no more.

Nathaniel S. Prime wrote in his *History of Long Island* (1845) that the preceding lines of verse were:

> [W]orse than doggerel poetry. Our grave yards abound with similar examples of bad grammar and contemptible trash, called poetry:
>> Enough to rouse a dead man into rage,
>> And warm with red resentment the wan cheek.

Prime's poetic quote is from the poem "The Grave," by Robert Blair (1699-1746). These are a few more of Blair's lines:

> Perchance some hackney hunger-bitten scribbler
> Insults thy memory, and blots thy tomb
> With long flat narrative, or duller rhymes,
> With heavy halting pace that drawl along;
> Enough to rouse a dead man into rage,
> And warm with red resentment the wan cheek.

So outraged were Long Islanders at the doggerel carved on the monument that they demanded an explanation from Peter T. Hewlett, chairman of the monument committee, who responded:

> The committee finally adopted the [poem] in question,
> simply for the reason, that the individual who prepared it,
> had pledged a liberal subscription toward the monument,
> on condition that it should secure the preference.

Sadly, the dead of the *Bristol* and the *Mexico* were victimized again, and not just by bad poetry. Over the years, as space became tight at the renamed Rockville Cemetery, the operators—under cover of the New York Cemetery Trust law—appropriated all the unused portion of the Mariners plot, and used it for burials having nothing to do with deaths at sea. Worse, the operators appear to have reused the very graves where the 139 wreck victims are buried. On at least two occasions over the last forty years, discarded, old, human bones have been traced to the Rockville Cemetery. In one case, bones turned up at a landfill in Freeport; in another, bones were discovered at the cemetery itself, in a heap of debris. The cemetery operators claimed the bones were old "Indian remains."

The Mariners Burying Ground has been encroached upon despite the boundary dimensions originally carved on the monument. To cover their mischief, the operators of the cemetery resorted to the original meaning of the word "chiseler." They literally chiseled the plot's dimensions off the monument, leaving a horrid gash. They were probably unaware that Nathaniel Prime had long ago written the monument's full text in his book, *The History of Long Island*, published in 1845. The book still exists, and it spells out the amount of land set aside for the Mariners Burying Ground, as originally carved on the south base:

The Inhabitants of the County
impelled by A generous sensibility
have Purchased thirty feet front and rear
by One hundred and Sixty one feet deep[39]
of this yard and set it apart exclusively
as a Mariners Burying Ground.

Grave markers from recent burials have been shoehorned in to within inches of the monument. Today there is nothing left to indicate either the location of the long burial trenches that hold the *Bristol's* and the *Mexico's* victims, or the separate grave of the *Mexico's* black sailors. Only the monument remains.

---

[39] This fourth line was obliterated from the monument.

Walt Whitman
and the Wrecks of the *Bristol* and the *Mexico*

Walt Whitman's Favorite Photograph (1887)
George C. Cox, photographer

In 1836, the year the *Bristol* and the *Mexico* crossed the Atlantic on their final voyages, Walt Whitman (1819-1892) was seventeen, living for a time with his parents in the village of Hempstead, and later that year in Babylon. Hempstead is only twenty miles from the *Bristol's* wreck site at Rockaway Beach, ten miles from the *Mexico's* at Long Beach, and five miles from the

Mariners Burying Ground in Lynbrook. Whitman was not an eyewitness to either of the wrecks, but he undoubtedly read the shocking firsthand accounts that were printed in the *Long Island Democrat*—a newspaper he aspired to write for—and the *Hempstead Inquirer*. Indeed, the wrecks were the biggest news of the year on Long Island—and perhaps of the decade. They made a big impression on him.

Walt Whitman developed into a modern poet with epic ambitions, but he had no popular American legends or myths available to interpret for his readers, so he created a mythology based on his own past, and placed himself at the center as observer and participant. This mythology was often drawn from his boyhood experiences on Long Island, and included his immersion in what he called "the atmosphere and traditions" of the Island's seacoast, including its natural beauty, its clammers and fishermen, and its tragic shipwrecks.

Seashore Fancies [40]

Even as a boy, I had the fancy, the wish, to write a piece, perhaps a poem, about the sea-shore—that suggesting, dividing line, contact, junction, the solid marrying the liquid . . . Hours, days, I haunted the shores of Rockaway or Coney Island, or away east to the Hamptons or Montauk. Once, at the latter place (by the old lighthouse, nothing but sea-tossings in sight in every direction as far as the eye could reach) I remember well, I felt that I must one day write a book expressing this liquid, mystic theme. Afterward, I recollect, how it came to me that instead of any special lyrical or epical or literary attempt, the sea-shore should be an invisible influence, a pervading gauge and tally for me, in my Compositions. . .

Whitman achieved his youthful wish when he included poems such as "The Sleepers" and "As I Ebb'd with the Ocean of Life" in the collection *Leaves of Grass*. Whitman acknowledges in one of his prose works that "The Sleepers" alludes to the wreck of the *Mexico*:

Paumanok, and My Life on It as Child and Young Man [41]

Worth fully and particularly investigating indeed this Paumanok (to give the spot its aboriginal name) stretching east through

---

[40] This selection and the following one are from Walt Whitman's *Specimen Days & Collect* (1882).

[41] Paumanok, literally, "land of tribute," is an Algonquian word for Long Island. Whitman used this word in many of his poems.

Kings, Queens and Suffolk counties, 120 miles altogether—on the north Long Island sound, a beautiful, varied and picturesque series of inlets, "necks" and sea-like expansions, for a hundred miles to Orient point. On the ocean side the great south bay dotted with countless hummocks, mostly small, some quite large, occasionally long bars of sand out two hundred rods to a mile-and-a-half from the shore. While now and then, as at Rockaway and far east along the Hamptons, the beach makes right on the island, the sea dashing up without intervention. Several light-houses on the shores east; a long history of wrecks tragedies, some even of late years. As a youngster, I was in the atmosphere and traditions of many of these wrecks—of one or two almost an observer. Off Hempstead beach for example, was the loss of the ship "Mexico" in 1840 (alluded to in "the Sleepers" in L. of G.) [42]

Dramatic details of the wreck of the *Mexico* help make "The Sleepers" one of Whitman's best poems, and perhaps his most haunting work. The fourth stanza captures the horrific scene of the wreck so accurately that it gives the sense that Whitman was an eyewitness both at the Hempstead Beach and at Lott's barn—where the dead were laid out—although there is no evidence that he was at either scene.

The Sleepers
Stanza Four, from *Leaves of Grass* (1891-92 edition)

The beach is cut by the razory ice-wind, the wreck-guns sound,
The tempest lulls, the moon comes floundering through the drifts.

I look where the ship helplessly heads end on, I hear the burst as
 she strikes, I hear the howls of dismay, they grow fainter
 and fainter.

I cannot aid with my wringing fingers,
I can but rush to the surf and let it drench me and freeze
 upon me.

I search with the crowd, not one of the company is wash'd to us
 alive,
In the morning I help pick up the dead and lay them in rows in
 a barn.

---

[42] Whitman is referring to *Leaves of Grass* when he writes, "in L. of G." He errs when he dates the wreck as 1840, instead of 1837. The cemetery monument was erected in 1840.

The details in the poem match the contemporaneous news accounts—the "razory ice-wind," the "wreck guns," the "howls of dismay growing fainter." Even the direction of the ship is correct, as it "helplessly heads end on"—i.e., bow-first. Whitman is both an observer and a participant in the poem. This allows him to connect to the shipwreck victims in an intense and personal way. Step by step he draws himself (and the reader) into the scene, first passively, then actively: "I cannot aid with my wringing fingers," "I can but rush to the surf and let it drench me and freeze upon me," "I search with the crowd," and "I help pick up the dead and lay them in rows in a barn."

"The Sleepers" was first published in 1855, eighteen years after the wrecks; but the terrible facts of the slow deaths by freezing of 115 men, women, and children were still remembered by his readers. For Long Islanders—especially those who witnessed the dead lying in rows in a barn, or who accompanied the bodies in a cortege of three hundred carriages—the poem must have taken on a powerful meaning.

Whitman's identification of the *Mexico* as an inspiration for "The Sleepers" also suggests that a new interpretation may be given to the poem's puzzling opening lines—a darker, colder meaning, related to the victims of the wreck:

> I wander all night in my vision,
> Stepping with light feet, swiftly and noiselessly stepping and stopping.
> Bending with open eyes over the shut eyes of sleepers,
> Wandering and confused, lost to myself, ill-assorted, contradictory,
> Pausing, gazing, bending and stopping.
>
> How solemn they look there, stretch'd and still,
> How quiet they breathe, the little children in their cradles.
>
> The wretched features of ennuyés,[43] the white features of corpses . . .

The above stanza evokes images from the letter written by a visitor to Lott's barn. That letter appears in full on pages 202-204 of this book. It describes in poignant detail the visitor's impressions as he wanders among the dozens of frozen bodies recovered from the *Mexico*. The letter was published in February 1837. It was reprinted that same month in the *Long Island Democrat*, and was almost certainly read by Whitman.

It is possible to interpret the first stanza of "The Sleepers" without reference to the children lying in Lott's barn, but once the connection is made, the contrasting images of children fast asleep in bed, and of life-like

---

[43] Ennuyés: bored people.

corpses from the wreck, take their place alongside Whitman's numerous mixed images of life, death, and the sea.

The following poem is one of Whitman's most beautiful. It is one which evokes his memories of Long Island's sandy beaches, sea-life, and shipwreck dirges:

As I Ebb'd with the Ocean of Life

1

As I ebb'd with the ocean of life,
As I wended the shores I know,
As I walk'd where the ripples continually wash you Paumanok,
Where they rustle up hoarse and sibilant,
Where the fierce old mother endlessly cries for her castaways,
I musing late in the autumn day, gazing off southward,
Held by this electric self out of pride of which I utter poems,
Was seiz'd by the spirit that trails the lines underfoot,
The rim, the sediment that stands for all the water and all the land of
    the globe.

Fascinated, my eyes reverting from the south, dropt, to follow those
    slender windrows,
Chaff, straw, splinters of wood, weeds, and the sea-gluten,
Scum, scales, from shining rocks, leaves of salt lettuce, left by the
    tide,
Miles walking, the sound of breaking waves the other side of me,
Paumanok there and then as I thought the old thought of likenesses,
These you presented to me you fish-shaped island,
As I wended the shores I know,
As I walk'd with that electric self seeking types.

2

As I wend the shores I know not,
As I list to the dirge, the voices of men and women wreck'd,
As I inhale the impalpable breezes that set in upon me,
As the ocean so mysteriously rolls toward me closer and closer,
I too but signify at the utmost a little wash'd-up drift,
A few sands and dead leaves to gather,
Gather, and merge myself as part of the sands and drift. . .

3

I too Paumanok,
I too have bubbled up, floated the measureless float, and been
    wash'd on your shores,

I too am but a trail of drift and debris,
I too leave little wrecks upon you, you fish-shaped island.

In the following lines of "Song of Myself" (stanza 33), Whitman may have been inspired by the heroes of the *Mexico* and the *Bristol*, and the people that were saved from certain death.

How he saved the drifting company at last,
How the lank loose-gown'd women look'd when boated from
     the side of their prepared graves,
How the silent old-faced infants and the lifted sick, and the
     sharp-lipp'd unshaven men;
All this I swallow, it tastes good, I like it well, it becomes mine,
I am the man, I suffer'd, I was there.

Some of Whitman's most accessible works are his prose reminiscences. "Paumanok, and My Life on It as Child and Young Man" (in *Specimen Days*) recounts his days fishing, clamming, and wandering the bays and coasts of Long Island. It is no wonder he wrote that he was "almost a witness" to the wrecks of the *Bristol* and the *Mexico*, for he had walked the bay ice in winter just as rescuer Raynor Smith and his sons had, and he had sailed along the South Shore barrier beaches on the bay and the ocean side. He also had, as he put it, a "plentiful acquaintance" with the New York pilots and discussed "marine incidents" with them.

Paumanok, and My Life on It as Child and Young Man[44]

Inside the outer bars or beach this south bay is everywhere comparatively shallow; of cold winters all thick ice on the surface. As a boy I often went forth with a chum or two, on those frozen fields, with hand-sled, axe and eel-spear, after messes of eels. We would cut holes in the ice, sometimes striking quite an eel-bonanza, and filling our baskets with great, fat, sweet, white-meated fellows. The scenes, the ice, drawing the hand-sled, cutting holes, spearing the eels, &c., were of course just such fun as is dearest to boyhood. The shores of this bay, winter and summer, and my doings there in early life, are woven all through L. of G. One sport I was very fond of was to go on a bay-party in summer to gather sea-gulls' eggs. (The gulls lay two or three eggs, more than half the size of hen's eggs, right on the sand, and leave the sun's heat to hatch them.)

---

[44] The author, a dyed-in-the wool Long Islander, must be excused for quoting Whitman at such length about the island they both love.

The eastern end of Long Island, the Peconic bay region, I knew quite well too—sail'd more than once around Shelter Island, and down to Montauk—spent many an hour on Turtle hill by the old light-house, on the extreme point, looking out over the ceaseless roll of the Atlantic. I used to like to go down there and fraternize with the blue-fishers, or the annual squads of sea-bass takers. Sometimes, along Montauk peninsula (it is some 15 miles long, and good grazing) met the strange, unkempt, half-barbarous herdsmen, at that time living there entirely aloof from society or civilization, in charge, on those rich pasturages, of vast droves of horses, kine or sheep, own'd by farmers of the eastern towns. Sometimes, too, the few remaining Indians, or half-breeds, at that period left on Montauk peninsula, but now I believe altogether extinct.

More in the middle of the island were the spreading Hempstead plains, then (1830–'40) quite prairie-like, open, uninhabited, rather sterile, cover'd with kill-calf and huckleberry bushes, yet plenty of fair pasture for the cattle, mostly milch-cows, who fed there by hundreds, even thousands, and at evening (the plains too were own'd by the towns, and this was the use of them in common) might be seen taking their way home, branching off regularly in the right places. I have often been out on the edges of these plains toward sundown, and can yet recall in fancy the interminable cow-processions, and hear the music of the tin or copper bells clanking far or near, and breathe the cool of the sweet and slightly aromatic evening air, and note the sunset.

Through the same region of the island, but further east, extended wide central tracts of pine and scrub-oak (charcoal was largely made here) monotonous and sterile. But many a good day or half-day did I have, wandering through those solitary cross-roads, inhaling the peculiar and wild aroma. Here, and all along the island and its shores, I spent intervals many years, all seasons, sometimes riding, sometimes boating, but generally afoot (I was always then a good walker) absorbing fields, shores, marine incidents, characters, the bay-men, farmers, pilots—always had a plentiful acquaintance with the latter, and with fishermen—went every summer on sailing trips—always liked the bare sea-beach, south side, and have some of my happiest hours on it to this day.

As I write, the whole experience comes back to me after the lapse of forty and more years—the soothing rustle of the waves, and the saline smell—boyhood's times, the clam-digging, barefoot, and with trowsers roll'd up—hauling down the creek—the perfume of the sedge-meadows—the hay-boat, and the chowder and fishing excursions;—or, of later years, little voyages down and out New York bay, in the pilot boats. Those same later years, also, while living in Brooklyn (1836–'50) I went regularly every week in the mild seasons down to Coney island, at that time a long, bare unfrequented shore, which I had all to myself, and where I loved, after bathing, to race up and down the hard sand, and declaim Homer or Shakspere to the surf and sea-gulls by the hour. But I am getting ahead too rapidly, and must keep more in my traces. [45]

---

[45] Whitman's memory for dates is sometimes suspect. He lived in Brooklyn in 1835, working as a printer's apprentice, but moved back to Long Island after the great fire of December, 1835 destroyed much of New York City. He did not move back to Brooklyn until 1841. Whitman here uses an alternate spelling for *Shakespeare.*

Nathaniel Currier's Print
and
Hanington's Dioramas

The New York City firm of Currier & Ives had its start in 1834 as Stoddard and Currier. In 1835, Nathaniel Currier went it alone and called the firm N. Currier, Lithographer. The name everyone is familiar with today, Currier & Ives, was adopted in 1857 and lasted until 1907. The business of the firm was just what their slogan said it was: "Printmakers to the People." They employed artists to draw subjects of everyday American life—sports, entertainment, and children playing. Lithographs of these drawings were sold directly to the public for framing and display in their homes.

The firm also produced prints of newsworthy events, and sold them as inserts in newspapers in the days before photography. Although Currier did not create a lithograph of the wreck of the *Bristol*, the firm was literally "on the spot" for the wreck of the *Mexico*. Just days after the wreck, the artist H. Sewell left Currier's Manhattan office at Nassau and Spruce Streets and went by ferry, stagecoach, carriage, and boat out to Hempstead Beach.

Sewell did not arrive at the scene in time to observe the action that he wanted to include in his drawing. Indeed, the barque was nearly in splinters by the time he got there. Instead, he interviewed eyewitnesses in order to construct a dramatic re-creation of Raynor Smith's and his boat crew's rescue. The accuracy of Sewell's detail is remarkable: powerful wind, giant waves, torn sails, drifting sea-ice, a smashed yawl near the beach, the foremast and main both down, the mizzen barely standing, and passengers at the rail waving desperately for help. The print was published as an insert in the *New York Sun* on January 25, 1837. In a sense, this was a forerunner of journalistic photography.

Dreadful WRECK of the MEXICO on HEMPSTEAD BEACH, Jany 2nd 1837; As now Exhibiting at HANINGTONS DIORAMAS.
(Copy-Right Secured.)
Pub'd at the Sun Office by Bi ijs
Drawn on the Spot by H Sewel.
N Currier's Lith cor of Nassau & Spruce St
Perished in all—115 Souls.

Nathaniel Currier's "Dreadful Wreck of the *Mexico* on Hempstead Beach"
"Drawn on the spot" by H. Sewell
Published as an insert in the *New York Sun*, January 25, 1837.

Sewell's drawing was also used to illustrate posted handbills for Hanington's Dioramas. Between 1832 and 1856, the visionary artists William and Henry Hanington anticipated the popularity of newsreels by one hundred years, when they produced "peristrephic dioramas," sometimes called "moving panoramas," of current events. The Hanington brothers' broadside (an advertisement printed on one large sheet of paper) invited the public to come each evening at half-past eight to the City Saloon, on lower Broadway, across from St. Paul's Church.

For twenty-five cents, the public saw eight different dramatic scenarios. Large, multi-colored, canvas paintings were sewn together and attached to giant rollers. As the various lighted scenes were slowly revealed to the seated viewers, appropriate piano music was played by "Professor of the Piano, Monsieur Foures, from Paris."

The *Mexico* diorama created a New York sensation. A three-masted vessel was seen fighting her way through heavy seas; flakes of artificial snow fell from above; sound effects came from behind the canvas; there were howling winds, sails flapping in the breeze, bells ringing, wreck guns firing, and women and children screaming for help. Some in the audience were so taken by the drama as it unfolded that they shouted out, "No!" and "Save them!" It was reported that people in the audience rushed toward the rolling canvas and had to be restrained by their neighbors.

Can Newydd
Llong-DDrylliad Y *Mexico*

Despite the large number of Irish, Scottish, English, and Welsh citizens lost in the wrecks of the *Bristol* and the *Mexico*, overseas reports simply repeated straightforward statistical facts about the wrecks, taken verbatim from New York newspapers. A search of newspaper collections in libraries in Ireland, England, Scotland, and Wales, uncovered only one item that appeared to be an independent reaction to the wrecks. It was a Welsh broadside, *Can Newydd*, published in 1837. However, the Welsh piece is, in fact, a translation of a lengthy poem—since lost—published in New York's *Weekly Chronicle* newspaper. The broadside is described in the catalog of the National Library of Wales as follows:

> This song depicts the tragic conditions that led to the shipwreck of the *Mexico*. When the ship ran aground 26 miles from Sandyhook, Hempstead, only the captain and 7 seamen were rescued out of the 104 migrants and 12 seamen on board. The song conveys the stormy conditions and the grim fate of the migrants.[46]

The artist, who may be Welsh, takes liberties with the facts: there was no lighthouse near the wreck; the *Mexico*—a U.S. ship—would not have been flying what appears to be an English flag at the stern; and two of the masts had already been chopped down by the time Raynor Smith launched his surfboat. Even so, the print wonderfully captures the drama of a rescue at sea. The unanswered question is: Why did a Welsh broadside present such a difficult poetic translation, along with such an elaborately composed image

---

[46] The National Library of Wales' catalog description does not match the *Mexico's* actual numbers, except for persons rescued—the captain and 7 seamen.

of the wreck? It is known that the *Bristol* had Welshmen aboard who died.
Perhaps the *Mexico* did as well.

**Can Newydd,
Yn Rhoddi Hannes
Llong-DDrylliad Y Mexico,
Ar Ei Thaith I America**

(New Piece of Poetry /
Tells the Actual Story /
Of a Ship-wreck *Mexico*, /
On its Journey to America)

National Library of Wales.

The Supreme Court Decides *U.S. v. Coombs*

When valuable freight washed ashore from the wreck of the *Bristol* and was seized by onlookers, five of the alleged thieves were taken into custody. They were indicted in federal court under the ninth section of the *Congressional Act of 1825*, Chapter 276:

> That if any person shall plunder, steal, or destroy any money, goods, merchandise, or other effects from, or belonging to, any ship or vessel, or boat, or raft which shall be in distress, or which shall be wrecked, lost, stranded, or cast away upon the sea, or upon any reef, shoal, bank, or rocks of the sea, or in any place within the admiralty or maritime jurisdiction of the United States; or if any person or persons shall willfully obstruct the escape of any person endeavouring to save his or her life from such ship or vessel, boat or raft, or the wreck thereof; or if any person shall hold out or show any false light or lights, or extinguish any true light, with intention to bring any ship or vessel, boat or raft, being or sailing upon the sea, into danger or distress, or shipwreck; every person so offending, his or their counsellors, aiders or abettors, shall be deemed guilty of felony; and shall, on conviction thereof, be punished by a fine, not exceeding five thousand dollars, and imprisonment and confinement at hard labour, not exceeding ten years, according to the aggravation of the offence.

One of the indicted men, Lawrence Coombs, appealed to the New York Southern District circuit court on the grounds that the 1825 federal law went beyond Congress' constitutional powers. Coombs claimed that when a wreck took place at sea, it was unconstitutional for the federal government to extend the reach of its "maritime jurisdiction" beyond the high tide mark. He went on to say that any valuables that washed up on shore above that mark were in the jurisdiction of a state—New York State in this case, where the penalty would be less severe.

The circuit court judges were unable to agree on the constitutionality of the charges, so they agreed to submit a rare non-finding—a "division of opinion" it was called—in other words, a tie. Thus, the case was automatically appealed to the U.S. Supreme Court and its newly appointed Chief Justice, Roger B. Taney.

In 1838, when the Coombs case was heard, the court was still mindful of its influential previous Chief Justice, John Marshall, who had repeatedly confirmed the supremacy of federal law over state law. The Taney court followed Justice Marshall's lead in the Coombs case. Their decision firmly established the federal government's jurisdiction over piracy whether committed at sea or on shore, and whether or not it was also a state crime. The transcript also provided certain details of the actual crime committed at Rockaway Beach, details not recorded elsewhere.

Ref: U.S. Supreme Court – U.S. v. COOMBS, 37 U.S. 72
January Term, 1838

This is a case, certified upon a division of opinion of the judges of the circuit court, for the southern district of New York. The case, as stated in the record, is as follows:

Lawrence Coombs was indicted . . . for having, on the 21st of November, 1836, feloniously stolen, at Rockaway Beach, in the southern district of New York, one trunk of the [nominal] value of five dollars, one package of yarn of the value of five dollars, one package of silk of the value of five dollars, one roll of ribbons of the value of five dollars, one package of muslin of the value of five dollars, and six pairs of hose of the value of five dollars, which said goods, wares and merchandise, belonged to the ship *Bristol*, the said ship then being in distress, and cast away on a shoal of the sea, on the coast of the state of New York, within the southern district of New York. On this indictment the prisoner was arraigned, and pled not guilty; and put himself upon his country for trial.

It was admitted, that the goods mentioned in the indictment, and which belonged to the said ship *Bristol*, were taken above the high water mark, upon the beach, in the county of Queens; whereupon, the question arose whether the offence committed was within the jurisdiction of the court; and on this point the judges [of the circuit court] were opposed in opinion.

Justice Story delivered the opinion of the court, which found against defendant Coombs. Story first discussed salvage cases from English Common Law and *Blackstone's Commentary,* which concluded that, "in cases of salvage . . . no process of the court could be served on land, but only on the water." Justice Story then brushed the English cases aside when he described them as "wholly inapplicable to the courts of the United States." The court's central finding was that Congress and the federal courts *did* have jurisdiction in the *Coombs* case even though the crime was committed *above* the high water mark. The decision was based on the Constitution's delegation of powers to Congress in the "Commerce Clause," which Justice Story cited as follows:

> [the power] to regulate commerce with foreign nations, and among the several states; and, as connected with these, the power to make all laws which shall be necessary and proper for carrying into execution the foregoing power, &c.

Justice Story applied this general principle to the *Coombs* case, as follows:

> The plundering, stealing, or destroying need not, then, be [taken directly] from any ship or vessel. It is sufficient if it be of property "belonging to any ship or vessel." It is nowhere stated that this property, belonging to any ship or vessel, shall be in any of the enumerated places [i.e., "upon the sea, or upon any reef, shoal, bank, or rocks"] when the offence is committed; but only that it shall be property belonging to the ship or vessel, which is in distress, or wrecked, lost, stranded, or cast away. Locality, then, is attached to the ship or vessel, and not to the property plundered, stolen, or destroyed. And this qualification is important, because it is manifest congress possess no authority to punish offences of this sort generally, when committed on land; but only to punish them when connected with foreign trade and navigation, or with trade and navigation among the several states.

> In the next place, the mischiefs intended to be suppressed by the section are precisely the same, whether the offence be committed on the shore, or below high water mark. There is, and there can be, no sound reason why congress should punish the offence when committed below high water mark, which would not apply equally to the offence when committed above high water mark. In such case, the wrong and injury to the owners, and to commerce and navigation, is the same; and the public policy of affording complete protection to property, commerce, and navigation,

against lawless and unprincipled freebooters, is also in each case
the same.

Coombs established precedent for later expansions of federal power
pursuant to the Commerce Clause. See, for example, *United States v. E. C.
Knight Co.*, 156 US 1, 13 (1895) ("Contracts to buy, sell, or exchange goods
to be transported among the several States, the transportation and its
instrumentalities . . . may be regulated").

The Sea Rescue Mission of the U.S. Coast Guard

The funnel-shaped New York Bight—with shoals along its sides and at its end—was determined to be so dangerous to shipping that, in 1831, the U.S. Treasury Department ordered the revenue cutter *Rush* to cruise the coast of Long Island from Sandy Hook to Montauk, and the cutter *Alert* to cruise the Jersey coast from Sandy Hook to Cape May. Their task was to assist "vessels found on the coasts in distress." Within a month, the *Rush* was herself wrecked on Long Island, and the plan was dropped. The coastal cutters returned to their mission of law enforcement and military readiness.

On February 11, 1837, with the wrecks of the *Bristol* and the *Mexico* clearly in mind, the New York Chamber of Commerce sent a "memorial" to Congress asking the federal government to take steps to prevent such tragedies. The Chamber asked that the revenue cutters' sea rescue service be permanently reinstituted. A bill was passed by Congress on December 22, 1837, under which cutters once again were sent out "to cruise upon the coast, in the severe portion of the season . . . to afford such aid to distressed navigators as their circumstance and necessities may require; and such public vessels shall go to sea prepared fully to render such assistance." Furthermore, the cutters were required to be "prepared to afford aid in case of shipwreck." From that day forward, the United States Coast Guard has performed sea rescues as a vital part of its mission. (Source: John Spears "Story of Beneficent Shipwrecks," *New York Times* July 24, 1907)

U.S. Coast Guard Sea Rescue Mission 1837 to today

U.S. Coast Guard District 8

The U.S. Lifesaving Service

Many authorities cite 1848 as the year when the U.S. Lifesaving Service was created by the federal government, following some awful wrecks off the New Jersey coast. Indeed, that was when Congress authorized $10,000 to provide "surfboats, rockets, carronades and other necessary apparatus for the better preservation of life and property from ship-wrecks on the coasts." But it can be argued that the date of origin should in fact be 1837, and that the service arose as a result of the wrecks of the *Bristol* and the *Mexico*. In 1837, Congress issued a redefinition of the mission of the U.S. Lighthouse Service, when it required lighthouse keepers to meet a new standard by having "fitness for life saving in the surf" (Spears, *New York Times,* July 24, 1907). Raynor Rock Smith, the hero of the wreck of the *Mexico,* was named keeper of the Fire Island Light. No one could argue that Smith lacked fitness for "life saving in the surf." Daniel Treadwell wrote in his journal, *Personal Reminiscences* (1842) that the rescue of the *Mexico*, led to the "incorporation of the Life Saving Benevolent Association." This organization still exists today. Operating out of the Seamen's Church Institute in New York City, the association continues to make monetary rewards to rescuers.

Surf Man on Patrol
www.wreckhunter.net/gal-marhist.htm

The Ambrose Lightship

When the twin Navesink Lights were constructed on the New Jersey Highlands in 1828, their visibility from a masthead fifty miles at sea was thought to make the Sandy Hook Lightship redundant; and so it was moved from the New York Bight to the Delaware Cape, where the need was deemed to be greater. Immediately following the wrecks of the *Bristol* and the *Mexico*, the Department of the Treasury received numerous complaints about the removal of the lightship. The complainants argued that if the lightship had been on station in the Bight, the captains of the *Bristol* and the *Mexico* could have used the lightship's bell and lights as references in keeping safely out to sea, and yet not too distant from the coasts. Within months of the two wrecks, the 230-ton lightship *W-W* was placed on station seven miles out in the Bight. Lightships remained there until 1967, when the station known as the Ambrose Lightship was discontinued.

Passing Ambrose Lightship
Edward Moran (1829-1901)

Conclusion

The story of the wrecks of the *Bristol* and the *Mexico* concludes where the Preface and Chapter One of this book began, at the Mariners Burying Ground in the Old Sand Hole Cemetery (now called the Rockville Cemetery). That is where, even today, the impact of the tragedies can be felt. The four-foot-high mound on which the Mariners Monument rests was piled there in 1837 by church sexton Thomas Shore and his helpers. The soil came from the mass grave where the bodies of passengers Judy and William Pepper are buried in an eternal embrace. They lie near their two daughters, and shoulder to shoulder with the other victims of the two wrecks, 139 bodies in all.

Go to the monument. Climb the steep mound without any feeling of disrespect. Touch the weather-worn biblical quotation and the poetic inscriptions carved into the white marble. Pass your hand over the south face, the one with the *Bristol's* text, and imagine the claustrophobic horror of the tall ship's watery deathtrap. Recall the infamous acts of the body robbers on shore, but remember also the brave deeds of the Rockaway boatmen and of Captain McKown, whose name is written there.

Examine the inscriptions on the monument's north face, where even on a summer day you can feel the coldness of the stone. Captain Winslow's name is carved there. It recalls Raynor Smith's desperate rescue of just eight people, and the agony of the men, women, and children left to freeze to death on the *Mexico's* open deck off Long Beach.

Look around and try to imagine where the long trenches lay, and where the black sailors from the *Mexico* are buried. The wooden markers that once identified their graves rotted away more than a century ago, so the precise location is not known.

Two hundred and fifteen lives were lost in the two wrecks. Their deaths were the result of the greed and self-interest of politicians, shipowners, harbor pilots, passenger brokers, and one of the captains, all of whom saw emigrants as less valuable than cargos. It is sadly true that the two wrecks, the worst accidental mass deaths in the history of the United States up to 1837, have been virtually forgotten after the passage of almost 175 years. However, the deaths of all these passengers—Irishmen, Englishmen, Welshmen, and Scots—and sailors were not in vain. That is because the story of the twin tragedies, as presented by artists, poets, and newspapermen, helped alter the consciousness of rich and powerful men of New York, New Jersey, and Washington, D.C. As a result, steps were soon taken to make sea travel safer for the millions of emigrants to follow.

The farmers and baymen of Long Island should be remembered, too. Without the monument they erected, this story would not have been rediscovered.

Appendix

Place-names:

Since 1644, the **Town of Hempstead** has had local jurisdiction over much of the southwestern quadrant of today's Nassau County. The **village of Hempstead**, a smaller, separate governmental entity from the town, was also established in 1644, and has been the seat of Hempstead Town government ever since that date. The **Village of Hempstead** was incorporated in 1853.

Near Rockaway first appeared in Town of Hempstead records in 1670, as Nere Rocoway, from the Indian name, Rechquaakie (a sandy place). The name Near Rockaway described those town lands lying *nearer* to the town seat at Hempstead village, while **Far Rockaway**, indicated town lands lying *farther* away, i.e., toward the ocean and **Rockaway Beach**. For the next two hundred years, the name Near Rockaway continued to be used to describe the area that today comprises **East Rockaway**, **Lynbrook**, **Oceanside**, and **Rockville Centre**. The name Near Rockaway disappeared from use in the late nineteenth century, unlike some other Long Island regional names such as the Five Towns, the North Fork, the Three Villages, and the Hamptons.

The Mariners Burying Ground was laid out in 1837, at the **Old Sand Hole Cemetery** adjacent to the **Old Sand Hole Church** in Near Rockaway. The origin of the name Old Sand Hole is uncertain, but it probably refers to the slightly elevated sandy grounds that made the site a good place for burials and for obtaining sand for making bricks. The last of three churches at the site burned down in 1912, but the **Old Sand Hole Cemetery** continues to be used for a limited number of burials. The Old Sand Hole name persisted well into the twentieth century, when the operators of the cemetery trust renamed it the **Rockville Cemetery**, for marketing reasons. The cemetery occupies a small piece of land between today's incorporated villages of **Lynbrook** and **Rockville Centre**. The cemetery is mostly on an unincorporated parcel of the Town of Hempstead, with a small sliver in Lynbrook. It has a Lynbrook postal address.

Steamboats:

The first steam-driven tugboat in New York Harbor—that is, a vessel used to pull or push other sea-going vessels and not just canal barges—was the *Nautilus*, a side-wheeler used as a passenger and freight ferry between Staten Island and New York. The steam-tug business happened by accident. In the winter of 1818, the *Nautilus* was tied up at her dock in Staten Island when a ship in the Narrows, the *Corsair*, was seen to be in trouble. The *Nautilus* got under steam, went out, and towed the *Corsair* to port. In 1828, the first regular commercial tug in New York Harbor came into being when the *Rufus W. King* was put in service. The *King* performed a variety of jobs such as transporting pilots to their pilot boats and news reporters to their news boats off the Hook, towing sailing ships out to the Hook, and moving passengers between the Battery and ships laying-to off the Hook.

On October 26, 1825, a Finger Lakes steamboat, the *Seneca Chief,* left Buffalo, New York, filled with upstate dignitaries. This was the first boat ever to attempt a transit of the full 363-mile length of the Erie Canal. On her arrival ten days later at New York Harbor, the vessel was hailed with the cry, "Whence came you and where are you bound?" The answered shout was, "From Lake Erie, bound for Sandy Hook!" The ensuing celebration was the most spectacular the city had ever experienced, with fireworks and parades attracting 100,000 people, almost two-thirds of the city's population. This was the largest public gathering that had ever been seen in North America.

The celebration was justified, for the opening of the Erie Canal turned New York City into an economic engine, and set it apart from any other city in the world. By 1836, when the *Bristol* and the *Mexico* set out on their fateful voyages, the port city of New York was unquestionably America's greatest city, leaving Boston, New Orleans, Philadelphia, and Baltimore as distant competitors. "The Ditch," only four feet deep and forty feet wide, with eighty-three locks, created easy access to the rapidly developing interior of Western New York, Western Pennsylvania, Ohio, and the Great Lakes. The economics were simple: freight rates from Buffalo to New York fell from one hundred dollars a ton to six dollars a ton.

The same year that the Erie Canal opened, in 1825, the 153-ton steamer *Henry Eckford* was built according to specifications dictated by the width and depth of the canal. Her task, which she faithfully executed until she exploded and sank in New York Harbor in 1841, was to tow grain barges through the canal and down the Hudson River. By 1836, steamboats and canals were still a profitable combination, but railroads were already undermining the Erie Canal's economic advantage in transporting goods from America's interior, and steamboats were moving their business away from the canals and out to sea.

Glossary
Nineteenth-Century Sailing Terms

Abaft – Toward the rear of a boat, or behind an area of the boat.

Barque - A sailing ship with three or (less commonly) four masts whose sails are fixed breadthways (square) except for the last mast, which has its sail running lengthwise (fore-and-aft). Also spelled *bark*.

Beat - To sail as nearly as possible in the direction from which the wind is blowing.

Bight - A narrowing bend or indentation in a shoreline.

Boom - A beam to which the bottom edge of a sail is attached in order to hold the sail at an advantageous angle to the wind.

Bowsprit - A spar that projects forward from the stem (the main upright timber at the bow) of a ship, to which the stays of the foremast are fastened.

Brig - A vessel having two masts, fore and main. The masts are square rigged, but the main mast has, in addition, a gaff main sail.

Brigantine - A vessel having two masts, fore and main. The foremast is square and the main mast is fore-and-aft rigged.

Broach - To be turned broadside to the wind, for example, by heavy seas, with a risk of capsizing.

Bull's-eye - A small round window, especially a disk of thick glass in a ship's sides or deck for letting in light below deck.

Bulwark - The sides of a ship projecting above the deck.

Capstan - A rotating machine with spindles used to pull ropes and chains.

Chock - Oval-shaped castings, either open or closed on top, and fitted with or without rollers, through which hawsers and lines are passed.

Cleat - A wood or metal fitting having two projecting arms or horns to which a sheet, halyard, or other rope is tied.

Clipper - A ship with a sharp bow, designed for speed.

Crosstrees - The horizontal struts near the upper end of the topmast. On modern sailboats the same function is provided by spreaders.

Cutter - A ship's boat, powered by oars and used for transporting passengers and light cargo. Also a small, lightly armed patrol boat used by the Coast Guard or customs department. Also a single-masted sailing vessel on which the mast is positioned farther aft than on a sloop.

Displacement - The amount of water (by weight) that is forced to move by a ship floating or submerged in it.

Entrepot - A port where merchandise can be imported and re-exported without paying import duties.

Fathom - Depth of water. One fathom equals six feet.

Fore and aft rigged - Type of sails that run lengthwise, instead of across the ship.

Foremast - The mast nearest the front or bow of a vessel with two or more masts.

Freeboard - The distance between the deck of a ship and the level of the water.

Gaff rigged – A boat with a fore-and-aft, four-sided sail extending aft of the mast. The upper edge of the sail is held up by a spar (the gaff) which extends aft from the mast.

Gig - A light rowboat carried on board a sailing ship.

Grog - A heated mixture of rum, water, and sugar.

Halyard - A rope used to raise or lower, for example, a sail or flag.

Hawser - A heavy rope that is used when mooring a ship or for towing.

Heel - To lean over to one side, e.g., a ship heeling.

Holystone - A piece of soft sandstone used for scouring the decks of ships.

Jib - A triangular, fore and aft sail attached to a foremast stay.

Keelson - A timber fastened along (and above) the keel of a ship or boat for stiffness and strength.

Kedge - To move a vessel by pulling on a rope or cable attached to a light anchor. Also, the anchor itself.

Kid - A wide, high-sided bowl containing the crew's meal.

Knee timbers - A block of wood (often live oak) having a natural angular shape and used for connecting the deck beams to the frames in a wooden vessel.

Knot - A measurement of speed at sea, equal to 1.15 statute miles per hour.

Larboard - the port or left side of a vessel.

Lee, Leeward - The side of a boat that lies away from the direction of the wind.

Lighter - A flat-bottomed open cargo boat, used especially for taking goods to or from a larger vessel.

Log line - A line used to determine a ship's speed in knots, for entry in the ship's log. The line was on a large spool and had knots tied into it every 47' 3". A wedge of wood about 18" in size was tied to one end of the rope. The end was thrown overboard at the ship's stern. One man held the spool of rope as it played out; another man started a sandglass filled with thirty seconds of sand; and a third man counted the knots as they passed over the stern board. When the thirty seconds of sand expired, the time keeper called out and the counting stopped.

Longboat - A large pulling boat with a square stern, intended for general utility.

Mainsail - The principal sail carried by the main mast.

Mainmast - The principal mast on a sailing ship with more than one mast, usually either the foremost mast or the second from the bow. On the *Bristol* and the *Mexico*, the main was the middle of the three masts.

Marlinspike - A tapering pointed metal implement used by riggers and sail makers to open the strands of rope in splicing and as a general-purpose lever.

Mizzenmast - On a ship with three or more masts, the third mast from the front.

North River - The lower Hudson River, alongside Manhattan.

Overhead - The top surface of an enclosed space on a ship.

Packet - Any vessel sailing on a schedule, whether a clipper, schooner, barque, etc.

Painter - A rope attached to the front of a small boat, and used to tie it to something such as a mooring.

Prize - A ship or its contents taken by another ship in wartime.

Reef - To reduce a sail's area by rolling or folding that portion adjacent to a yard or boom and securing it. In square sails this reduction is made at the top of the sail, while in fore-and-aft sails it is done at the bottom. Additional reductions are accomplished through double-reefing and triple-reefing.

Round-to - To turn the bow of a ship toward the wind, thus slowing it.

Schooner - A sailing ship with at least two masts and with sails set lengthways (fore and aft).

Sheet - A line used to change the sail's position. It is attached to a bottom corner of the sail.

Shears (or sheers) - An apparatus rigged up for raising and moving heavy weights where a crane is not available.

Ship - Generally, any large vessel; specifically, a vessel with three or more masts all square-rigged.

Sloop - A single-masted sailboat, rigged fore and aft, with an additional forward sail extending from the foremast to the bowsprit.

Sovereign - A British gold coin worth one pound sterling, worth $115 today.

Spar - A pole serving as a mast, boom, gaff, yard, bowsprit, etc.

Spencer - A trysail carried at the foremast or mainmast, often set with a gaff and no boom.

Square-rigged - Rectangular sails running across the ship instead of fore and aft.

Stays - The ropes, whether hemp or wire, that support the lower masts, topmasts, top-gallant masts, etc.

Staysails - Triangular fore-and-aft sails attached to the stays.

Steerage - The part of a passenger ship, whether in the area near the rudder and steering gear or not, that was allotted to those passengers who traveled at the cheapest rate.

Stunsail - An additional sail on an extra yard and boom at either side of a square sail, for use in light winds. (Also called a studding-sail.)

Supercargo - The person aboard a ship in charge of all financial matters relating to the cargo.

Tack - To sail a ship against the direction of the wind by moving in a zigzag pattern from one tack to another, bringing her bow across the wind at each turn.

Taffrail - The upper, flat, and often carved part of a ship's stern, and the rail around it.

Topgallant - Relating to the mast, yard, rigging, or sails of the third mast-section up from the deck, the one above the top mast.

Topsails - Relating to the mast, yard, rigging or sails of the second mast-section up from the deck, the one above the main mast.

Trysail - A strong sail used in stormy weather, either square or triangular, and set to run parallel to the length of the ship (fore and aft).

'Tween deck - The between deck, shortened to 'tween deck, was the deck immediately below the main deck of a sailing ship. It was frequently used for cargo, given a cursory cleaning after the cargo was discharged, and then fitted-out with temporary partitions and bunks for steerage accommodation.

Yard - A spar attached at its middle portion to a mast and running across a vessel as a support for a square sail. The end of the yard is the yardarm.

Yawl - A small boat kept on a ship, rowed by four or six people.

Bibliography

Books, Articles, eBooks, Maps, and Manuscripts

Albion, Robert Greenhalgh. *The Rise of the Port of New York*. New York: Charles Scribner's Sons, 1939.

_____ . *Square-Riggers on Schedule*, Princeton, NJ: Princeton University Press, 1938.

Barber, John Warner and Henry Howe. *Historical Collections of the State of New York,* New York: S. Tuttle, 1842. (A public domain book at Books.Google.com.)

Basset, Preston and Arthur L. Hodges. *History of Rockville Centre*. Uniondale, NY: Salisbury Printers, 1969.

Bingley, Thomas. *Shipwrecks and Other Disasters at Sea*. Boston: Tappan and Dennet, 1842.

Bolster, W. Jeffrey. *Black Jacks – African American Seamen in the Age of Sail*. Cambridge, MA: Harvard University Press, 1997.

Bromwell, William J. *History of Immigration to the United States*. New York: Redfield, 1856. (A public domain book at Books.Google.com.)

Burrows, Edwin G. and Mike Wallace. *Gotham: A History of the City of New York*. New York: Oxford University Press, 1999.

Chambers, Whittaker. *Witness*. 1952. Reprint: Washington, DC: Regnery Gateway, 1987.

Colton, J.H. *Travelers Map of Long Island*, 1848. Long Island Studies Institute at Hofstra University, Hempstead, NY.

Cooper, James Fenimore. *Ned Myers; or, A Life Before the Mast*, 1843. (Published online at Project Guttenberg: www.gutenberg.org/etext/9788.)

Cornell, Frederick William. "The Raynor Family," 1946. Freeport, NY: Manuscript at the Freeport Historical Society.

Cutter, William Richard, ed. *Genealogical and Personal Memories Relating to the Families of the State of Massachusetts*, Vol. 4. New York: Lewis Historical Publishing, 1910. (A public domain book at Books.Google.com.)

Dana, Richard. *Two Years Before the Mast*. 1840. Cornwall, NY: Dodd Mead & Co., 1946. (Project Guttenberg: www.gutenberg.org/etext/4277)

Douglas, Frederick. The Life and Times of Frederick Douglass, Written by Himself. Boston: De Wolfe & Fiske Co., 1892. (http://docsouth.unc.edu/neh/dougl92/ menu.html)

Durant, John and Alice. *Pictorial History of Ships on the High Seas and Inland Waters*. Toronto: A.S. Barnes and Co., 1953.

Ellms, Charles. *Tragedies of the Seas*. Philadelphia: Carey & Hart, 1841. (A public domain book at Books.Google.com.)

Fairburn, William Armstrong. *Merchant Sail*. Vol. II. Lovell, ME: Fairburn Marine Educational Foundation Center, 1945-1955.

Funell, Bertha H. *Walt Whitman on Long Island*. Port Washington, NY: Kennikat Press, 1971.

Gibbs, George, *Map of an Estate Belonging to M. Hogan, Esq.* Located in New-York Historical Society Map File.

Gribben, Arthur, ed. *The Great Famine and the Irish Diaspora in America.* Amherst: University of Massachusetts Press, 1999.

Hendrickson, Robert. *The Ocean Almanac.* New York: Doubleday, 1984.

Hewlett, Peter T. *The Property of Peter T. Hewlett – Near Rockaway.* An unpublished journal in the private collection of John Hewlett.

History of Queens County, with illustrations, Portraits & Sketches of Prominent Families and Individuals. New York: W.W. Munsell & Co.; 1882. <http://www.bklyn-genealogy-info.com/Queens/history/hempstead.html>

Holland, F. Ross. *Lighthouses.* New York: MetroBooks, 1995.

Holton, David Parsons and Frances K. Holton, *Winslow Memorial – Family Records of Winslows and their Descendants.* Vol. II. New York: Mrs. Frances K. Holton, 1888.

Isachsen, Y.W. et al. *Geology of New York: A Simplified Account. The State Education Department Educational Leaflet No. 28.* The University of the State of New York, 1991.

Johnson, Stanley C. *A History of Emigration to North America, 1763-1912.* London: George Routledge & Sons, Ltd., 1913. (A public domain book at Books.Google.com.)

Junger, Sebastian. *The Perfect Storm.* New York: Norton, 1997.

Kapp, Friedrich. *Immigration and the Commissioners of Emigration.* New York: The Nation Press, 1870. (A public domain book at Books.Google.com.)

Koch, Tom. *The Wreck of the William Brown: A True Tale of Overcrowded Lifeboats and Murder at Sea.* Camden, ME: McGraw-Hill Marine, 2004.

Krieg, Joann, P. "Walt Whitman, Paumanok's Son." *The Nassau County Historical Society Journal.* Vol. 60. 2005: 1-9.

Labaree, Benjamin W. *America and the Sea—A Maritime History.* Mystic, CT: Mystic Seaport Museum, 1998.

Lindsay, W.S. *History of Merchant Shipping.* Kessinger Publishing, 1876 (reprint: 2006).

MacGregor, David. *Merchant Sailing Ships 1815-1850.* Annapolis: Naval Institute Press, 1984.

Maddocks, Melvin. *The Atlantic Crossing. (The Seafarers).* Chicago: Time-Life Books, 1981.

Maritime History of New York, A. WPA Writers' Project, 1941. Reprint: New York: Haskell House, 1973.

Martin, J.H. *Pictorial History of Ships*. Norwalk, CT: Longmeadow Press, 1979.

Mattson, Arthur S. *The History of Lynbrook*. Lynbrook, NY: Lynbrook Historical Books, 2005.

McKay, Richard C. *South Street, A Maritime History*. Riverside, CT: 7 C's Press, 1969.

Melville, Herman. *Redburn – His First Voyage*, 1849. Project Gutenberg eBook. A public domain book at http://www.gutenberg.org/dirs/etext05/8redb10h.htm.

Metz, Clinton E. "Raynor Family History." Freeport, NY: Manuscript at the Freeport Historical Society, 1970.

Morse, Samuel Finley Breese. *Imminent Danger to the Free Institutions of the United States through Foreign Immigration*. 1835 Reprint; New York: Arno Press, 1969.

Nicholson, Asenath. *Annals of the Famine in Ireland*. New York: E. French, 1851. (Includes Patrick M'Kye's memorial of 1837.)

Paine, Ralph D. *The Old Merchant Marine, A Chronicle of American Ships and Sailors*, 1921. <http://www.authorama.com/old-merchant-marine-7.html>

Pennington, William, Joseph C. Hormblower, John S. Darcy, and Archer Gifford. *A Statement of the Facts and Circumstances Relative to the Operation of the Pilot Laws of New York*. Newark, NJ: M.S. Harrison & Co.,1840; Reprint: Whitefish, MT: Kessinger Publishing. 2008. (A public domain book at Books.Google.com.)

Prime, Nathaniel S. *A History of Long Island, from its First Settlement by Europeans, to the Year 1845, with Special Reference to its Ecclesiastical Concerns*. New York and Pittsburgh: R. Carter, 1845.

Rattray, Jeanette Edwards. *Perils of the Port of New York*. New York: Dodd, Meade, 1973.

Shaw, David W. *The Sea Shall Embrace Them – The Tragic Story of the Steamship Arctic*. New York: The Free Press Division of Simon & Schuster, 2002.

Smith, Valentine. *The Rock Smith Family*. Freeport. NY: Self-published manuscript at the Freeport Historical Society, 1937.

Spears, John R. "A Story of Beneficent Shipwrecks." *New York Times,* Jul 24, 1904: SM 3.

Styles, Michael. *Captain Hogan – Sailor, Merchant, Diplomat – On Six Continents*. Fairfax Station, VA: Six Continents Horizons, 2003.

Thompson, Benjamin F. *History of Long Island*. New York: E. French, 1839. (A public domain book at Books.Google.com.)

_____. *History of Long Island*. Vol. II. New York: Gould Banks & Co., 1843. (A public domain book at Books.Google.com.)

Treadwell, Daniel. *Personal Reminiscences of Men and Things on Long Island* (1842-1873), 2 vols. Brooklyn: Charles Andrew Ditmas, 1912.

Tumey, Harold. E. "The *Bristol* and *Mexico* Tragedies." *Long Island Forum,* Nov, 1943: 215+

Welsh, Frank. *The Four Nations, a History of the United Kingdom*. New Haven: Yale University Press, 2003. (A public domain book at Books.Google.com.)

Whitman, Walt. *Leaves of Grass* (reprint of 1891-92 edition). New York: Mitchell Kennerley, 1914. A public domain book at Books.Google.com <http://books.google.com/books?id=fWk1AAAAMAAJ&printsec=frontcover&dq=leaves+of+grass#PPP11,M1>

_____. *Specimen Days & Collect*, 1882. Reprint; New York: Dover Publications, 1995.

_____. *Whitman – The Laurel Poetry Series*. Leslie A. Fielder, ed. New York: Dell Publications, Inc., 1959.

Wilner, Steven. *Lynbrook Legacy, The Story of Our Community*. Valley Stream, New York: Maileader Publishing Corp., 1960.

Winsche, Richard A. *The History of Nassau County Community Place-Names*. Interlaken, NY: Empire State Books, 1999.

Wood, Dr. Clarence A. "Findin's Keepin' Was the Rule." *Long Island Forum*, Oct 1950: 189+.

Newspapers (From 1835-37, except as shown)

Albion News - Liverpool Library.

Dublin Evening Post - Dublin Library.

Hempstead Inquirer - Long Island Studies Institute at Hofstra University, Hempstead, NY.

Liverpool Mercury - Liverpool Library.

London Illustrated News, July 6, 1850. Church of Jesus Christ of Latter-day Saints, Family History Library, Salt Lake City.

Long Island Democrat - Long Island Studies Institute, Hofstra University, Hempstead, NY.

Morning Courier and New York Express - New York Public Library.

New York American - New York Public Library.

New York Commercial Advertiser - New York Public Library.

New York Daily Times, Dec 13, 1891. "Days of the Old Packet - Contrast between Present and Past Atlantic Liners" - <http://www.theshipslist.com/accounts/packets.htm>

New York Gazette - New York Public Library.

New York Herald - New York Public Library.

New York Sun - Supplement to the *New York Sun*, January 12, 1837, "Two Late Awful Shipwrecks." Long Island Studies Institute, Hofstra University, Hempstead, NY.

New York Sun - New York Public Library.

New York Times - New York Public Library (This is a newspaper unrelated to today's *New York Times*, which got its start in 1851.)

Sunday Morning News - New York Public Library.

The Times of London - On-line access at New York Public Library.

The Williamsburgh Gazette - Brooklyn Public Library and the private collection of Brian Merlis.

<u>Websites</u>

"Act for the establishment and support of Lighthouses, Beacons, Buoys, and Public Piers (1789)." *United States Statutes at Large - Volume 1- 1st Congress - 1st Session/Chapter. Chap. IX.* <http://en.wikisource.org/wiki/United_States_Statutes_at_Large/Volume_1/ 1st_Congress/1st_Session/Chapter_9>

Baker, Sean. "Nativism: American Anti-Catholic Sentiment, 1830-1845." *The American Religious Experience – Anti-Catholic Sentiment, 1830-1845.* West Virginia University. <http://are.as.wvu.edu/baker.htm>

Dysthe, Kristian B., Harald E. Krogstad, Hervé Socquet-Juglard, and Karsten Trulsen. "Freak waves, rogue waves, extreme waves and ocean wave climate." Matematisk Institutt. (Norway). 2005. <http://www.math.uio.no/~karstent/waves/index_en.html>

"Early History of the LIRR." *Long Island Rail Road History Website.*

Flags of The World (FOTW) - 2009 <http://flagspot.net/flags/>

Harper, Douglas. "Emancipation in New York." Slavery in the North. 2003. <http://www.slavenorth.com/nyemancip.htm>

Haver, Sverre. "Freak Wave Event at Draupner Jacket." Matematisk Institutt (Norway). 2003. <www.math.uio.no/~karstent/seminarV05/Haver2004.pdf >

The Institute of Chartered Shipbrokers. (Plimsoll mark information) <http://www.ics.org.hk/doc%5CMER0509.pdf>

"Joseph Grinnell" and "Robert Bowne Minturn." *Virtual American Biographies.* <http://famousamericans.net/robertbowneminturn/>

"Liverpool Docks in 1834." *Picture of Liverpool: Stranger's Guide* (1834). <http://www.old-liverpool.co.uk/Docks.html>

Measuringworth.org <http://www.measuringworth.com/exchange/> (Provides historical conversions from U.K. pounds to U.S. dollars.)

M'Kye, Patrick. "The Memorial of Patrick M'Kye." From Nicholson, Asenath. *Annals of the famine in Ireland (1851)* The University of Wisconsin Digital Collection. <http://digicoll.library.wisc.edu/cgi-bin/History/History-idx?type=HTML&rgn=DIV1 &byte=21763758>

"Religion and the Early Republic – American Catholics." *History Online – The Gilder Lehrman Institute of American History.* <http://www.class.uh.edu/gl/Religion8.htm>

"Square Rigging." *Sailing Ships.* <http://sailing-ships.oktett.net/square-rigging.html>

"Statement of the facts and circumstances relative to the operation of the pilot laws of the U.S. with particular reference to New-York. (1840)" *Internet Archive.* <http://www.archive.org/stream/statementoffacts00newyiala/statementoffacts00newyial a_djvu.txt>

Stephens, Mitchell. "History of Newspapers – Article for *Collier's Encyclopedia*." New York University. <http://www.nyu.edu/classes/stephens/Collier's%20page.htm>

Stoffer, Phil and Paula Messina. "Dynamics of Beaches and Barrier Islands." *Geology and Geography of New York Bight Beaches*. <http://www.geo.hunter.cuny.edu/bight/>

"Tide of Immigration to the United States and the British Colonies, The." *London Illustrated News*, July 6, 1850 (An account of emigration from the Port of Liverpool.) <http://vassun.vassar.edu/~sttaylor/FAMINE/ILN/Tide/Tide.html>

"United States Passenger Act of 1819." Norway-Heritage. <http://www.norwayheritage.com/articles/templates/historic_documents.asp?articleid=21&zoneid=18>

"University of Wisconsin Digital Collection" <http://uwdc.library.wisc.edu/Collections.shtml>

"Wind Chill." *NOAA Magazine.* <http://www.noaanews.noaa.gov/stories2004/s2154.htm>

Research Libraries and Museums

The author is grateful for the help of research librarians at the following institutions:

East Rockaway and Lynbrook Historical Society (Access to Journal of Peter T. Hewlett and original print of Nathaniel Currier print)

Family History Library of the Church of Jesus Christ of Latter-day Saints, Salt Lake City. (Genealogical research and emigrant issues.)

Freeport Historical Society. (Information on Raynor Smith.)

Liverpool Library. (Newspapers on microfilm.)

Long Beach Historical Society. (Interviews regarding location of the wreck of the *Mexico*.

Long Island Studies Institute, Hofstra University, Hempstead, New York. (Rare books, articles, vintage maps, and newspapers on microfilm.)

Lynbrook Public Library. (Rare books.)

Merseyside Maritime Museum Research Library, Liverpool (British Maritime regulations, Prince's Dock images, and descriptions.)

National Archives, New York City. (Port of New York crew lists.)

National Library of Ireland, Dublin. (Newspapers on microfilm.)

New-York Historical Society. (New York City history.)

New York City Public Library. (Newspapers on microfilm.)

Phillips House Museum, Rockville Centre, NY. (Painting and relic of the wreck of the *Mexico*)

Stephen B. Luce Library, New York Maritime College, SUNY, Fort Schuyler, NY (Ship technology.)

Acknowledgements

The author wishes to acknowledge the assistance of my family, friends and associates whose guidance, encouragement, and unflinching criticism influenced everything from spelling and style to the content and arrangement of the book. They helped me set a straight course. If *Water and Ice* is successful, it is largely because of their invaluable contributions. If there are mistakes, they are mine.

Dr. Gerard Barker, Susan Barry, Thomas Canavan, Jr., Esq., Dr. Geoffrey Clark, Dr. Arthur Liebman, and Donald MacLean helped steer my early manuscripts in the right direction. Ron and Faith Hailparn cured my writer's block by means of a generous invitation to their retreat in St. Croix, where I was also able to research the 1836 sugar trade. Thanks go to my many friends at PEIR (Personal Enrichment In Retirement) at Hofstra University for their unfailing encouragement.

Special thanks go to Dr. Stanley Feld, for his exacting proof reading and his softly administered admonitions.

I am deeply indebted to Natalie Naylor, Professor Emerita at Hofstra University, who offered much wise counsel and encouragement. I hope that a glimmer of her vast love of the history of Long Island is reflected in this book.

Last, but not least, this book is a family effort. My daughter Kirstin and son Gregory worked tirelessly over the manuscript at various stages, as has my wife Nori. I owe so much to her, for she is my traveling companion to far-off archives, the patient reader and critic of every word I have ever had published, and still, after forty-one years, the love of my life.

Index

D

E

For inquires, or to purchase copies of *Water and Ice*:

Website

www.Lynhistory.com

Publisher's Mailing Address

Lynbrook Historical Books
28 Hart Street
Lynbrook, NY 11563-1711

Telephone

(516) 887-7673

Email

Lynhistory@AOL.com

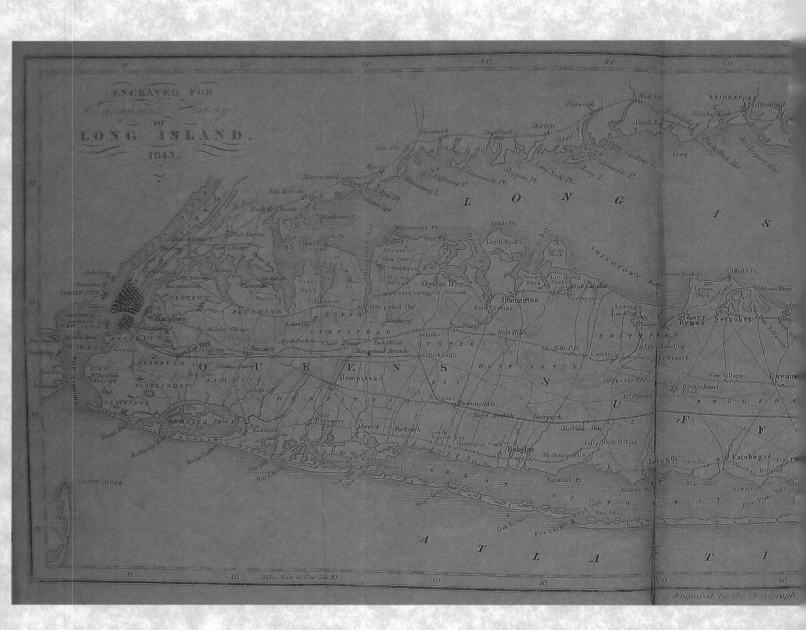

ENGRAVED FOR
Prime's History
OF
LONG ISLAND.
1843.